HANNAH WHITALL SMITH from
GOD IS ENOUGH

The life of faith is no speculative theory, neither is it a dream of romance. There is such a thing as having one's soul kept in perfect peace, now and here in this life; and childlike trust in God is the key to its attainment. We cannot earn it; we can do nothing but ask for it and receive it. It is the gift of God in Christ Jesus.

GOD
IS
ENOUGH

Hannah Whitall Smith

Edited by Melvin E. Dieter
and Hallie A. Dieter

BALLANTINE BOOKS • NEW YORK

Library of Congress Catalog Card Number: 86–15879

ISBN 0–345–36111–3

This edition published by arrangement with Zondervan Publishing
House, a division of Zondervan Corporation.

Manufactured in the United States of America

First Ballantine/Epiphany Books Edition: April 1990

PREFACE

From the time of her conversion in 1858 until her death more than sixty years later in 1911, Hannah Whitall Smith served as a spiritual guide for thousands of Christians around the world. The persistent popularity of her *Christian's Secret of a Happy Life*, first published in 1875, has kept her name before the Christian public from then until the present. The book has become one of the classics of Christian devotional literature. This volume introduces the reader to excerpts from that classic as well as from her other lesser-known writings.

Hannah Whitall (1832–1911) and her husband Robert Pearsall Smith (1827–1898) were birthright Quakers. She was a favorite daughter of a prosperous family who owned a large New Jersey glass plant; he was the first son of a family of comfortably placed Philadelphia Quakers whose roots reached back to the well-known James Logan, personal secretary to William Penn. The dramatic spiritual and life pilgrimage which followed the wedding of this promising young couple in 1851 is one of the most remarkable in the annals of Christian history. It eventually led the Smiths out of what they felt to be the barrenness of mid-nineteenth-century Quakerism into the more vital spirituality of the now-famed revival of 1858 and, subsequently, into the "higher Christian life" teachings of the Methodist holiness movement. Eager for "real Christianity," both Hannah and Robert experienced a second crisis of personal commitment and cleansing at the camp meetings of the Methodist-sponsored National Holiness Association.

Hannah's persistent "optimism of grace" is the first of several themes that stand out in bold patterns throughout her teachings. This firm confidence in the possibilities of grace and victorious

Christian life supported the vision of the fully consecrated and sanctified life which lay at the heart of the spirituality of the Christian holiness/higher-life revival of their time. These concepts were undergirded by her Quaker belief that God's Spirit was working with every man and woman to bring them to himself; they became dominant notes in her spiritual song.

A second pervasive theme in all Hannah Whitall Smith's spiritual counsel is the centrality of "faith" to any true knowledge and experience of God. She learned this reality both from the ultimate frustration of her own extended efforts to prove her relationships with God by an emotional or even physical evidence of some kind, and from her husband Robert's life of stormy emotional highs and lows. She finally came to the unshakable conviction that faith in Jesus Christ as we know Him in the sure and true words of the Bible is the only steady foundation for the Christian life.

A third note that dominates her writings is their practical orientation. She would have nothing to do with a Christianity that is not in line with the way God made us and His world. As warped as humans and creation are because of sin, she believed we can still see God's patterns and intentions in it, and true Christianity and our sense of God must square with these. God's work in us will affirm the goodness and fullness of His work in nature. Redemption and the natural order, when stripped of its sinful perversions, can show us God.

The fourth major thread that weaves its pattern throughout the whole is the image of God as the gracious loving Father. Hannah's own experience in a home where she felt absolutely secure as the object of care of loving generous parents ultimately became the focal point of her concept of God and the Christian life. Her own father loved her so much that he had never failed to do anything in his finite power to help her to be good and joyful. It became easy for her to ask, "How much more will our heavenly Father in His infinite love and mercy do for us if we will trust ourselves to Him unreservedly as children do to a loving earthly parent?" She had found, as a daughter, that having such a father as she had was enough. In the midst of her life and her intense struggle for spiritual reality, she discovered that by the same wholehearted faith in God, He too would be enough—here, anywhere, now, and always!

LIST OF ABBREVIATIONS

All of the following were written by Hannah Whitall Smith (Mrs. R. Pearsall Smith):

COG	*Chariots of God* (pamphlet)
DIARIES	Diaries
EDR	*Every-Day Religion: The Common-Sense Teaching of the Bible.* London: James Nisbet & Co., Limited, 1902.
GAC	*The God of All Comfort and the Secret of His Comforting.* London: James Nisbet & Co., Limited, 1906.
KK	*Kings and Kingdoms* (pamphlet)
OTT	*Old Testament Types and Teachings.* New York: Fleming H. Revell Company, 1878.
SEC	*The Christian's Secret of a Happy Life.* New York: Fleming H. Revell Company, 1888.
VU	*The Veil Uplifted; or, The Bible Its Own Interpreter.* London: 79–81 Fortress Road, N.W., n.d.
WS	*Wings* (pamphlet)

THE SEEKER

God is a Father. I a weary child. He is beyond all thought or reach of mine, but if I come to Him, He will lead me blind and weak among the dangers—guiding on, I follow through the strangest winding paths: and He will lead me to His own belief. I trust everything to Him. (*Diaries*, 1856 [age 23])

JANUARY 1
GOD IS ENOUGH

"My soul, wait thou only upon God; for my expectation is from him. He only is my rock and my salvation: he is my defense; I shall not be moved. In God is my salvation and my glory: the rock of my strength, and my refuge, is in God" (Ps. 62:5–7).

The greatest lesson a soul has to learn is that God, and God alone, is enough for all its needs. This is the lesson that all God's dealings with us are meant to teach, and this is the crowning discovery of our entire Christian life. GOD IS ENOUGH!

No soul can really be at rest until it has given up dependence on everything else and has been forced to depend on the Lord alone. As long as our expectation is from other things, nothing but disappointment awaits us. Feelings may change, doctrines and dogmas may be upset, the Christian work may come to nought, prayers may seem to lose their fervency, promises may seem to fail, everything that we have believed in or depended on may seem to be swept away, and only God is left—just God, the bare God, if I may be allowed the expression, simply and only God.

If God is what He would seem to be from his revealings; if He is indeed the "God of all comfort" (2 Cor. 1:3); if He is our Shepherd; if He is really and truly our Father; if, in short, all the many aspects He has told us of His character and His ways are actually true, then we must come to the positive conviction that He is, in himself alone, enough for all our needs and that we may safely rest in Him absolutely and forever. (*GAC*, 242–43)

JANUARY 2
THE BEGINNING AND THE ENDING

The thing that helped me most to come to a conviction that God was really enough for me was an experience I had some years ago. It was at a time in my religious life when I was passing through a great deal of questioning and perplexity. There happened to be staying near me for a few weeks a lady who was considered to be a deeply spiritual Christian and to whom I had been advised to apply for spiritual help. I summoned my courage and went to see her and poured out my troubles, expecting that she would be at great pains to do all she could to help me.

She listened patiently, but when I had finished my story and had paused, expecting sympathy and consideration, she simply said, "Yes, all you say may be very true, but then, in spite of it all, there is God." I waited a few minutes for something more, but nothing came, and my friend and teacher had the air of having said all that was necessary. "But," I continued, "surely you did not understand how very serious and perplexing my difficulties are." "Oh yes, I did," replied my friend, "but then, as I tell you, there is God." And I could not induce her to make any other answer. We got Doubts, Fears, troubles

It seemed to me most disappointing and unsatisfactory. I felt that my peculiar and harrowing experiences could not be met by anything so simple as the mere statement, "Yes, but there is God." (*GAC*, 248–49)

JANUARY 3
DETACHING AND EMPTYING

The old mystics used to teach what they called "detachment," meaning the cutting loose of the soul from all that could hold it back from God. This need for detachment is the secret of much of our instability. We cannot follow the Lord fully so long as we are tied fast to anything else, any more than a boat can sail out into the boundless ocean so long as it is tied fast to the shore.

If we want to reach the "city which hath sure and steadfast foundations" (Heb. 1:10, para.), we must go out like Abraham from all other cities and be detached from every earthly attachment. Everything in Abraham's life that could be shaken was shaken. He was, as it were, emptied from vessel to vessel, here today and gone tomorrow; all his resting places disturbed and no settlement or comfort anywhere. We, like Abraham, are looking for a city with foundations, whose builder and maker is

2

God; and therefore we too need to be emptied from vessel to vessel.

But we do not realize this, and when the overturnings and shootings come, we are in despair and think we will never reach the city that has foundations. But it is these very shakings that make it possible for us to reach it. The psalmist had learned this, and after all the shakings and emptyings of his eventful life, he cried, "In God is my salvation and my glory: the rock of my strength, and my refuge, is in God" (Ps. 62:7). At last God was everything to him; he found that God was enough. It is the same with us: when only that which cannot be shaken remains, we learn to have our expectation from Him alone. (GAC, 155–56)

God's Love—God's Grace—It's God himself Enough for you

JANUARY 4

BELIEVING AND RESTING

God is all we need—

My need was so great that I did not give up with my first trial but went to my friend again and again, always with the hope that she would begin to understand the importance of my difficulties and give me adequate help.

It was of no avail. I was never able to draw forth any other answer. Always, with an air of entirely dismissing the subject, she would give the simple reply, "Yes, I know; but there is God." And at last, by dint of her continual repetition, I became convinced that my friend really and truly believed that the mere fact of the existence of God as the Creator and Redeemer of mankind, and of me as a member of the race, was an all-sufficient answer to every possible need of His creatures. At last, because she said it so often and seemed so sure, I began dimly to wonder whether God might really be enough, even for my need, overwhelming and peculiar as I felt it to be. From wondering I came gradually to believing, that, being my Creator and Redeemer, He must be enough; and finally a conviction burst upon me that He really was enough, and my eyes were opened to the all-sufficiency of God.

My troubles disappeared like magic, and I did nothing but question how I could ever have been such an idiot as to be troubled by them, when all the while there was God, the almighty and all-seeing God, the God who had created me and who was therefore on my side, eager to care for me. I had found out that God was enough, and my soul was at rest. (*GAC*, 250)

JANUARY 5
DEPENDING, NOT FEELING

Let us think of a man accused of a crime standing before a judge. Which would be the important thing for that man: his own feelings toward the judge, or the judge's feelings toward him? Would he watch his own emotions and try to see whether he felt that the judge was favorable to him, or would he watch the judge and try to discover from his looks or his words whether or not to expect a favorable judgment? Of course the man's own feelings are not of the slightest account in the matter; only the opinions and feelings of the judge are worth a moment's thought. The man might have all the "glows" and all the "experiences" conceivable, but these would avail absolutely nothing. On the judge only would everything depend. This is what we would call a self-evident fact. In the same way, if we look sensibly at the subject, we will see that the only vital thing in our relations with the Lord is not what our feelings toward Him are but what His feelings toward us are.

This, then, is what I mean by God being enough. It is that we find in Him, in the facts of His existence and His character, all that we can possibly want for everything. "GOD IS," must be our answer to every question and every cry of need. If there is any lack in the One who has undertaken to save us, nothing we can do will help to make it up; and if there is no lack in Him, then He, of himself and in himself, is enough. (*GAC*, 247–48)

God is – our everything – in Him
there is NO Lack

JANUARY 6
HAVING, BUT NOT HAVING

The apostle Paul gives us this paradox as one of the foundation principles of the Christian life: "Having nothing, and yet possessing all things" (2 Cor. 6:10). It is a saying of the deepest significance, for it strikes a blow at the whole fabric of the ordinary Christian life.

The ambition of most Christians, so far from being an ambition to have nothing, is, on the contrary, an ambition to have a vast number of things; and their energies are all wasted in the vain effort to get possession of these things. Some strive to get possession of certain experiences, some seek after ecstatic feelings, some try to make themselves rich in theological views and dogmas, some store up a long list of works done and results achieved, some seek to acquire illuminations or to accumulate gifts and graces. In short, Christians, almost without exception, seek to possess a store of something or other, which they fancy will serve to recommend them to God and make them worthy of His love and care.

Could we but understand clearly the meaning of Paul's words, "having nothing, and yet possessing all things," all this would be at an end. For we would see that the one thing God wants of us is for us to empty ourselves of all our own things in order that we may depend on Him for everything, to discover that His purpose is to bring us to the place where we have nothing apart from Him. (*EDR*, 121–22)

JANUARY 7
KNOWING AND RESTING

The all-sufficiency of God ought to be as complete to the child of God as the all-sufficiency of a good mother is to her child. We all know the utter rest of a young child in his mother's presence and love. That his mother is there is enough to make all fears and troubles disappear. He does not need his mother to make any promises; she herself, just as she is, without promises and without explanations, is all that the child needs.

My own experience as a child taught me this beyond any possibility of question. My mother was the remedy for all my own ills and, I fully believed, for the ills of the whole world, if only they could be brought to her. And when anyone expressed doubts as to her capacity to remedy everything, I remember with what fine scorn I used to annihilate them by saying, "Ah! but you don't know my mother."

Now when any troubled soul fails to see that God is enough, I feel like saying not with scorn but with infinite care, "Ah, dear friend, you do not know God! If you knew Him you could not help seeing that He is the remedy for every need of your soul. God is enough, even though no promise may seem to fit your case nor any inward assurance give you confidence. The Promiser is more than His promises; and His existence is a surer ground of confidence than the most fervent inward feelings.''

> *Oh, utter but the name of God*
> *Down in your heart of hearts,*
> *And see how from the soul at once*
> *All anxious fear departs. (GAC, 250–51)*

JANUARY 8
TRIUMPHING IN TRUSTING

God's saints in all ages have known that God was enough for them. Job said out of the depths of sorrow and trials that few can equal, "Though he slay me, yet will I trust in him" (Job 13:15). David could say in the moment of his keenest anguish, "Yea, though I walk through the valley of the shadow of death, I will fear no evil: for thou art with me" (Ps. 23:4). And again he could say, "God is our refuge and strength, a very present help in trouble. Therefore will not we fear though the earth be removed, and though the mountains be carried into the midst of the sea; though the waters thereof roar and be troubled, though the mountains shake with the swelling thereof" (46:1–3).

In the midst of many and grievous trials, Paul could say triumphantly, "For I am persuaded that neither death, nor life, nor angels, nor principalities, nor powers, nor things present, nor things to come, nor height, nor depth, nor any other creature, shall be able to separate us from the love of God, which is in Christ Jesus our Lord" (Rom. 8:38–39).

Therefore, doubting and sorrowful Christian, in the face of all we know about the God of all comfort, cannot you realize with Job, David, Paul, and the saints of all ages, that nothing else is needed to quiet all your fears but that God is? (GAC, 254–55)

JANUARY 9
VIEWING AND COMPREHENDING

In our different understandings of God's Book, we are all like people climbing up a high mountain to see the view. Our views differ according to the different degrees of height we may each have reached. The man at the foot of the mountain, who has just begun to climb, will have a very limited view, true as far as it goes, but hedged in on all sides by the surrounding obstructions unless his knowledge is greater than his view.

But as he climbs higher he will see the country beyond and the distant windings of the river or road. The dividing lines so strongly marked at the foot of the mountain will gradually flatten into the surrounding landscape until they are almost lost to sight in the wideness and grandeur of the climber's vision. And so on and on as the mountain is climbed, stretch after stretch of the landscape will unfold to his wondering gaze, until finally, when he reaches the top, he will see as far as human eyesight can reach, over hill, valley, forest, and river, one grand sweep of land, water, and sky, a view limited only by his own powers of vision.

One can see at a glance how different is the view from the top of a mountain from that at the mountain's foot, and can easily understand that should two gazers, looking from these two widely separated standpoints, undertake to compare views, they would find that although they have been looking over the very same landscape, their descriptions of what they saw would differ widely. It is in this progressive way that we learn to understand God's truth. (*OTT*, 11–12)

JANUARY 10
RECEIVING HIS ASSURING

The "record" God has given us of His Son has been given for the purpose of making us know that in His Son we have eternal life. "This is the record, that God hath given to us eternal life in Christ, and whoever believes in Christ has this life; and

7

of course, ought to know it. If we do not believe this record, and consequently do not know that we have eternal life, we are making God a liar" (1 John 5:10–11, para.). These are solemn words, yet when one doubts God's record, isn't he making a liar of God? If I doubt the record of one of my friends, I do in effect make that friend a liar, although I may never dare to use the word. The only way in which we can really honor God is to declare that what He says is always true and that we know it to be true and are therefore sure that we have eternal life.

Nowhere in the Bible are we given the slightest intimation that God's children were to be anything but perfectly sure of their relationship to Him as children and of His relationship to them as Father. The flood of doubt and questioning that so often overwhelms Christian hearts in these days was apparently never so much as conceived of in Bible times nor by Bible Christians, and consequently it was nowhere definitely provided against. The foundation on which all commands and exhortations were based was that those to whom the commands and exhortations were addressed knew without question that they were God's children and that He was their Father. (*EDR*, 3–4)

JANUARY 11
REJOICING IN KNOWING

The thing I want to say, and to say in such a way that no one can fail to understand it, is not a mistake. That thing is this: Our religious lives ought to be full of joy, peace, and comfort, and if we become better acquainted with God, they will be full. (*GAC*, 10)

No one can read the history of the words and deeds of the apostles and early Christians without seeing that they were saturated with an utter certainty of their salvation in the Lord Jesus Christ. Their salvation was as much a part of them as was their nationality as Jews and was no more open to question.

Let us try to imagine the apostles and early Christians as being filled with as many doubts and questionings as modern Christians, and think what effect it would have had on their preaching and work. We can see in a moment that it would have been fatal to the spread of the gospel. A church founded on doubts and questionings could have made no headway in an unbelieving world.

If we run through the Epistles we will invariably find that they also, like the Gospels and Acts, are saturated with assurance. Nowhere is a doubt or question of the believer's standing in the family of God even so much as hinted at or supposed possible. (*VU*, 42–43)

JANUARY 12
LOOKING, NOT AVOIDING

Someone may say, "All this about God's sufficiency is no doubt true, and I could easily believe it if I could only be sure it applied to me. But I am so good for nothing and so full of sin that I do not feel as if I have any claim to such riches of grace."

If you are good for nothing and full of sin, you have all the more a claim on the all-sufficiency of God. Your very good-for-nothingness and sinfulness are your strongest claims. The Bible declares that Christ Jesus came into the world to save sinners— not to save the righteous, the fervent, and the earnest workers, but simply and only to save sinners (cf. Matt. 9:13). Why then should we spend our time and energy trying to create a claim, which after all is no claim but only a hindrance?

As long as our attention is turned on ourselves and our own experiences, it is turned away from the Lord. It is not that He hides himself; He is always there in full view of all who look unto Him; but if we are looking in another direction, we cannot expect to see Him.

It may be that our eyes have been so exclusively fixed on ourselves, that all our questioning has been directed toward our own condition—Is my love for God warm enough? Am I enough in earnest? Are my feelings toward Him what they ought to be? Have I enough zeal? And we have been miserable because we have never been able to answer these questions satisfactorily. Although we do not know it, it has been a mercy that we never could answer them satisfactorily, for, if we had, the self in us would have been exalted and we would have been filled with self-congratulation and pride. (*GAC*, 251–53)

JANUARY 13
DEPENDING, NOT DEMANDING

If we want to see God, our inner questioning must be not about ourselves but about Him. How does God feel toward me? Is His love for me warm enough? Has He enough zeal? Does He feel my need deeply enough? Is He sufficiently in earnest? Although these questions may seem irreverent to some, they simply embody the doubts and fears of a great many doubting hearts, and they only need to be asked in order to prove that these doubts and fears are in themselves the real irreverence. We know what the triumphant answers to such questions would be. No doubts could withstand their testimony; and the soul that asks and answers them honestly will be shut up to a profound and absolute conviction that God is and must be enough.

Because God is, all must go right for us. Because the mother is, all must go right, up to the measure of her ability, for her children; and infinitely more must this be true of the Lord. To the child there is behind all that changes and can change the one unchangeable fact of the mother's existence. While the mother lives, the child must be cared for; and while God lives, His children must be cared for as well. What else could He do, being what He is? Neglect, indifference, forgetfulness, ignorance, are all impossible to God. He knows everything, He cares about everything, He can manage everything, and He loves us. What more could we ask? (*GAC*, 253–54)

JANUARY 14
DISCOVERING AND TASTING

I will never forget the hour when I first discovered that God was really good. I had of course always known that the Bible said He was good, but I had thought it only meant He was religiously good, and it had never dawned on me that it meant He was actually and practically good, with the same kind of goodness He has commanded us to have. The expression "the goodness of God" had seemed to me nothing more than a sort of heavenly statement that I could not be expected to understand.

And then one day I came across the words, "O taste and see that the LORD is good" (Ps. 34:8), and suddenly they meant something. The Lord is good, I repeated to myself. What does it mean to be good? To live up to the best and highest that one knows. To be good is exactly the opposite of being bad. To be bad is to know the right and not to do it, but to be good is to do the best we know. And I saw that, since God is omniscient, He must know what is the best and highest good of all, and that therefore His goodness must necessarily be beyond question.

I can never express what this meant to me. I had such a view of the real goodness of God that I saw nothing could possibly go wrong under His care, and it seemed to me that no one could ever be anxious again. And over and over since, when appearances have been against Him and when I have been tempted to question whether He had not been unkind or neglectful or indifferent, I have been brought up short by the words, "The Lord is good"; and I have seen that it was simply unthinkable that a God who was good could have done the bad things I had imagined. (*GAC*, 90–91)

JANUARY 15
UNDERSTANDING FATHERING

One of the most illuminating names of God is the one especially revealed by our Lord Jesus Christ—Father. I say especially revealed by Christ, because while God has been called throughout the ages by many other names expressing other aspects of His character, Christ alone has revealed Him to us under the all-inclusive name of Father, a name that holds within itself all other names of wisdom and power, a name that embodies for us a perfect supply for all our needs. In the Old Testament God was not revealed as the Father so much as He was a great warrior fighting for His people or as a mighty king ruling over them and caring for them. The name of Father is only given to Him a very few times there, while in the New Testament it is given between two and three hundred times.

But do we in the least understand what the word means? All

11

the discomfort and unrest of the religious life of so many of God's children, come, I feel sure, from this very thing, that they do not understand that God is actually and truly their Father. They think of Him as a stern judge or a severe taskmaster or, at best, as an unapproachable dignitary seated on a far-off throne, dispensing exacting laws for a frightened and trembling world. In their terror lest they should fail to meet His requirements, they hardly know which way to turn. But of a God who is a father, tender and loving and full of compassion, who will be on their side against the whole universe, they have no conception. Discomfort and unrest are impossible to souls who come to know that God is their Father. (*GAC*, 62–63)

JANUARY 16
FATHERING AND MOTHERING

God is a father like the best of earthly fathers ought to be. Sometimes earthly fathers are unkind, tyrannical, selfish, or even cruel, or they are merely indifferent and neglectful; but none of these can by any stretch of charity be called good fathers. But God, who is good, must be a good father or not a father at all. We all have known good fathers in this world or at least can imagine them. I knew one, and he filled my childhood with sunshine by his loving fatherhood. I can remember vividly with what confidence and triumph I walked through my days, absolutely secure in the knowledge that I had a father. And I am very sure that I have learned to know a little about the perfect fatherhood of God because of my experience with this earthly father.

But God is not only a father, He is a mother as well, and we all have known mothers whose love and tenderness have been without bound or limit. God who created them both and who is himself father and mother in one, could never have created earthly fathers and mothers who were more tender and more loving than He is himself. Therefore if we want to know what sort of a father He is, we must heap together the best of all the fathers and mothers we have ever known or can imagine, and we must tell ourselves that this is only a faint image of our Father in heaven. (*GAC*, 63–64)

JANUARY 17
COMFORTING AND MOTHERING

We all know how a mother comforts her children, and most of us have tasted the sweetness of this comforting.

God is called the "God of all comfort" (2 Cor. 1:3).

The Holy Spirit is called the Comforter (John 14:26).

Christ, when He was leaving His disciples, provided for their comfort when He should be gone.

If God is like a mother and comforts as mothers comfort, why is it that His children are not comforted? Have you never seen a young child sitting up stiff in his mother's lap, refusing to be comforted in spite of all his mother's coaxing? And do we not often act in very much the same way?

Even a mother's love and tenderness cannot comfort a child who refuses to be comforted, and neither can God's. But no sorrow can be too great for His comfort to reach, if we will only consent to be comforted.

When a child cries, the mother runs and listens to the story of his sorrows and needs, and then relieves them. And God does the same for His children.

"Here I am" is a mother's unfailing answer to a child's cry of "Mother, Mother, where are you?" And God answers the same.

How alert is the ear of the mother to the feeblest cry of her baby in the night. Even if she is sleeping soundly, she will hear the tiny cry. How comforted and quieted the little one is when he realizes the mother's presence and can go to sleep in her care. (*VU*, 92, 94)

JANUARY 18
PARENTING IS PROTECTING

A mother carries her child in her arms and folds him to her bosom. Do we not act sometimes as though we are carrying the Lord rather than He carrying us? Do we not go bowed down under this fancied burden when we ought to be resting peacefully in His arms? A baby, safe in his mother's arms, will sometimes make little clutches of fright, as though his safety depended on the strength of his tiny grasp on his mother's neck. But the mother knows how useless these are and that it is her grasp, not the baby's, that secures his safety. Surely this is true of us in the arms of God.

The baby carried in the arms of his mother knows no fear even though their path may lie through a howling wilderness or through raging enemies. The mother's arms are his impregnable fortress. The "everlasting arms" (cf. Deut. 33:27) of God can be no less.

Even the eagle knows this secret of motherly love. When the eaglets are old enough to learn to fly, in love the mother stirs up the nest and thrusts them out so that they will be driven to find the use of their wings. But she floats in the air under them and watches them with eyes of love, and when she sees any little eaglet showing signs of weariness, she flies beneath it and spreads out her great strong mother wings to bear it up until it is rested and ready to fly again. The Lord does the same for His children.

We cannot make any mistake, then, in believing that the Lord carries us in His arms and folds us to His bosom with far more tenderness and watchful care than any mother ever could. (*VU*, 95–96)

JANUARY 19
LISTENING AND ATTENDING

We are sometimes tempted to think that the Lord does not hear our prayers. But let the mother teach us. Could she possibly let the cry of her child go unheeded? Is the earthly mother more tender than the heavenly Father?

We are tempted to think that trouble shuts God's ears. In times of prosperity we find it easy to believe that He hears us, but when the dark days come we moan and complain because we think our prayers do not reach Him. Which cry catches the mother's ear the soonest—the cry of joy or the cry of sorrow? There can be but one answer to this. Happy noises of children in the nursery often pass by a mother unnoticed, but the slightest cry of pain or trouble reaches her ear at once. And is a mother more alert to the suffering of her children than God is to His?

An infant may not know why he cries, but his mother does not refuse, because of this, to listen to his cry. She seeks all the more to discover the cause of his discomfort and to remedy it. And surely, so must God.

Let us never grieve our heavenly Father again by doubting that He hears us, however faint and feeble may be our cry. Let us be encouraged to ask as children do for everything we need, sure that He will always hear and answer either in kind or in kindness. (*VU*, 94–95)

JANUARY 20
MOTHERING IS GIVING

The mother is always ready to feed her hungry child and would starve herself before she would allow the child to starve.

It is not always the food the child asks for that the wise mother gives. Sometimes such food would be fatal to his health. Rather she gives her child the most nutritious food she can procure. And we may be perfectly sure that our God always gives us that which is best, whether it is what we ask for or not. Therefore we must be satisfied.

What our Father gives may look to us like a "serpent" or a "scorpion," but since He gives it, we may be sure it cannot be anything but the best thing for us. For if parents know how to give good gifts, how "much more" must He (Luke 11:11–13)?

The child does not have to supply or prepare his own food; that is the mother's responsibility. All the child has to do is eat and live, without care and without cost.

What, then, is the summing up of the whole matter? Simply this: If God is only as good as the mothers He has made, where can there be any room left for a thought of care or of fear? And if He is as much truer to the ideal of motherhood than an earthly mother can be, as His infiniteness is above hers, then what oceans and continents of bliss are ours for the taking!

Shall we not take them? (*VU*, 102, 107)

15

JANUARY 21
NAMING IS REVEALING

When our Lord was teaching His disciples how to pray, the only name by which He taught them to address God was "Our Father which art in heaven" (Matt. 6:9). And this surely meant that we were to think of Him only in this light. Millions upon millions of times during all the centuries since then, this name has been uttered by the children of God everywhere, yet it has been greatly misunderstood. Had all who used the name known what it meant, it would have been impossible for the misrepresentations of His character and the doubts of His children throughout all the ages to have crept in. Tyranny, unkindness, and neglect might perhaps be attributed to a God who was only a king or judge or lawgiver, but of a God who is before all else a father, and since He is God, a good father, no such things could possibly be believed.

It is inconceivable that a good father could forget or neglect or be unfair to his children. A savage or wicked father might, but a good father never! In calling our God by the blessed name of Father, we ought to know that if He is a father at all, He must be the very best of fathers, and His fatherhood must be the highest ideal of fatherhood we can conceive. It is, as I have said, a fatherhood that combines both father and mother in one, in our highest ideals of both. It comprises all the love, tenderness, compassion, yearning, and self-sacrifice that we recognize to be the inmost soul of parentage, even though we may not always see it carried out by all earthly parents. (*GAC*, 64–65)

JANUARY 22
FATHERING IS DEFINING

But what about the other names of God; do they not convey other and more terrifying ideas? They only do so because the name Father is not added to them. This name must underlie every other name by which He has ever been known. Has He been called a judge? Yes, but He is a father judge, one who judges as a loving father would. Is He a king? Yes, but He is a king who is at the same time the Father of His subjects and who rules them with a father's tenderness. Is He a lawgiver? Yes, but He is a lawgiver who gives laws as a father would, remembering the weakness and ignorance of His helpless children. Scripture doesn't say, "as a judge judges, so the Lord judges," nor "as a lawgiver imposes laws, so the Lord imposes laws," but "as a father pitieth . . . , so the LORD pitieth" (Ps. 103:13).

Never, never must we think of God in any other way than as our Father. We must base and limit all of our conceptions of Him, all of the titles we give Him, on the fact that He is our Father. What a good earthly father would not do, God who is our Father would not do either; and what a good father ought to do, God who is our Father is absolutely sure to do.

Christ has declared to us the name of the Father in order that we may discover that the Father loves us as He loves His Son. If we believed this, could we ever have an anxious or rebellious thought again? Would we not believe in every conceivable circumstance that the divine Father would care for us in the best possible way and meet our every need? (*GAC*, 65–66)

JANUARY 23
FATHERING MEANS BLESSING

Our Lord draws the comparison between earthly fathers and our heavenly Father in order to show us, not that He is less good, tender, and willing to bless, but much more. Can we conceive of a good earthly father giving a stone or a serpent to a hungry child instead of bread or fish? Would not our souls revolt at the thought of a father who could do such things? And yet, I fear, there are a great many of God's children who actually think that their heavenly Father does this sort of thing to them: gives them stones when they ask for bread or curses them when they ask for blessings. Perhaps these very people may belong to the "Society for the Prevention of Cruelty to Children," a society which is the nation's protest against such behavior on the part of earthly fathers; yet they have never thought of the dreadful wickedness of charging their heavenly Father with things which they are banded together to punish earthly fathers for!

17

But it is not only that our heavenly Father is willing to give us good things; He is far more than willing. There is no grudging in His giving; He likes to give. He wants to give you the kingdom far more than you want to have it. Those of us who are parents know how eager we are to give good things to our children, often far more eager than our children are to have them. Why, then, should we ask God in such fear and trembling, and why should we torment ourselves with anxiety lest He should fail to grant what we need?

There can be only one answer to these questions, and that is that we do not know the Father. (*GAC*, 67–68)

JANUARY 24
FATHERING BRINGS RESTING

We are told that we are of the "household of God" (Eph. 2:19). The principle is announced in the Bible, that if any man provides not for his own household, he has "denied the faith, and is worse than an infidel" (1 Tim. 5:8). Since we are of the "household of God," this principle applies to God, and if He should fail to provide for us, His own words would condemn Him. I say this reverently but emphatically, for so few people seem to have realized it.

In my own case it was a distinct era of immense importance when I first discovered this fact. In a single moment the burden of life was lifted from my shoulders and laid on His, and all my fears, anxieties, and questionings dropped into the abyss of His loving care. I saw that the instinct of humanity, which demands that parents are bound by every law, both human and divine, to care for and protect their children according to their best ability, is a divinely implanted instinct. It is meant to teach us the magnificent fact that the Creator, who has made human parents responsible toward their children, is himself equally responsible toward His children. I could have shouted for joy! From that glad hour my troubles were over.

With such a God, who is at the same time a father, there is no room for anything but rest. And when, ever since that glad day, temptations to doubt or anxiety or fear have come to me, I have not dared to listen to them, because I have seen that to do

18

so would be to cast a doubt on the trustworthiness of my Father in heaven. (*GAC*, 68–69)

JANUARY 25
TRUSTING HIS FATHERING

We may think that our doubts and fears are because of our own unworthiness, and arise from humility. We may even take them as a sign of special piety, believing they are in some way pleasing to God. But if, in their relations with their earthly parents, children should let in doubts of their parents' love and fears that their care should fail, would these doubts and fears be evidences of filial piety on the children's part, and would they be at all pleasing to their parents?

If God is our Father, the only thing we can do with doubts, fears, and anxious thoughts is cast them all behind our backs forever. We can do this. We can give up our doubts just as we would urge a drunkard to give up his drink. We can take a pledge against doubting, just as we try to induce the drunkard to take a pledge against drinking. And if once we see that our doubts are a sin against God and that we are questioning His trustworthiness, we will be eager to do it.

We may have cherished our doubts heretofore because perhaps we have thought they were a part of our religion and a becoming attitude of soul in one so unworthy; but if we now see that God is in very truth our Father, we will reject every doubt with horror, as a libel on our Father's love and care. No good earthly father would want his children to take on their young shoulders the burden of his duties, and surely much less would our heavenly Father want to lay on us the burden of His. We are told to cast all our care on Him (1 Peter 5:7). (*GAC*, 69–71)

JANUARY 26
KNOWING HIM IS TRUSTING HIM

God cares for us. It is His business as a father to do so. All He asks of us is to let Him know when we need anything and then leave the supplying of that need to Him. He assures us that if we do this the "peace of God, which passeth all understanding, shall keep [our] hearts and minds" (Phil. 4:7).

The children of a good human father are at peace because they trust in their father's care, but the children of the heavenly Father too often have no peace because they are afraid to trust in His care. They make their requests known to Him, but that is all they do. It is a sort of religious form they feel is necessary to go through with. But as to supposing that He really will care for them, no such idea seems to cross their minds; and they go on carrying their cares and burdens on their own shoulders as if they had no Father in heaven and had never asked Him to care for them.

What utter folly this is! So few of His children trust Him because they have not yet found out that He is really their Father. Or perhaps although they call Him Father in their prayers, they have never seen that He is the sort of father a good human father is, a father who is loving, tender, and full of kindness toward the helpless beings He has brought into existence. This sort of father no one could help trusting; but the strange and far-off Creator, whose fatherhood stops at our creation, who has no care for our fate after we are launched into the universe, no one could be expected to trust. (*GAC*, 71–73)

JANUARY 27
RECEIVING OR REJECTING

"Ye have not received the spirit of bondage again to fear; but ye have received the Spirit of adoption, whereby we cry, Abba, Father" (Rom. 8:15), says the apostle Paul. Is it this "spirit of adoption" that reigns in your heart, or is it the "spirit of bondage"? Your comfort in the religious life depends on which spirit you have. No amount of wrestling or agonizing, no prayers and no effort, can bring you comfort while the "spirit of adoption" is lacking in your heart.

But how are we to get this "spirit of adoption"? I can only say that it is not a thing to be got. It comes, and it comes as the necessary result of the discovery that God is in very truth a real Father. When we have made this discovery, we cannot help feeling like a child. This is what the "spirit of adoption" means. It is nothing mystical or mysterious; it is the simple natural result of having found a father where you thought there was only a judge.

The great need for every soul, therefore, is it to make this supreme discovery. To do this we have only to see what Christ tells us about the Father and then believe it. "Verily, verily," He declares, "I say unto thee, We speak that we do know, and testify that we have seen"; but, He adds sadly, "ye receive not our witness" (John 3:11). In order to come to the knowledge of the Father, we must receive the testimony of Christ. The whole authority of Christ stands or falls with this. If we receive His testimony, we acknowledge that God is true. If we reject that testimony, we make Him a liar (cf. 1 John 5:10). (*GAC*, 73)

JANUARY 28
KNOWING IS RESTING

Because we do not know God, we naturally get all sorts of wrong ideas about Him. We think He is an angry judge watching for our slightest faults, or a harsh taskmaster determined to exact from us the uttermost service, or a self-absorbed deity demanding His due of honor and glory, or a far-off sovereign concerned only with His own affairs and indifferent to our welfare. Who can wonder that such a God can neither be loved nor trusted? And who could expect Christians, with such ideas concerning Him, to be anything but full of discomfort and misery?

I can assert boldly and without fear of contradiction that it is impossible for anyone who really knows God to have any such uncomfortable thoughts about Him. There may be plenty of outward discomforts and many earthly sorrows and trials, but through them all, the soul who knows God will live inwardly in

21

a fortress of perfect peace. "Whoso hearkeneth unto me," He says, "shall dwell safely, and shall be quiet from fear of evil" (Prov. 1:33). This is a statement no one dares question. If we would really hearken unto God, which means not only hearing Him, but believing what we hear, we could not fail to know that just because He is God, He cannot do other than care for us as He cares for the apple of His eye. All that the tenderest love and divinest wisdom can do for our welfare must be and will be unfailingly done. Not a single loophole for worry or fear is left to the soul who knows God. (*GAC*, 5–6)

JANUARY 29
ABOUNDING BELIEVING

Have we never been taunted with the discouraging thought that God is "much less" able to deliver us than His promises would lead us to expect? And when we have looked at the things of our need, has it not sometimes seemed to us as if it would be equivalent to giving ourselves over to "die by famine and thirst" if we had absolutely no one else to trust but the Lord alone? I remember hearing of a Christian who was in great trouble, who said to a friend in utmost despair, "Well, there is nothing left for me now but to trust the Lord." "Alas!" exclaimed the friend in consternation, "is it possible it has come to that?"

If we are honest with ourselves, I believe we must confess that sometimes we have indulged in just this feeling. To come to the point of having nothing left but to trust the Lord has seemed to us, at times, a desperate condition. But God is able to do "exceeding abundantly above all that we can ask or think" (Eph. 3:20).

We are told that "eye hath not seen, nor ear heard, neither have entered into the heart of man, the things which God hath prepared for them that love him" (1 Cor. 2:9). God has prepared more for us than it has ever entered into our hearts to conceive. Surely we can have no question about obtaining much more. (*GAC*, 123)

JANUARY 30
OVERADVERTISING OR UNDERTRUSTING

The religion of the Lord Jesus Christ was meant to be full of comfort. Every newly converted soul, in the first joy of conversion, fully expects it. And yet it seems as if for a great number of Christians, their religious lives are the most uncomfortable part of their existence. Does the fault of this state of things lie with the Lord? Has He promised more than He is able to supply?

We know what overadvertisement is. It is a twentieth-century disease from which we all suffer. Everything is overadvertised. Is it the same with the kingdom of God? Has He deceived us? There is a feeling abroad that Christ offered more in His gospel than He has to give. People claim that they have not realized what was predicted as the portion of the children of God.

But why is this so? Has the kingdom of God been overadvertised, or is it only that it has been underbelieved? Has the Lord Jesus Christ been overestimated, or has He only been undertrusted? I firmly believe that the kingdom of God cannot possibly be overadvertised nor the Lord Jesus Christ overestimated, for "eye hath not seen, nor ear heard, neither have entered into the heart of man, the things which God hath prepared for them that love him" (1 Cor. 2:9). The difficulty arises from the fact that we have underbelieved and undertrusted. (*GAC*, 3–4)

JANUARY 31
GLORYING IN HIS WORKING

"Why have you made me like this?"

This is a question we are very apt to ask. There is, I imagine, hardly one of us who has not been tempted at one time or another to question God in reference to the matter of our own personal make-up. We do not like our peculiar temperaments or our special characteristics, and we long to be like someone else, who has, we think, greater gifts of appearance or talent. We are discontented with our make-up and feel sure that all our

23

failures are due to our unfortunate temperaments; and we are inclined to blame our Creator for having made us as He has.

I remember vividly a time in my life when I was tempted to be very rebellious about my own make-up. My natural temperament was far too energetic and outspoken for any appearance of saintliness, and many a time I said upbraidingly in my heart to God, "Why have you made me like this?"

But one day I came across a sentence in an old mystic book that seemed to open my eyes. It was as follows: "Be content to be what thy God has made thee"; and it flashed on me that God had made me and that He must know the sort of person He wanted me to be. If He had made me a potato vine, I must be satisfied to grow potatoes and must not want to be a rosebush and grow roses. We are God's "workmanship" (Eph. 2:10), and God is good, and we may securely trust that before He is done with us, He will make out of us something that will be to His glory, no matter how unlike this we may appear. (*GAC*, 98–99)

FEBRUARY 1
SAVING IN DELIVERING

All of God's children feel instinctively, in their moments of divine illumination, that a life of inward rest and outward victory is their inalienable birthright. Remember the shout of triumph your soul gave when you first became acquainted with the Lord Jesus and had a glimpse of His mighty saving power? How sure you were of victory then! How easy it seemed to be more than a conqueror through Him who loved you (cf. Rom. 8:37)! And yet, to many of you, how different has been your real experience! Your victories have been few and fleeting, your defeats many and disastrous.

Your heart has sunk within you as day after day and year after year your early visions of triumph have grown dimmer and dimmer and you have been forced to settle down to the conviction that the best you can expect from your religion is a life of alternate failure and victory, one hour sinning and the next repenting, a never ending cycle.

In the very outset, then, settle down on this one thing: Jesus came to save you, now, in this life, from the power and dominion of sin and to make you more than a conqueror through His power. Search your Bible and collect together every declaration concerning the purpose of His death on the cross. You will be astonished to find how full they are. Everywhere and always His work is said to be to deliver us from our sins, from our bondage, from our defilement; and not a hint is given anywhere that this deliverance was to be the limited and partial one with which many Christians so continually try to be satisfied. (*SEC*, 15–18)

FEBRUARY 2
LOVING AND LAVISHING

He loves us—loves us, I say—and the will of love is always blessing for its loved one. Some of us know what it is to love, and we know that could we only have our way, our beloved ones would be overwhelmed with blessings. All that is good and sweet and lovely in life would be poured out on them from our lavish hands.

If this is the way of love with us, how much more must it be so with our God, who is love itself? Could we but for one moment get a glimpse into the mighty depths of His love, our hearts would spring out to meet His will and embrace it as our richest treasure. We would abandon ourselves to it with an enthusiasm of gratitude and joy that such a wondrous privilege could be ours.

A great many Christians seem to think that all their heavenly Father wants is a chance to make them miserable and to take away all their blessings. They imagine, poor people, that if they hold on to things in their own will, they can hinder Him from doing this.

Better and sweeter than health, friends, money, fame, ease, or prosperity is the will of our God. It gilds the darkest hours with a divine halo and sheds brightest sunshine on the gloomiest paths. He always reigns who has made it his kingdom, and nothing can go amiss to him.

The first step into the life hid with Christ in God is that of entire consecration. You must do it gladly, thankfully, and en-

thusiastically. You will find it the happiest place you have ever
entered. (*SEC*, 49, 51)

FEBRUARY 3
UNDERSTANDING GOD

The only thing that can bring unfailing joy to the soul is to
understand and know God. Everything for us depends on what
He is. He has created us and put us in our present environment,
and we are absolutely in His power. If He is good and kind, we
will be well cared for and happy; if He is cruel and wicked, we
will be miserable. Just as the welfare of any possession depends
on the character, temper, and knowledge of its owner, so does
our welfare depend on the character, temper, and knowledge of
God.

The child of a drinking father can never find any lasting joy
in material possessions, for at any minute the father may destroy
them all. A good father would be infinitely more to the child
than the most costly possessions. Similarly, none of our possessions would be of the slightest worth to us if we were under the
dominion of a cruel and wicked God. Therefore, for us to have
any lasting joy, we must come to the place where we understand
and know "the Lord which exerciseth loving-kindness, judgment, and righteousness, in the earth" (Jer. 9:24). (*EDR*, 82)

FEBRUARY 4
KNOWING IS REJOICING

We must have a clear comprehension of what spiritual joy and
gladness really are. Some people seem to look on spiritual joy
as a thing, a sort of lump or package of joy, stored away in one's
heart to be looked at and rejoiced over. But joy is not a thing at
all: it is only the gladness that comes from the possession of
something good or the knowledge of something pleasant. The
Christian's joy is simply his gladness in knowing Christ and in
his possession of such a God and Savior. We do not on an earthly
plane rejoice in our joy but in the thing that causes our joy. And
on the heavenly plane it is the same. We are not to rejoice in our

joy, but we are to "rejoice in the LORD, and joy in the God of our salvation" (Hab. 3:18, para.). No man or devil can take this joy from us, and no earthly sorrows can touch it.

All the spiritual writers of past generations have recognized this joy in God, and all of them have written concerning the stripping process that seems necessary to bring us to it. They have called this process by different names—"inward desolation," "winter of the soul," "dispensation of darkness"—all meaning the same thing, which is the experience of finding all earthly joys strained or taken away in order to drive the soul to God alone. (*EDR*, 91)

FEBRUARY 5
THANKING, NOT DESPAIRING

It is not because things are good, but because He is good, that we are to thank the Lord. We are not wise enough to judge whether some things are really, in their essence, joys or sorrows; but we always know that the Lord is good and that His goodness makes it absolutely certain that everything He provides or permits must be good and must therefore be something for which we would be heartily thankful if only we could see it with His eyes.

The trouble is that very often God's gifts come to us wrapped up in such rough coverings that we are tempted to reject them as worthless; or the messengers who bring them come in the guise of enemies, and we want to shut the door against them and not give them entrance. But we lose far more than we know when we reject even the most unlikely.

We are commanded to enter into God's gates with thanksgiving and into His courts with praise (Ps. 100:4), and I am convinced that the giving of thanks is the key that opens these gates more quickly than anything else.

The last verse of the Book of Psalms, taken in connection with the vision of John in the Book of Revelation, is very significant. The psalmist says, "Let every thing that hath breath praise the LORD" (Ps. 150:6). In the Book of Revelation, John tells us that he heard this: "And every creature which is in heaven, and on the earth, and under the earth, and such as are in the sea, and all that are in them, heard I saying, Blessing, and honour, and glory, and power, be unto him that sitteth upon the throne, and unto the Lamb, for ever and ever'' (Rev. 5:13). (*GAC*, 215–21)

FEBRUARY 6
BELIEVING IS KNOWING

You say, ''But how am I to get to know Him? Other people seem to have some kind of inward revelations that make them know Him, but I never do; and no matter how much I pray, everything seems dark to me. I want to know God, but I do not see how to do it.''

Your trouble is that you have a wrong idea of what knowing God is—or, at least, the kind of knowing I am referring to. For I do not mean any mystical interior revelations. Such revelations are delightful when one has them, but they are not always at your command, and they are often variable and uncertain. The kind of knowing I mean is the plain matter-of-fact knowledge of God's nature and character that comes to us by believing what is revealed to us in the Bible concerning Him.

It is believing the thing that is written, not the thing that is inwardly revealed, that gives life; and the kind of knowing I mean is the knowing that comes from believing the things that are written.

When I read in the Bible that God is love, I am to believe it just because it is written, and not because I have had any inward revelation that it is true. When the Bible says that He cares for us as He cares for the lilies of the field and the birds of the air (Matt. 6:26–29), and that the very hairs of our heads are all numbered (Matt. 10:30), I am to believe it, just because it is written, regardless of whether I have any inward revelation of it or not. (*GAC*, 6–7)

FEBRUARY 7
READING AND KNOWING

It is of vital importance for us to understand that the Bible is a book not of theories but of actual facts. Things are not true because they are in the Bible, but they are only in the Bible because they are true. A little boy said to his father one day, "If I had been Columbus I would not have taken all that trouble to discover America." "Why, what would you have done?" asked the father. "Oh," replied the little boy, "I would just have gone to the map and found it." This little boy did not understand that maps are only pictures of known places. He failed to see that America did not exist because it was on the map and that it could not be on the map until it was known to exist. The Bible, like the map, is a simple statement of facts. When it tells us that God loves us, it is only telling us something that is a fact and would not be in the Bible if it had not been known to be a fact.

It was a great discovery to me when I grasped this idea. It seemed to take all uncertainty and speculation out of the revelation given us in the Bible of the salvation of the Lord Jesus Christ. It made all that is written concerning Him to be simply a statement of incontrovertible facts. Inward revelations we cannot manage, but anyone can believe the thing that is written. Although this may seem very dry and bare to start with, it will, if steadfastly persevered in, result in very blessed inward revelations and will sooner or later lead us out into such a knowledge of God that it will transform our lives. (*GAC*, 7–8)

FEBRUARY 8
WILLING AND BELIEVING

The Bible is God's own book, containing an authoritative and inspired record of His mind and His ways. We must come to it, then, with this one thought: He has spoken and we must believe. Whether we understand it or not, is no matter; whether its revelations look reasonable or consistent or even possible, is of no account. He has spoken, and we must believe what He says.

Where we cannot understand, we must set it down to our limited power of comprehension and be content to wait until the eyes of our understanding are enlightened by the divine Spirit.

I do not mean, however, to ignore or look down on the honest doubts of earnest seekers. I know from my own experience that they must be met with loving sympathy rather than with scoldings or contemptuous condemnation. If it will help any soul in this direction, I am quite willing to confess that the difficulties and questionings of the generation to which I belong have not left me unmolested. I know what it is to have been compelled to lift up the shield of faith against many an assault of doubt that has come like an army to overwhelm me.

But I have never found argument to help me here. The Devil can outargue any human reasoner in a debate of this kind and is likely to come off as the conqueror. Doubts are to be overcome not by reasoning but by faith. "I will believe; I choose to believe," have been the weapons with which I have conquered in many a fierce battle. For the will has far more to do with our believing than most people think. (*OTT*, 7–8)

FEBRUARY 9
BELIEVING BY CHOOSING

The will is king in our nature, and what the will decides, all else must submit to and follow. If we shall will to believe, turning resolutely away from every suggestion of doubt, we cannot fail to get the victory in the end.

This will sound unreasonable to human philosophy, but nevertheless it is a fact, and to me it is a fact that attests the divinity of the Bible more than anything else. For unless the Bible is a divine book, no effort of will in believing it, after once doubts have entered, will amount to anything at all. When once we have cause to doubt a friend, no effort of will to trust again will help us. In all human relations we must have proofs of trustworthiness before we can trust. If the Bible were a human book, it would require human proofs of its authenticity and authority before it could be believed or rested on. But to believe God, requires no proofs and no reasonings, only a choice of the will. For when the will is put on His side, He takes possession of it by His Holy Spirit. In an omnipotent way and independent of any proofs, He convinces the soul of the truth of that which it has chosen to believe.

This may seem like stepping off of a precipice into an apparently bottomless abyss. But it is safe to step because God is there and will receive us. Because God is, and is in His truth, there is no risk. Whoever will do His will, shall sooner or later know of the doctrine (see John 7:17). (*OTT*, 8–9)

FEBRUARY 10
COMFORTING IN MOURNING

The God who exists is the God who so loved the world that He sent His Son not to judge the world but to save it (John 3:16–17). He is the God who "anointed" the Lord Jesus Christ "to bind up the brokenhearted, to proclaim liberty to the captives, and the opening of the prison to them that are bound; . . . and to comfort all that mourn" (Isa. 61:1–2). Please notice the word "all." He comforts not only a few select ones, but all. Every captive of sin, every prisoner in infirmity, every mourning heart must be included in this "all." It would not be "all" if even one were left out, no matter how insignificant or unworthy or even feeble-minded that one might be.

I have always been thankful that the feeble-minded are especially mentioned by St. Paul in his exhortations to the Thessalonian Christians when he is urging them to comfort one another. In effect he says, "Do not scold the feeble-minded, but comfort them" (cf. 1 Thess. 5:14). The very ones who need comfort most are the ones God wants to comfort—not the strong-minded ones but the feeble-minded.

This is the glory of a religion of love, the religion of the Lord Jesus Christ. The "God of all comfort" (2 Cor. 1:3) sent His Son to be the Comforter of a mourning world. Throughout His life on earth He fulfilled His divine mission. When His disciples asked Him to call down fire from heaven to consume some people who refused to receive Him, He turned and rebuked them (Luke 9:54–55). He welcomed Mary Magdalene when all men turned from her. Always and everywhere He was on the side of sinners. He came to save sinners. He had no other mission. (*GAC*, 30–31)

FEBRUARY 11
TRUSTING, NOT FEELING

Some people can never believe that God loves them when their circumstances are contrary. If we rely on circumstances, in the slightest degree, as the groundwork of our confidence or our joy, we are sure to come to grief.

What I mean is that we are to hold ourselves absolutely independent of circumstances, resting only in the magnificent fact that God as our Savior is sufficient. Our inner life prospers just as well and is just as triumphant without ecstatic personal experiences or great personal doings. We are to find God, the fact of God, sufficient for all our spiritual needs, whether we feel ourselves to be in a desert or in a fertile valley. We are to say with the prophet, ''Although the fig tree shall not blossom, neither shall fruit be in the vines; the labour of the olive shall fail, and the fields shall yield no meat; the flock shall be cut off from the fold, and there shall be no herd in the stall: yet I will rejoice in the LORD, I will joy in the God of my salvation'' (Hab. 3:17–18).

The soul is made for this and can never find rest short of it. All God's dealings with us are shaped to this end; if necessary, He is obliged to deprive us of all joy in everything else in order that He may force us to find our joy only in himself. (*GAC*, 246)

Joy in Him

FEBRUARY 12
BELIEVING, NOT EARNING

All Spiritual things by faith divine God

Faith is the only door into the kingdom of heaven, and there is no other. If we will not go in by the door, we cannot get in at all, for there is no other way.

God's salvation is not a purchase to be made, nor wages to be earned, nor a summit to be climbed, nor a task to be accomplished; it is simply and only a gift to be accepted and can only be accepted by faith. Faith is a necessary element in the acceptance of any gift, whether earthly or heavenly. My friends may put their gifts on my table or even place them in my lap, but unless I believe in their friendliness and honesty of purpose enough to accept their gifts, the gifts can never become really mine.

It is therefore plain that the Bible is simply announcing, as it always does, the nature of things, when it declares that "according to your faith" it shall be unto you (Matt. 9:29). The sooner we settle down to this the better. All our wavering comes from the fact that we do not believe in this law. We acknowledge of course that it is in the Bible, but we think it cannot really mean what it says, that there must be some additions made to it, such as, for instance, "according to our fervency it shall be unto us," or "according to our importunity," or "according to our worthiness." We are inclined to think that these additions of ours are by far the most important part of the whole matter. Consequently, our attention is mostly directed to getting these matters settled, and we overlook the one fundamental principle of faith, without which nothing can be done. (*GAC*, 165–66)

FEBRUARY 13
WAVERING AND DOUBTING

Can't
fight A
Giant

A wavering Christian trusts in the love of God one day and doubts it the next, and is thus alternately happy and miserable. He mounts to the hilltop of joy at one time, only to descend at another time into the valley of despair. He is driven to and fro by every wind of doctrine, is always striving and never attaining, and is a prey to each changing circumstance, such as his health, influences around him, and even the weather.

You would suppose that even the most ignorant child of God would know that to waver in one's faith after such a fashion is wrong, that it dishonors the Lord, impugning His truth and faithfulness. But there are many Christians whose eyes are so blinded in the matter that they actually think this tendency to waver is a tribute to the humility of their spirits. They exalt every fresh attack of doubt into a secret and most pious virtue.

A wavering Christian will say complacently, "Oh, I am so unworthy; I am sure it is right for me to doubt," and he will imply by his tone of superiority that his hearer, if truly humble, would doubt also. In fact, I knew one devoted Christian whose religious life was one long torment of doubt. Once after I had been urging him to have more faith, he said to me in solemn earnestness, ''My dear friend, if once I should be so presumptuous as to feel sure that God loved me, I should be certain I was on the direct road to hell.''

What a misapprehension of God's will for us! (*GAC*, 159–60)

FEBRUARY 14
ENDING WAVERING

doubting) sin
wavering)

The one question for all whose faith wavers is how to put an end at once and forever to wavering. I am thankful to say that I know a perfect remedy. The only thing you have to do is to *give it up*. Your wavering is caused by your doubting. Give up your doubting, and your wavering will stop. Keep on with your doubting, and your wavering will continue. The whole matter is as simple as day and night; and the choice is in your own hands.

Perhaps you may think this is an extreme statement, for it has probably never entered into your mind that you could give up doubting altogether. But you can. You can simply refuse to doubt. You can shut the door against any suggestion of doubt that comes and can by faith declare exactly the opposite. Your doubt says, ''God does not forgive my sins.'' Your faith must say, ''He does forgive me; He says He does, and I choose to believe Him. I am His forgiven child.'' You must assert this steadfastly until all your doubts vanish. You have no more right to say that you are of such a doubting nature that you cannot help doubting, than to say you are of such a thieving nature that you cannot help thieving. One is as easily controlled as the other. You must give up your doubting just as you would give up your thieving. You must treat the temptation to doubt exactly as an alcoholic must treat the temptation to drink: you must take a pledge against it. (*GAC*, 167–68)

FEBRUARY 15
SURRENDERING OUR DOUBTING

To be free from unbelief, the most effectual process is to lay our doubts, just as we lay our other sins, on God's altar and make a total surrender of them. We must give up all liberty to doubt and must consecrate our power of believing to Him. We must trust Him to keep us trusting. We must make our faith in His Word as inevitable and necessary a thing as is our obedience to His will. We must be as loyal to our heavenly Friend as we are to our earthly friends, refusing to question His love or His faithfulness, and putting our absolute faith in His Word.

Of course temptations to waver will come, and it will sometimes seem impossible that the Lord can love such disagreeable, unworthy beings as we feel ourselves to be. But we must turn as deaf an ear to these insinuations against the love of God as we would to any insinuations against the love of our dearest friend. The fight to do this may sometimes be severe and may even seem almost unendurable. But our declaration must continually be, "Though he slay me, yet will I trust in him" (Job 13:15). Our steadfast faith will unfailingly bring us, sooner or later, a glorious victory. (*GAC*, 168)

FEBRUARY 16
PARTAKING AND CONFORMING

In order to become conformed to the image of Christ, we must of necessity be made "partakers of the divine nature" (2 Peter 1:4). Our tastes, our wishes, our purposes, will become like Christ's tastes, wishes, and purposes; we will see things as He sees them. This is inevitable; for where the divine nature is, its fruit cannot fail to be manifest; and, where it is not manifest, we are forced to conclude that that individual, no matter how loud his profession, has not yet been made a partaker of the divine nature.

I can hear someone asking, "But do you really mean to say that, in order to be made partakers of the divine nature, we must

35

cease from our own efforts entirely and must simply by faith put on Christ, letting Him live in us and work in us to will and to do of His good pleasure? And do you believe He will then actually do it?"

Yes, I mean just that. I mean that if we abandon ourselves entirely to Him, He comes to abide in us and is himself our life. We must commit our whole lives to Him—our thoughts, our words, our daily walk, our downsittings, our uprisings. By faith we must abandon ourselves and, as it were, move over into Christ and abide in Him. By faith we must put off the old man, and by faith we must put on the new man (cf. Col. 3:9–10). By faith we must reckon ourselves dead unto sin and alive unto God—as truly dead as alive (cf. Rom. 6:11). By faith we must realize that our daily life is Christ living in us; and, ceasing from our own works, we must suffer Him to work in us to will and to do of His good pleasure (cf. Phil. 2:13). (*GAC*, 238–39)

FEBRUARY 17
WORKING AND PERFECTING

No longer is it truth about Christ that must fill our hearts, but it is himself, the living, loving, glorious Christ. If we let Him, he will make us His dwelling place, to reign and rule within us and "subdue all things unto himself" (Phil. 3:21).

It was no mere figure of speech when our Lord, in His wonderful Sermon on the Mount, said to His disciples, "Be ye . . . perfect, even as your Father which is in heaven is perfect" (Matt. 5:48). He meant the reality of being conformed to His image to which we have been predestined. In the Epistle to the Hebrews we are shown how that reality is to be brought about. "Now the God of peace, that brought again from the dead our Lord Jesus, that great shepherd of the sheep, through the blood of the everlasting covenant, make you perfect in every good work to do his will; working in you that which is well-pleasing in his sight, through Jesus Christ: to whom be glory for ever and ever. Amen" (Heb. 13:20–21).

It is to be by His working in us, not by our working in ourselves, that this purpose of God in our creation is to be accomplished. If it looks that some of us are too far removed from any

36

conformity to the image of Christ for such a transformation ever to be wrought, we must remember that our Maker is not done making us yet. The day will come when the work begun in Genesis will be finished in Revelation. The whole creation, as well as ourselves, will be "delivered from the bondage of corruption into the glorious liberty of the children of God" (Rom. 8:21). (*GAC*, 239–40)

[handwritten: christ alone!]

FEBRUARY 18
WAITING AND TRUSTING

[handwritten: desires Him alone!]

Most Christians have sung more often than they could count, these words in one of our most familiar hymns: "Thou, O Christ, art all I want, More than all in Thee I find." But I doubt whether all of us could honestly say that the words have expressed any reality in our own experience. Christ has not been all we want. We have wanted fervent feelings about Him or realizations of His presence with us or an inner revelation of His love; or else we have demanded satisfactory schemes of doctrine or successful Christian work or something of one sort or another. Jesus Christ himself, Christ alone, without the addition of any of our experiences concerning Him, has not been enough for us, in spite of all our singing.

In Old Testament times the psalmist said, "My soul, wait thou only upon God; for my expectation is from him" (Ps. 62:5). But now the Christian says, "Soul, wait on my sound doctrines, for my expectation is from them"; or, "Soul, wait on my good frames and feelings, or on my righteous works, or on my fervent prayers, or on my earnest striving, for my expectation is from these." To wait on God only seems one of the most unsafe things they can do, and to have their expectation from Him alone seems like building on the sand. They reach out on every side for something to depend on, and not until everything else fails will they put their trust in God alone. George Macdonald says: "We look upon God as our last and feeblest resource. We only go to Him when we have nowhere else to go. And then we learn that the storms of life have driven us, not upon the rocks, but into the desired haven." (*GAC*, 243–44)

[handwritten: Storms of Life - take us there]

FEBRUARY 19
BEING AND PROMISING

We say sometimes, "If I could only find a promise to fit my case, I could then be at rest." But promises may be misunderstood or misapplied, and at the moment when we are leaning all our weight on them, they may seem utterly to fail us. But the Promiser, who is behind His promises and is infinitely more than His promises, can never fail or change. The young child does not need to have any promises from his mother to make him content; he has his mother herself, and she is enough. His mother is better than a thousand promises.

In our highest ideal of love or friendship, promises do not enter. One party may love to make promises, just as our Lord does, but the other party does not need them; the personality of lover or friend is better than all his promises. Should every promise be wiped out of the Bible, we would still have God left, and God would be enough. Again I repeat it: Only God, He himself just as He is, without the addition of anything on our part, whether it be feelings, experiences, good works, sound doctrines, or any other thing either outward or inward, is enough.

I do not mean by this that we are not to have feelings or experiences or good works or sound doctrines. We may have all of these, but they must be the result of salvation and never the procuring cause, and they can never be depended on as being any indication of our spiritual condition. They are all things that come and go and are often dependent on our health, our surroundings, or even the direction of the wind. (*GAC*, 244–45)

FEBRUARY 20
REJOICING WITHOUT FEELING

It is all very well, perhaps, to rejoice in God's promises or in the revelations He may have granted us or in the experiences we may have realized; but to rejoice in the Promiser himself—Him alone—is the crowning point of Christian life. This is the only place we can know the peace which passes all understanding and where nothing can disturb.

It is difficult to explain just what I mean. We have so accustomed ourselves to consider all these accompaniments of the spiritual life as being the spiritual life itself, that it is hard to detach ourselves from them. And when we talk about finding our all in God, we generally mean that we find it in our feelings or our views about Him. If, for instance, we feel a glow of love toward Him, then we can say heartily that He is enough; but when this glow fails, as sooner or later it is almost sure to do, then we no longer feel that we have found our all in Him. The truth is that what satisfies us is not the Lord but our own feelings about the Lord. But we are not conscious of this, and consequently when our feelings fail, we think it is the Lord who has failed, and we are plunged into darkness.

Of course, all this is very foolish, but it is such a common experience, that very few can see how foolish it is. (*GAC*, 246–47)

FEBRUARY 21
LOVING IS BINDING

There are many relations in life that require from the different parties only very moderate degrees of devotion. We may have pleasant friendships with one another yet spend a large part of our lives in separate interests and widely differing pursuits. When together, we may greatly enjoy one another and find many congenial points; but separation is not any special distress to us, and other and more intimate friendships do not interfere. There is not enough love between us to give us either the right or the desire to enter into and share one another's most private affairs. A certain degree of reserve and distance seems to be the suitable thing in such relations as these.

But there are other relations in life where all this is changed. The friendship becomes love. The two hearts give themselves to each other, to be no longer two, but one. A union of soul takes place, making all that belongs to one the property of the other. Separate interests and separate paths in life are no longer possible. Things that were lawful before become unlawful now because of the nearness of the tie that binds. The reserve and distance suitable to mere friendship become fatal in love. Love gives all and must have all in return. The wishes of one become binding obligations to the other, and the deepest desire of each heart is that it may know every secret wish or longing of the other, in order that it may fly on the wings of the wind to gratify it. (*SEC*, 211–12)

FEBRUARY 22
TRUSTING, NOT CARING

What are the characteristics of a young child, and how does he live? He lives by faith, and his chief characteristic is freedom from care. His life is one long trust from year's end to year's end. He trusts his parents, he trusts his teachers; he sometimes even trusts people who are utterly unworthy of trust. And this trust is abundantly answered. The child provides nothing for himself, yet everything is provided. He takes no thought for the morrow and forms no plans, yet all his life is planned out for him, and he finds his paths made ready, opening out as he comes to them day by day and hour by hour.

Who is the best cared for in every household? Isn't it the children? And doesn't the least of all, the helpless baby, receive the largest share? The baby doesn't toil or spin, yet he is fed, clothed, loved, and rejoiced in more tenderly than the hardest worker.

The life of faith, then, consists in just this—being a child in the Father's house. This is enough to transform every weary, burdened life into one of blessedness and rest. Leaving yourselves in His hands, learn to be literally "careful for nothing," and you will find that the peace of God which passes all understanding will keep (as within a garrison) your hearts and minds through Christ Jesus (Phil. 4:6–7). (*SEC*, 43–44)

FEBRUARY 23
WALKING AND TRUSTING

It may be you have not passed this way before; but today it is your happy privilege to prove, as never before, your loyal confidence in Jesus, by starting out with Him on a life and walk of faith lived moment by moment in absolute and childlike trust in Him.

You have trusted Him in a few things, and He has not failed you. Trust Him now for everything and see if He does not do for you exceeding abundantly, above all that you could ever have asked or even thought, not according to your power or capacity, but according to His own mighty power, working in you all the good pleasure of His most blessed will.

It is not hard, you find, to trust the management of the universe and all of the outward creation to the Lord. Can your case then be so much more complex and difficult than these, that you need to be anxious or troubled about His management of you? Away with such unworthy doubtings! Take your stand on the power and trustworthiness of your God and see how quickly all difficulties will vanish before a steadfast determination to believe.

Trust in the dark, trust in the light, trust at night, and trust in the morning, and you will find that the faith that may perhaps begin by a mighty effort, will sooner or later become the natural habit of the soul. It is a law of the spiritual life that every act of trust makes the next act less difficult, until at length, if these acts are persisted in, trusting becomes, like breathing, the natural unconscious action of the redeemed soul. (*SEC*, 76–77)

FEBRUARY 24
SAVING FROM SINNING

When the angel of the Lord appeared to Joseph in a dream to announce the coming birth of the Savior, he said, "And thou shalt call his name Jesus: for he shall save his people from their sins" (Matt. 1:21).

When Zacharias was "filled with the Holy Ghost, and prophesied" at the birth of his son (Luke 1:67), he declared that God had visited his people in order to fulfill the promise and the oath He had made them, "that he would grant unto us, that we being delivered out of the hand of our enemies might serve him without fear, in holiness and righteousness before him, all the days of our life" (vv. 74–75).

When Peter was preaching in the porch of the temple to the wondering Jews, he said, "Unto you first, God, having raised up his Son Jesus, sent him to bless you in turning away every one of you from his iniquities" (Acts 3:26).

It is sometimes overlooked that in the declarations concerning the death of Christ, far more mention is made of a present salvation from sin than of a future salvation in heaven beyond, showing plainly God's estimate of the relative importance of these two things.

Can we for a moment suppose that the holy God who hates sin in the sinner is willing to tolerate it in the Christian and that He has even arranged the plan of salvation in such a way as to make it impossible for those who are saved from the guilt of sin to find deliverance from its power? (SEC, 18–21)

FEBRUARY 25
WILLING AND OBEYING

The true kingdom of God within us can only be set up in the region of our will. It is not a question of splendid talents, great deeds, fervent emotions, or wonderful illuminations; it is simply to will what God wills, always and in everything without reservation. We have nothing under our own control but our wills. Our feelings are controlled by many other things—our health, the weather, the influence of other personalities on us—but our will is our own. All that lies in our power is the direction of our will. The important question is not what we feel or what we experience, but whether we will whatever God wills. This was the crowning glory of Christ: that His will was set to do the will of His Father.

Francois Fenelon says: "I do not ask from you a love that is tender and emotional; but only that your will should lean towards love. The purest of all loves is a will so filled with the will of God that there remains nothing else." We "delight" to do the will of God, not because our piety is so exalted, but because we have the sense to see that His will is the best; and therefore what He wants we want also. This sort of delight, while it may not be as pleasing to ourselves, is far more satisfactory to Him than any amount of delight in joyous emotions or gratifying illuminations. (*EDR*, 74–75)

FEBRUARY 26
HIS WILLING IS BLESSING

The apostle Paul tells us that the will of God is "good, and acceptable, and perfect" (Rom. 12:2). The will of a good God cannot help being "good." In fact, it must be perfect. When we come to know this, we always find it "acceptable"; that is, we come to love it. I am convinced that all trouble about submitting to the will of God would disappear if once we could see clearly that His will is good. We struggle and struggle in vain to submit to a will that we do not believe to be good, but when we see that it is good, we submit to it with delight. We want it to be accomplished. Our hearts spring out to meet it.

> *I worship you, sweet Will of God!*
>   *And all your ways adore;*
> *And, every day I live, I seem*
>   *To love you more and more.*
>
> *I love to kiss each print where you*
>   *Have set your unseen feet;*
> *I cannot fear your blessèd Will!*
>   *Your empire is so sweet.* (*GAC*, 101–2)

FEBRUARY 27
SURRENDERING, NOT DESTROYING

Someone will ask whether we are not told to give up our wills. To this I answer yes. But in giving up our wills we are not meant to become empty of will power, to be left poor, flabby, nerveless creatures who have no will. We are simply meant to substitute for our own foolish misdirected wills of ignorance and immaturity, the perfect, beautiful, and wise will of God. It is not will power in the abstract we are to give up, but our misguided use of that will power. The will we are to give up is our will as it is misdirected and so separated from God's will, not our will when it is one with God's will. For when our will is in harmony with His, it would be wrong for us to give it up.

The child is required to give up the misdirected will that belongs to him as an ignorant child, and we cannot let him say ''I will'' or ''I will not,'' but when his will is in harmony with ours, we want him to say ''I will'' or ''I will not'' with all the force of which he is capable.

Our will is a piece of splendid machinery, a sort of governor, such as in a steam engine to regulate the working of the steam; everything depends on the intelligence that guides its action— our ignorance or God's wisdom. As long as our own ignorance is the guide, the whole machinery is sure to go wrong, and it is dangerous for us to say ''I will'' or ''I will not.'' But when we have surrendered the working of our wills to God, we are letting Him work in us ''to will and to do of his good pleasure'' (Phil. 2:13). (*EDR*, 75–76)

FEBRUARY 28
WILLING IS ASSURING

''Doing the will of God from the heart'' (Eph. 6:6) is the only kind of doing His will that is of any value. The soul who has surrendered his will to God, is the only soul who can do His will ''from the heart.'' It is for this reason that we say that the essence of true virtue consists, not in the state of our emotions nor in the greatness of our illuminations nor in the multitude of our good works, but simply and only in the attitude of the will.

The practical bearing of all this on our religious experience is of vital importance. We are so accustomed to consider the state of our emotions as being the deciding test of our religious life, that we very often neglect to notice the state of our will. The moment, however, that we recognize that the will is king, our common sense will teach us to disregard the clamor of our emotions and claim as real the decision of our will, however contrary it may be to the voice of our emotions.

The real thing in your experience is not the verdict of your emotions but the verdict of your will. You are far more in danger of hypocrisy and untruth in yielding to the assertions of your feelings than in holding fast to the decisions of your will. If your will then at bottom is on God's side, you are no hypocrite at this moment in claiming your position as belonging altogether to Him and as being entirely submitted to His control, even though your feelings may all declare the contrary. (*EDR*, 76–78)

FEBRUARY 29
WILLING OVER FEELING

We must *choose*, without any regard to the state of our emotions, what attitude our will will take toward God. We must recognize that our emotions are only the servants of our will (which is the real interior king in our being), and that it is the attitude, not of the servant but of the master that is important. Is our choice deliberately made on God's side? Is our will given up to Him? Does our will decide to believe and obey Him? Are we "steadfastly minded" to serve Him and follow Him? If this is the case, then, no matter what our feelings may be, we ourselves are given up to Him, we ourselves decide to believe, we ourselves decide to obey. For my will is myself, and what my will chooses, I choose.

Your attitude toward God is as real where only the will acts as when every emotion coincides. It does not seem as real to us, but in God's sight it is as real, and often I think all the more real, because it is unencumbered with a lot of unmanageable feelings. When, therefore, this wretched feeling of unreality or hypocrisy comes, do not be troubled by it. It is only in the region of your emotions and means nothing, except perhaps that your digestion is out of order or that there is an east wind blowing. Simply see to it that your will is in God's hands; that your true inward personality is abandoned to His working; that your choice, your decision, is on His side; and there leave it. (*EDR*, 79–80)

MARCH 1
WILLING AND CONTROLLING

Our will can control our feelings if only we are steadfastly minded to do so. Many times when my feelings have declared contrary to the facts, I have changed those feelings entirely by a steadfast assertion of their opposite. Similarly, I have been able many times to control my rebellious feelings against the will of God by a steadfast assertion of my choice to accept and submit to His will. Sometimes it has seemed to drain my lips of all the will power I possessed to say, ''Thy will be done,'' so contrary has it been to the evidence of my senses or emotions. But invariably, sooner or later, the victory has come. God has taken possession of the will thus surrendered to Him and has worked in me to will and to do of His good pleasure (cf. Phil. 2:13).

Surging emotions—like a tossing vessel, which by degrees yields to the steady pull of the anchor—finding themselves attached to the mighty power of God by the choice of your will, must sooner or later give allegiance to Him. (*EDR*, 80)

MARCH 2
KNOWING, NOT WAVERING

In our moments of spiritual exaltation we may sometimes seem to ourselves to have great wisdom, strength, or spiritual riches of one kind or another in which to glory; but when we come down from the ''mount of vision'' into the humdrum routine of everyday life, these grand spiritual possessions all seem to disappear, and we are left with nothing of them to glory in.

God alone is unchangeable; what we call "spiritual blessings" are full of the element of change. The prayer that is answered today may seem to be unanswered tomorrow; the promises once so gloriously fulfilled may cease to have any apparent fulfillment; the spiritual blessing that was at one time such a joy may be utterly lost; and nothing of all we once trusted in and rested on may be left but the hungry and longing memory of it all. But when all else is gone, God is still left. Nothing changes Him. He is "the same yesterday, and to day, and for ever" (Heb. 13:8), and in Him "is no variableness, neither shadow of turning" (James 1:17). The soul who finds his joy in Him alone can suffer no wavering.

To rejoice in the Lord is not a pious fiction, nor is it merely a religious phrase. Neither is it anything mysterious or awe-inspiring. It is just good plain commonsense happiness and comfort. It is something people around us can see and be glad about. When we are cast down, everything is a burden; when we are happy, we feel equal to anything. (*EDR*, 82–83, 87)

MARCH 3
DISCIPLINING FOR REJOICING

Our souls are of such a divine origin that no other joy but God can ever satisfy them. God made the soul for this high destiny, and His object, therefore, in all the discipline and training of life, is to bring us to the place where we will find our joy in Him alone. For this purpose He is obliged often to stain our pleasant pictures and thwart and disappoint our brightest anticipations. He detaches us from all else that He may attach us to himself, not from an arbitrary will, but because He knows that only so can we be really happy. I do not mean by this that it will be necessary for all one's friends to die or for all one's money to be lost; but I do mean that the soul will find itself, either from inward or outward causes, desolate and bereft and empty of all comfort, except in God. We must come to the end of everything that is not God in order to find our joy in God alone.

For every soul there must come a time to say, "Lo, this is [my] God; [I] have waited for him, . . . [I] will be glad and rejoice in his salvation" (Isa. 25:9). Through all the experiences of life this is what we are waiting for, and all our training and discipline is to lead us to this. I say "waiting for," not in the sense of any delay on God's part, but because of the delay on our own part. God is always seeking to make himself our "exceeding joy" (Ps. 43:4), but until we have been detached from all earthly joys and are ready to find our joy in Him alone, we must still wait for Him. We think that the delay is altogether on His part, but in reality it is He who waits for us. (*EDR*, 87–89)

MARCH 4
CHASTENING BUT LOVING

We think of punishment as retribution or vengeance. But God's idea of punishment is the parental idea of chastening. To chasten means, according to Webster, "to inflict pain upon anyone in order to purify from errors or faults." God's chastening, therefore, is for purifying, not vengeance. "Whom he loves he chastens" (Heb. 12:6, para.), not whom He hates, or whom He is angry with. The purpose of our chastisement, therefore, is plainly that we may be made "partakers of his holiness" (v. 10). In other words, it is for character building, which is to us the most important thing in the whole universe. What happens to me is of no account compared to what I am. If I will only pay attention to what God is trying to teach me through chastisement, I will see that no present ease, comfort, or absence of trial is to be weighed for a moment against the building up of character for eternity.

Anything that is to do such a wonderful thing for us as to work out a "far more exceeding and eternal weight of glory" (2 Cor. 4:17) cannot be counted otherwise than as a blessing. All affliction would be so counted, I am very sure, if we had but eyes to see its outcome. The marble may quiver and shrink from the heavy blows of the mallet, but there can be nothing but joy and rejoicing over the beautiful statue that is wrought thereby. (*EDR*, 96–97)

or marble statue

48

MARCH 5
REFINING AND LOVING

To refine something does not mean to punish it, but only to purify it, to get rid of all its dross and rubbish and to bring out its full beauty and worth. It is a blessing, not a curse. Instead of its being something God demands of us, it really is something we ought to demand of God. We have a right to be made as pure as God can make us. He created us, and we have a right to demand that He make of us the best He can. It is His duty to burn up our dross and bring out our full beauty and worth. Love demands that He should.

George Macdonald speaks some strong words concerning this: "Man has a claim on God, a Divine claim for any pain, want, disappointment, or misery that will help to make him what he ought to be. He has a claim to be punished, and to be spared not one pang that may urge him toward repentance; he has a claim to be compelled to repent; to be hedged in on every side, to have one after another of the strong sheepdogs of the Great Shepherd sent after him, to thwart him in any desire, foil him in any plan, frustrate him of any hope, until he comes to see at length that nothing will ease his pain, nothing make life a thing worth having, but the presence of the living God; nothing noble enough for the desire of the heart of man but oneness with the eternal. For this God must make him yield his very being, that He himself may enter in and dwell with him." (*EDR*, 100–101)

MARCH 6
HEWING OUT BLESSING

The purpose of chastisement is to make us good. We have a right to be made good, for it is God's purpose concerning us. Let us therefore accept our trials as a part of our birthright and give thanks to the divine Potter that He has set His wheel whirring and is casting out, with a fine, separating hand, all the chips, stones, and sand that mar the perfect purity of our clay.

How changed would be the aspect of all our trials if we could see them in this light! How easy it would be to say, "Thy will be done," if we could once recognize that trouble meant only and always blessing for us! I think the psalmist understood this when he wrote that wonderful 107th Psalm, in which he tells us of how the Lord chastened Israel when they rebelled against Him and wandered away from Him, and how this chastening always brought them back to cry unto the Lord. He breaks out after each such recital with the exultant cry, "Oh that men would praise the LORD for his goodness, and for his wonderful works to the children of men!" (Ps. 107:21).

In view of all the blessings that troubles and trials have wrought for many of us, can we not also join with our whole souls in this triumphant cry? (*EDR*, 101–2)

MARCH 7
GUIDING BY THWARTING

The blessed chastening and refining work of sorrow and trouble has a higher purpose, and that is to thwart us in a course that our heavenly Father knows would be disastrous and to turn us into safer and more successful paths.

Disappointments are often direct gateways to prosperity in the very things we have thought they were going to ruin forever. Joseph's story is an illustration of this. He had the promise of a kingdom, but instead he received slavery, cruel treachery, and imprisonment. It looked as though all hope of a kingdom was over. But these very trials were the gateway into his kingdom, and in no other way could he have reached it.

God's thwartings are often our grandest opportunities. We start in a pathway that we think is going to lead us to a desired end, but God in His providence thwarts us. We then rashly conclude that all is over and give up in despair. But after a while we find that that very thwarting has been the divine opportunity for the success we desired; or, if not for just that, for a far better thing that we would infinitely rather have. He changes the very thing we thought was our sorrow into our crown of joy.

> 'Tis that I am not good—that is enough.
> I pry no farther—that is not the way.

Here, O my Potter, is Thy making stuff!
Set Thy wheel going; let it whirl and play.
The chips in me, the stones, the straws, the sand,
Cast them out with fine separating hand,
And make a vessel of Thy yielding clay. (EDR, 101)

MARCH 8
HIDING, STILL CARING

"Oh that I knew where I might find him!" (Job 23:3). This despairing cry was uttered fifteen centuries before Christ. That it should ever be uttered now, by any person who possesses the Bible and has even the slightest faith in Christ, would seem impossible if we did not know that it is only too often the cry of even Christian hearts. In fact, in the lives of many Christians, it is a great difficulty. God seems to hide himself from their longing gaze, and this hiding seems often to be in anger or in neglect. This is especially the case in our everyday lives; in the ordinary business and bustle of everyday life, we are apt to lose consciousness of God. Then, because we do not feel His presence, we think He cannot be there.

Because we cannot see the hand of God in our affairs, we rush to the conclusion that He has lost sight of them and of us. We look at the "seemings" of things and declare that because God is unseen He must necessarily be absent. This is especially the case if we are conscious of having wandered away from Him and forgotten Him. We judge Him by ourselves and think that He must have forgotten and forsaken us. We measure His truth by our falseness and find it hard to believe He can be faithful when we know ourselves to be so unfaithful. How foolish it is to make our feelings the test of God's actions, as if He comes and goes in response to the continual changes in our emotions! (*EDR*, 106–7)

MARCH 9
HIDING BUT REMEMBERING

That our emotions should determine God's response to us would turn the omnipotent, omnipresent God into a helpless puppet, pulled by the strings of our varying feelings! But this, of course, is inconceivable, for the God revealed to us in the Bible is a God who never leaves us or forgets us or neglects our interests.

God is shown to us as a tender Shepherd who performs with the utmost fidelity all a shepherd's duties. He does not forsake His sheep in the cloudy and dark day, nor desert them when the wolf comes. He always draws nearer in every time of need and goes after each wandering sheep until He finds it. The hireling flees when danger appears because he is only a hireling, but the Good Shepherd sticks closer than ever. It is impossible to imagine a good shepherd forgetting or forsaking his sheep. In fact, it is his duty to watch over them and care for them in all circumstances.

The God who is revealed to us as the "good shepherd" (John 10:14) must necessarily be as faithful to His responsibilities as an earthly shepherd is to his. His care of us may be hidden care, but it is nonetheless real, and all things in the daily events of our lives are made to work subservient to His gracious purposes toward us. He may seem to have forgotten us or neglected us, but it can never be anything but a seeming, for it would be impossible for the God who is revealed to us in the face of Jesus Christ to do such a thing. (*EDR*, 107–8)

MARCH 10
HAVING NOTHING, HAVING EVERYTHING

"I am their inheritance" (Num. 18:20, para.), God said of the tribe of Levi. What an amazing saying! No wonder the Levites were content to go without any other possessions! Having nothing, they truly possessed all things, for God was their possession! How slow we are to see that this is our privilege now, just as really as it was that of the Levites. Apart from Christ we have nothing, for moth and rust are sure to corrupt and thieves to break through and steal merely human possessions (Matt. 6:19-20). But if God is ours, then all things are eternally ours, for what belongs to God must of necessity belong to us, according to our need and measure.

When our hands are full of our own things, we cannot possibly get possession of the things of God. Only empty hands can grasp a gift, only empty vessels can receive the filling, and only the heart that is emptied of all its own things can receive the things of God.

Have any of us ever come to the place where we have honestly ceased to glory in our own possessions? Never, I believe, until we have been deprived of them. Human nature is so constituted that while it possesses anything, it can hardly help glorying in it. As long, for instance, as a Christian feels wise or strong or rich in spiritual things, that Christian will almost inevitably glory in his strength, wisdom, or riches. But if these are taken away from him, he will be driven to glory in the Lord alone simply because there will be nothing else for him to glory in. (*EDR*, 123-24)

MARCH 11
LOSING ALL, POSSESSING ALL

The contrast between our things and God's things is very striking. Our things all partake of the nature of "that which is not bread" and "that which satisfieth not" (Isa. 55:2). They are of the earth, earthy, and consequently cannot, in the very nature of things, satisfy the spirit that is from heaven.

We must lay aside our own wisdom and righteousness in order that Christ may be made wisdom and righteousness and sanctification unto us (1 Cor. 1:30). Practically, this means that if I want righteousness of any kind I must not try to get a store of it laid up within myself but must draw my supply of righteousness moment by moment from the Lord as I need it.

The loss of all things meant to Paul the gain of all things (Phil. 3:8). The loss of the nest to the young eaglet who is just learning to fly means the gain of the whole heavens for its home. The loss of our own strength means the gaining of God's strength in its place; the loss of our own wisdom means the gaining of God's wisdom; the loss of our own life means the gaining of God's life. Who would not make the exchange?

God declared to the tribe of Levi that He would be their inheritance and would give them no possession in Israel. He said that He would be their possession. Contrast His granting them no possession with His declaration that He would be their possession, and you will get a faint glimpse of what it means to have nothing yet possess all things (cf. 2 Cor. 6:10). (*EDR*, 124–29)

MARCH 12
FORSAKING FOR RETAINING

All that we have, whether outward or inward, must be forsaken if we would receive the hundredfold of God—forsaken, not in the sense of literally getting rid of everything, but in the sense of having everything only in and from the Lord. Only God knows how to take care of things as they ought to be taken care of, therefore nothing is really safe until it is handed over to His care. The most unsafe person in the universe to have charge of my things is myself; and never do I possess them so firmly as when I have transferred them into the hands of God.

Never am I so sure of my money as when I have transferred it out of my unsafe pockets into the safe custody of a trustworthy bank; and the same thing is true as regards the abandonment of all I possess into the custody of God. (*EDR*, 128–30)

MARCH 13
UNDERSTANDING CROSS-BEARING

A great deal of misunderstanding exists in regard to "taking up the cross." Most people think it means doing the will of God under a feeling of great trial, such as giving up something that we very much want to keep or performing some duty from which we exceedingly shrink. Consequently we often hear the expression used in reference to some act of obedience to what is thought

to be the will o...
and do it.'' The lo... Well, I suppose I must ...
''heavy'' this cross is. ...d accompanying sig...
   This falls far short of ...
said, ''If any man will come a... Lord really me...
take up his cross, and follow me, let him deny ...
ceivable to me that He could have m...att. 16:24). ... incon-
God was to be a hard yoke and a heavy ...hat doing the will of
God. In fact, He himself declared exactly the ...en to the child of
said that His yoke was easy and His burden light ...osite when He ...t. 11:30).
Taking up the cross, therefore, cannot mean that it is to ... hard
to do God's will. A careful study of the subject will show us that
it has a far deeper and wider significance. (*EDR*, 133)

MARCH 14
CRUCIFYING AND DYING

   As far as I can see, the cross in Scripture always means death.
The cross in connection with Christ always means the death of
Christ. The only use of the cross is to put to death, not to keep
alive. It may be a suffering death, but still it is sooner or later
death. In most cases this is manifest to everyone. Why some
have chosen to make it mean living in misery is hard to explain.
When our Lord told His disciples that they could not be His
disciples unless they took up the cross, He could not have meant
that they were to find it hard to do His will. He was, I believe,
simply expressing in figurative language that they were to be
made partakers of His death and resurrection by having their
old man crucified with Him and by living only in their new
man—in the resurrection life of the Spirit.
   To crucify means to put to death, not to keep alive in misery.
But so obscure has the subject become to the children of God,
that a great many feel as if they are crucifying self when they
are simply seating self on a pinnacle and tormenting it and making it miserable. They will undergo the most painful self-sacrifice
and call it ''taking up the cross'' (Matt. 16:24) yet will fail to
understand that the true cross consists in counting the flesh, or
the ''old man'' (Rom. 6:6), as an utterly worthless thing, fit
only to be put to death. (*EDR*, 134–37)

55

take up the cross is to die
not to live in mysery —

There is a subtle ...ent in torturing the outward self if
the inner self-life ec fed thereby. A man will make himself
a fakir if he ca_re in the glory. The flesh of man likes to
receive credi; cannot bear to be counted as dead and therefore
ignored. ~ all religions of legality the flesh has the opportunity
to be _xalted. This explains, I am sure, why there is so much
legality among Christians. If we read the Scriptures properly,
we will see that the carnal mind cannot serve God or enter into
His kingdom (cf. Rom. 8:6–8), no matter how much one may
try, by all sorts of asceticism, to make it fit.

When the apostle says here that they who are ''in the flesh''
cannot please God, he obviously does not mean that they who
are in the body cannot please God (Rom. 8:8), for it is to people
in the body that all his exhortations are addressed. The ''flesh''
here, therefore, must mean the lower nature in man, that part of
his nature that is called the ''carnal mind'' or the ''old Adam.''
It is the part of man's being that must die in order that the ''new
man'' or the spiritual nature may be born. If a caterpillar is to
become a butterfly, the only way is for the caterpillar life to die
in order that the butterfly life may evolve. And just as the caterpillar cannot live the butterfly life, so also the ''flesh,'' or
carnal nature in us cannot live the spiritual life. It is in this sense
that Paul says he is crucified with Christ (Gal. 2:20). (*EDR*,
137–38)

MARCH 16
DELIGHTING, NOT GRUDGING

If our affections are set on the will of God, we must love His
will. It is impossible that God's will should seem hard to a
person whose affections are set on it. It may be accompanied
with hard things, but in itself it must be a delight. Our Lord
could say with the psalmist David, ''I delight to do thy will, O
my God'' (Ps. 40:8), because He was dead to everything that

was contrary to His Father's will. Until our affe...
larly so set on the will of God as to delight in i...
"taken up the cross" (Matt. 16:24) in the Scriptur...

A good illustration of what I mean would be the...
takes place in the feelings of a little girl when she...
woman. As a child she loves to climb trees and make ...ud pies;
she hates to sit still and sew or learn long lessons or do hard
work. But when the little girl becomes a woman, her feelings
are reversed; she loves the things she once hated, and hates the
things she once loved. The woman "takes up the cross" to her
childish play; that is, she becomes dead to it and no longer finds
any pleasure in it. She delights in the pursuits of maturity and
leaves behind the pursuits of childhood, just as once she delighted in the pursuits of childhood and dreaded those of maturity.

There are a great many Christians who look at the Christian
life as I in my childish ignorance looked at adult life; they think
religion means to give up the things they love and to do the
things they hate. They call this "taking up the cross" and actually think God enjoys their grudging service. (*EDR*, 139–40)

MARCH 17
SUFFERING YET DELIGHTING

Grudging service is no more acceptable to God from us than
it would be to us from one another. Such an idea of the "cross"
as this is a poor substitute for the glorious truth of our death
with Christ and our resurrection into the triumphant spiritual
life hid with Christ in God. Surely, if we are born of God, we
must love the things God loves and hate the things He hates. If
we are one with Christ, it is out of the question that we should
chafe against His will or find His service hard! Is it a sign of the
highest sort of union between a husband and wife when the one
finds it a great trial to please the other? Ought it not rather to be
a joy to do so? And how much more is this true as regards our
relation to Christ?

Dying and death are definite words and can only mean that
that which is said to be "crucified," and is therefore called
dead, must be in a condition spiritually analogous to what death

...cally, that is, without life or feeling or capacity to suffer. ...erefore, the doing of God's will cannot cause suffering, for the part of the being that dislikes God's will and shrinks from doing it, is dead. Only that part is alive that loves God's will and delights to do it. (*EDR*, 140–41)

MARCH 18
DELIGHTING THROUGH DENYING

"Reckoning ourselves to be dead indeed unto sin" (cf. Rom. 6:11) is only another expression for "taking up our cross and denying ourselves" (cf. Matt. 16:24). It simply means that we are to look at ourselves as dead to the things of the flesh that once attracted us, and as alive only to the higher things of God. In other words, we are to live in the higher part of our nature instead of in the lower. There are always two attitudes of mind toward anything, between which we may choose. We may take hold of things on the plane of flesh, or we may take hold of them on the plane of spirit; and it is to do the latter that the apostle exhorts us when he tells us to reckon ourselves "alive unto God" (Rom. 6:11).

Fenelon tells us that true self-denial consists in looking at this "I," of whom we are all so fond, as a stranger in whom we take no interest. "I do not know you," we must say. "You may be the most interesting or the most ill-used person in the world, but you need not bring your tales to me, for you are a stranger to me, and I take no interest in you." If anyone objects that it is not possible to lose all interest in self after this fashion, I would ask him if he has never known what it was to be so overwhelmed by some strong emotion of love or of joy or sorrow, as to forget and deny self utterly, not even to notice what happens to self. We say at such times, "I entirely forgot myself," and what is this but to deny self in the most effectual sort of way? (*EDR*, 141–44)

MARCH 19
BLESSING IN SORROWING

Troubles come because of God's faithfulness, not, as so many seem to think, because of His unfaithfulness. We are taught this in a striking way in the story of Lazarus (John 11). Martha evidently thought their trouble had come because the Lord had failed to be present in the moment of need. "Lord," she cried, "if thou hadst been here, my brother had not died" (v. 21). But the Lord's absence had not been a mistake or an oversight. He had planned not to be there; and His absence was for a purpose of mercy.

He loved them, therefore He stayed away! It was His faithfulness, not His unfaithfulness, that permitted their sorrow to come on them without hindrance from Him. We may be sure that what was true of their sorrow is true of our sorrows also. We say in our ignorance, "If You had been here, this or that would not have gone wrong"; but if we could see into the heart of the Lord we would hear Him saying in reply, "I am glad for your sakes that I was not there" (cf. John 11:15). Love can never be glad of anything that hurts its loved ones, unless there is to come out of the hurt some infinitely greater blessing. Therefore, no matter how unlikely it may seem, hidden in every sorrow there is a blessing which would be a most grievous loss for us to miss. (*EDR*, 94–96)

MARCH 20
SERVING, NOT SEARCHING

When God's people complained that they fasted and afflicted their souls, yet He did not acknowledge them, He answered: "Is it such a fast that I have chosen? a day for a man to afflict his soul? is it to bow down his head as a bulrush, and to spread sackcloth and ashes under him? wilt thou call this a fast, and an acceptable day to the LORD?" (Isa. 58:5).

God is not pleased with the miseries of our self-examination. He does not want us to bow down our heads as a bulrush any

not self searching + afflicting. D

more than He wanted His people of old to do it. He calls on us, as He did on them, to forget our own miserable selves and to go to work to lessen the miseries of others. "Is not this the fast that I have chosen," He says, "to loose the bands of wickedness, to undo the heavy burdens, and to let the oppressed go free, and that ye break every yoke? Is it not to deal thy bread to the hungry, and that thou bring the poor that are cast out to thy house? when thou seest the naked, that thou cover him . . . ?" (Isa. 58:6–7).

Service for others is of infinitely greater value to the Lord than the longest seasons of self-examination and self-abasement. He has shown us here the surest way of deliverance out of the slough of misery, into which our habits of self-examination have plunged us. (*GAC*, 141–42)

MARCH 21
SEEING AND UNDERSTANDING

Much misunderstanding arises in reference to the life and walk of faith, because its two sides are not clearly seen. I refer, of course, to God's part and man's part in the work of sanctification. People are apt to think there is only one side and consequently have a distorted view of the matter.

Suppose two friends go to see some celebrated building and return home to describe it. One has seen only the north side, and the other only the south. The first says, "The building was built in such a manner and has such and such stories and ornaments." "Oh no," says the other, interrupting him, "you are altogether mistaken; I saw the building, and it was built in quite a different manner, and its ornaments and stories were so and so." A lively dispute might follow on the truth of the respective descriptions until the two friends discover that they have been describing different sides of the building. Then all would be reconciled at once.

There are two distinct sides to sanctification; and looking at one, without seeing the other, will be sure to create wrong views of the truth. (*SEC*, 26–27)

MARCH 22
TRUSTING, NOT TRYING

Our part is to trust, and God's part is to work. His work is to deliver us from the power of sin and make us perfect in every good work to do His will. "Beholding as in a glass the glory of the Lord," we are to be actually "changed into the same image from glory to glory even as by the Spirit of the Lord" (2 Cor. 3:18). We are to be transformed by the renewing of our minds, that we "may prove what is that good, and acceptable, and perfect, will of God" (Rom. 12:2). A positive work is to be wrought in us and on us.

Somebody must do this work. Either we must do it for ourselves, or another must do it for us. Most of us have tried to do it for ourselves and have grievously failed. Then we discovered from the Scriptures and from our own experience that it is something we are unable to do, but that the Lord Jesus Christ has come to do it and will do it for all who put themselves wholly in His hands and trust Him without reserve.

Now then, under these circumstances, what is the part of the believer, and what is the part of the Lord? Plainly the believer can do nothing but trust, while the Lord, in whom he trusts, actually does the work entrusted to Him. (*SEC*, 27–28)

MARCH 23
SURRENDERING AND DEVELOPING

Sanctification is both a step of faith and a process of works. It is a step of surrender and trust on our part, and it is a process of development on God's part. By a step of faith we get into Christ; by a process we are made to "grow up into him in all things" (Eph. 4:15). By a step of faith we put ourselves into the hands of the divine Potter; by a gradual process He makes us into a vessel unto His own honor, meet for His use, and prepared to every good work (2 Tim. 2:21).

What can be said about man's part in this great work but that he must continually surrender himself and continually trust?

61

When we come to God's side of the question, what is there that may not be said as to the manifold and wonderful ways in which He accomplishes the work entrusted to Him? It is here that the growing comes in. The lump of clay could never grow into a beautiful vessel if it stayed in the clay pit for thousands of years. But when it is put in the hands of a skillful potter it grows rapidly, under his fashioning, into the vessel he intends it to be. And in the same way the soul, abandoned to the working of the heavenly Potter, is made into a vessel of honor, sanctified and meet for the Master's use.

Having, therefore, taken the step of faith by which you have put yourself wholly and absolutely into His hands, you must now expect Him to begin to work. His way of accomplishing that which you have entrusted to Him may be different from your way; but He knows best, and you must be satisfied. (*SEC*, 30–33)

MARCH 24
GROWING AND MATURING

The maturity of a Christian experience cannot be reached in a moment, but is the result of the work of God's Holy Spirit, who, by His energizing and transforming power, causes us to grow up into Christ in all things. We cannot hope to reach this maturity in any other way than by yielding ourselves up to His mighty working. But the sanctification the Scriptures urge as a present experience for all believers does not consist in maturity of growth but in purity of heart, and it may be complete in our early, as well as later, experiences.

A baby may be all that a baby can be and may therefore perfectly please its mother; yet it is very far from being what that mother would wish it to be when the years of maturity come.

An apple in June is a perfect apple for June, the best apple that June can produce, but it is very different from an apple in October, which is a perfected apple.

God's works are perfect in every stage of their growth. Man's works are never perfect until they are in every respect complete.

All that we claim, then, in this life of sanctification is that by an act of faith we put ourselves into the hands of the Lord, and then, by a continuous exercise of faith, keep ourselves there. When we do it and while we do it, we are, in the Scripture sense, truly pleasing to God, although it may require years of training and discipline to mature us into a vessel that will be in all respects fit for every good work (see 2 Tim. 2:21). (*SEC*, 34–35)

MARCH 25
TRUSTING AND SANCTIFYING

Our part in sanctification is trusting; it is God's part to accomplish the results. When we do our part, He never fails to do His. No one ever trusted in the Lord and was confounded. Do not be afraid, then, that if you trust or tell others to trust, the matter will end there. Trust is the beginning and continuing foundation. When we trust, the Lord works, and His work is what is important.

This explains an apparent paradox that puzzles many. They say, "In one breath you tell us to do nothing but trust, and in the next you tell us to do impossible things. How can you reconcile such contradictory statements?" They are to be reconciled, just as we reconcile the statements concerning a saw in a carpenter's shop. We say at one moment that the saw has sawn a log in two, and the next moment we declare that the carpenter has done it. The saw is the instrument used; the power that uses it is the carpenter's. And so we, yielding ourselves to God, and our members as instruments of righteousness to Him, find that He works in us to will and to do of His good pleasure, and we can say with Paul, "I laboured . . . ; yet not I, but the grace of God which was with me" (1 Cor. 15:10).

In the divine order, God's working depends on our cooperation. During His earthly ministry, Jesus could do no mighty works in at least one city because of the people's unbelief. It was not that He would not, but that He could not. We often think that God will not, when in reality He cannot because of our unbelief. (*SEC*, 35–36)

MARCH 26
SURRENDERING AND WINNING

What are the chief characteristics of the life hid with Christ in God, and how does it differ from much in the ordinary Christian experience?

Its chief characteristics are an entire surrender to the Lord and a perfect trust in Him, resulting in victory over sin and inward rest of soul. It differs from the lower range of Christian experience in that it causes us to let the Lord carry our burdens and manage our affairs for us, instead of trying to do it ourselves.

In laying off your burdens, therefore, the first one you must get rid of is yourself. You must hand yourself, with your temptations, temperament, circumstances, feelings, and all your inward and outward experiences, into the care of your God, and leave it all there. He made you, and therefore He understands you and knows how to manage you; and you must trust Him to do it.

Say to Him, "Here, Lord, I abandon myself to You. I have tried in every way I could think of to manage myself and to make myself what I know I ought to be, but have always failed. Now I give it up to You. Take entire possession of me. Work in me all the good pleasure of Your will, according to Your promise, and make me into a vessel for Your own honor, 'sanctified, and meet for the master's use, and prepared unto every good work' " (2 Tim. 2:21).

Here you must rest, trusting yourself to Him, continually and absolutely. (*SEC*, 37–39)

MARCH 27
OBTAINING, NOT ATTAINING

The life of faith is no speculative theory, neither is it a dream of romance. There is such a thing as having one's soul kept in perfect peace, now and here in this life; and childlike trust in God is the key to its attainment. We cannot earn it; we can do nothing but ask for it and receive it. It is the gift of God in Christ Jesus.

When offered a gift, the only course for the receiver is to take it and thank the giver. We never say of a gift, "See what I have attained!" and boast of our skill and wisdom in having attained it. Instead we say, "See what has been given me," and boast of the love and wealth and generosity of the giver. Everything in our salvation is a gift. From beginning to end, God is the giver and we are the receivers; and it is not to those who do great things, but to those who "receive abundance of grace and of the gift of righteousness" (Rom. 5:17) that the richest promises are made.

In order, therefore, to enter into a practical experience of this inner life, the soul must be in a receptive attitude, fully recognizing that it is God's gift in Christ Jesus and that it cannot be gained by any effort or works of our own. This will simplify the matter greatly, and the only thing left to be considered then, will be to discover on whom God bestows this gift and how he is to receive it.

In short, God can bestow His gift only on the fully consecrated soul, and it is to be received by faith. (*SEC*, 45–47)

MARCH 28
CONSECRATING AND ABANDONING

Consecration is the first thing needed for us to receive a gift from God—not in any legal sense, not in order to purchase or deserve God's blessing, but to remove the obstacles and make it possible for God to bestow it. In order for a lump of clay to be made into a beautiful vessel, it must be entirely abandoned to the potter and must lie passive in his hands. Similarly, in order for a soul to be made into a vessel unto God's honor, "sanctified, and meet for the master's use, and prepared unto every good work" (2 Tim. 2:21), it must be utterly abandoned to Him and must lie passive in His hands.

To some minds the word "abandonment" might express this idea better than the word "consecration." But whatever word we use, we mean an entire surrender of the whole being to God—spirit, soul, and body placed under His absolute control, for Him to do with what He pleases. The language of our hearts, under all circumstances and in view of every act, is to be "Thy will be done."

To a soul ignorant of God, this way of consecration may look hard; but to those who know Him, it is the happiest and most restful of lives. He is our Father, and He loves us and knows just what is best. Therefore, of course, His will is the most blessed thing that can come to us under any circumstances. I do not understand how it is that the eyes of so many Christians have been blinded to this fact, but it seems as if some of God's own children are more afraid of His will than of anything else in life—His perfect will, which only means loving-kindnesses, tender mercies, and unspeakable blessings to their souls! (*SEC*, 47–49)

MARCH 29
BELIEVING AND CLAIMING

Faith is an absolutely necessary element in the reception of any gift. If a friend gives us something, it is not really ours until we believe it has been given and we claim it as our own. Above all, this is true in gifts that are purely mental or spiritual. Love may be lavished on us by another without measure, but until we believe that we are loved, it never really becomes ours.

I suppose most Christians understand this principle in reference to the matter of their forgiveness. They know that the forgiveness of sins through Jesus might have been preached to them forever, but it would never really have become theirs until they believed this preaching and claimed the forgiveness as their own. But when it comes to living the Christian life, they lose sight of this principle and think that, having been saved by faith, they are now to live by works and efforts. Instead of continuing to receive, they are now to begin to do. This makes our declaration that the life hid with Christ in God is to be entered by faith seem perfectly unintelligible to them. Yet it is plainly declared that, "as we have received Christ Jesus the Lord, so we are to walk in him" (Col. 2:6, para.). We received Him by faith and by faith alone. The faith by which we enter into this hidden life is the same as the faith by which we were translated out of the kingdom of darkness into the kingdom of God's dear Son. (*SEC*, 51–52)

MARCH 30
APPROPRIATING BELIEVING

Faith must be a present faith. No faith that is exercised in the future tense amounts to anything. We may believe forever that our sins will be forgiven at some future time, and we will never find peace. We have to come to the now belief and say by a present appropriating faith, "My sins are now forgiven," before our souls can be at rest. Similarly, no faith that looks for a future deliverance from the power of sin will ever lead a soul into the life we are describing. The Enemy delights in this future faith, for he knows it is powerless to accomplish any practical results. But he trembles and flees when the soul of the believer dares to claim a present deliverance and to reckon itself now to be free from his power.

Perhaps no four words in the language have more meaning in them than the following, which I would have you repeat over and over with your voice and with your soul, emphasizing each time a different word:

Jesus saves me now. (It is He.)

Jesus *saves* me now. (It is His work to save.)

Jesus saves *me* now. (I am the one to be saved.)

Jesus saves me *now*. (He is doing it every moment.)

In order to enter into this blessed inner life of rest and triumph, you have two steps to take: first, entire abandonment, and second, absolute faith. No matter what may be the complications of your particular experience or temperament, these two steps, definitely taken and unwaveringly persevered in, will bring you into the green pastures and still waters of the life hid with Christ in God. (*SEC*, 53–54)

MARCH 31
EMPOWERING FOR LIVING

You are a child of God and long to please Him. You love your divine Master and are sick and weary of the sin that grieves Him. You long to be delivered from its power. Everything you have hitherto tried has failed to deliver you; and now in your despair, you are asking if it can indeed be that Jesus is able and willing to deliver you. Surely you must know in your very soul that He is—that to save you out of the hand of all your enemies is, in fact, the very thing He came to do.

Then trust Him. Commit your case to Him without reserve and believe that He undertakes it; and at once, knowing what He is and what He has said, claim that He saves you now. Just as you believed at first that He delivered you from the guilt of sin because He said it, so now believe that He delivers you from the power of sin because He says it. Let your faith now lay hold of a new power in Christ. You have trusted Him as your dying Savior; now trust Him as your living Savior.

Just as much as He came to deliver you from future punishment, He also came to deliver you from present bondage. Just as truly as He came to bear your stripes for you, He has come to live your life for you. You are as utterly powerless in the one case as in the other. You could as easily have got rid of your own sins as you could now secure for yourself practical righteousness. Christ, and Christ only, must do both for you. Your part is simply to give the thing to Him to do, and then believe that He does it. (*SEC*, 54–55)

APRIL 1
BELIEVING THEN EXPERIENCING

Seekers after holiness are told that they must consecrate themselves, and they endeavor to do so. But at once they meet with a difficulty. They have done as they think they are instructed, yet they find no difference in their experience. Nothing seems changed, as they have been led to expect it would be. They are completely baffled and ask the question almost despairingly, "How are we to know when we are consecrated?"

The one chief temptation that meets the soul at this juncture is the same that assaults it at every step of its progress—namely, the question as to feelings. We cannot believe we are consecrated until we feel that we are; and because we do not feel that God has taken us in hand, we cannot believe that He has. As usual, we put feeling first, faith second, and the fact last of all. God's invariable rule in everything, however, is, fact first, faith second, and feeling last of all. We are striving against the inevitable when we seek to change this order.

The way, then, to meet this temptation in reference to consecration, is simply to take God's side in the matter, to adopt His order by putting faith before feeling. Give yourself to the Lord definitely and fully, according to your present light, asking the Holy Spirit to show you all that is contrary to Him, either in your heart or life. If He shows you anything, give it to the Lord immediately and say in reference to it, "Thy will be done." (*SEC*, 59-60)

APRIL 2
SEEING IS NOT BELIEVING

Because God is not visibly present to the eye, it is difficult to feel that a transaction with Him is real. If, when we consecrate ourselves to God, we could actually see Him present with us, we would feel as if it were a very real thing and would realize that we had given our word to Him and could not take it back. Such a transaction would have for us the binding power that a spoken promise to an earthly friend always has to a person of honor.

What we need, therefore, is to see that God's presence is a certain fact always and that every act of our soul is done before Him and every word spoken in prayer is as really spoken to Him as if our eyes could see Him and our hands could touch Him. Then we will cease to have such vague conceptions of our relations with Him and will feel the binding force of every word we say in His presence.

I know some will say here, "Ah, yes; but if He would only

speak to me and say that He took me when I gave myself to Him, I would have no trouble believing it." No, of course you would not; but then where would be the room for faith? Sight, hearing, and feeling are not faith; but believing when we can neither see, hear, nor feel, is faith; and everywhere the Bible tells us our salvation is to be by faith. Therefore we must believe before we feel, and often against our feelings, if we would honor God by our faith. Always the one who believes has the witness, not the one who doubts. (*SEC*, 63–64)

APRIL 3
CONSECRATING, THEN BELIEVING

After consecration comes faith. Here the soul immediately encounters certain forms of difficulty and hindrance because of a misunderstanding of faith. In reality, however, faith is the simplest and plainest thing in the world, the easiest of exercises: it is simply believing God. Like sight, it is nothing apart from its object. You may as well shut your eyes and look inside to see whether you have sight, as to look inside to discover whether you have faith. You see something and thus know that you have sight; you believe something and thus know that you have faith. For as sight is only seeing, so faith is only believing. As the only necessary thing about sight is that you see the thing as it is, so the only necessary thing about belief is that you believe the thing as it is. The virtue does not lie in your believing but in the thing you believe. If you believe the truth, you are saved; if you believe a lie, you are lost. The act of believing is the same in both cases; the things believed are exactly opposite, and this it is which makes the mighty difference.

Your salvation comes, not because your faith saves you, but because it links you to the Savior who saves; and your believing is really nothing but the link. (*SEC*, 69–70)

APRIL 4
TRUSTING AND WORRYING

Two things are more incompatible even than oil and water: trust and worry. Would you call it trust if you gave something to a friend to attend to for you and then spent your nights and days in anxious thought as to whether it would be rightly and successfully done? Can you call it trust when you have given the saving and keeping of your soul into the hands of the Lord, if day after day and night after night you are spending hours of anxious thought and questionings about the matter? When a believer really trusts, he ceases to worry about the thing he has entrusted. When he worries, it is proof that he does not trust.

Tested by this rule, how little real trust there is in the church of Christ! No wonder our Lord asked the pathetic question, "When the Son of man cometh, shall he find faith on the earth?" (Luke 18:8). He will find plenty of work, a great deal of earnestness, and doubtless many consecrated hearts; but will He find faith, the one thing He values more than all the rest? Every child of God, in his own case, will know how to answer this question. Should the answer for any of you be a sorrowful no, let this be the last time for such an answer; and if you have ever known anything of the trustworthiness of our Lord, may you henceforth affirm that He is true by the generous recklessness of your trust in Him! (*SEC*, 75)

APRIL 5
BELIEVING AGAINST SEEMING

You must put your will into your believing. Your faith must not be a passive imbecility, but an active energy. You may have to believe against every seeming, but no matter. Set your face like a flint to say, "I will believe, and I know I will not be confounded." We are told that all things are possible to God (Matt. 19:26) and that all things are possible also to him who believes (Mark 9:23). Faith has in times past "subdued kingdoms, wrought righteousness, obtained promises, stopped the mouths of lions, quenched the violence of fire, escaped the edge of the sword, . . . waxed valiant in fight, turned to flight the armies of the aliens'' (Heb. 11:33–34); and faith can do it again. For our Lord himself says unto us, ''If you have faith as a grain of mustard seed, ye shall say unto this mountain, remove hence to yonder place; and it shall remove; and nothing shall be impossible unto you'' (Matt. 17:20).

If you are a child of God, you must have at least as much faith as a grain of mustard seed, and therefore you dare not say again that you cannot trust because you have no faith.

Let your faith, then, throw its arms around all God has told you, and in every dark hour remember that ''though now for a season, if need be, ye are in heaviness through manifold temptations'' (1 Peter 1:6), it is only like going through a tunnel. The sun has not ceased shining because the traveler through the tunnel has ceased to see it; and the Sun of Righteousness is still shining, although you in your dark tunnel do not see Him. Be patient and trustful, and wait. This time of darkness is only permitted ''that the trial of your faith . . . might be found unto praise and honour and glory at the appearing of Jesus Christ'' (1 Peter 1:7). (*SEC*, 77–78)

APRIL 6
REIGNING IN OUR WILLING

Fenelon says that ''pure religion resides in the will alone.'' By this he means that as the will is the governing power in the man's nature, if the will is set right, all the rest of the nature must come into harmony. By the will, I do not mean the wish of the man or even his purpose, but the deliberate choice, the deciding power, the king to which all that is in the man must yield obedience.

Some say that the emotions are the governing power in our nature, but I think we all know from experience that there is within us, behind our emotions and behind our wishes, an independent self that decides everything and controls everything. Our emotions belong to us and are suffered and enjoyed by us, but they are not ourselves. If God is to take possession of us, it must be into this central will or personality that He enters. If, then, He is reigning there by the power of His Spirit, all the rest of our nature must come under His sway.

The decisions of our will are often so directly opposed to the decisions of our emotions, that if we are in the habit of considering our emotions as the test, we will be very apt to feel like hypocrites in declaring those things to be real which our will alone has decided. But the moment we see that the will is king, we will utterly disregard anything that clamors against it and will claim as real its decisions, let the emotions rebel as they may. (*SEC*, 80–81)

APRIL 7
BELIEVING IS CHOOSING

Stop considering your emotions and simply regard your will, which is the real king in your being. Is your will given up to God? Does your will decide to believe? Does your will choose to obey? If this is the case, then you are in the Lord's hands. You decide to believe and you choose to obey, for your will is yourself.

A transaction with God is as real when only your will acts as when every emotion coincides. It does not seem as real to you, but in God's sight it is as real. When you have discovered that you need not attend to your emotions but simply to the state of your will, obeying the Scripture commands to yield yourself to God, abide in Christ, and walk in the light will become possible to you. You will be conscious that in all these areas you will can act and can take God's side. If, however, your trusted in your emotions, you would, knowing them to be utterly uncontrollable, sink down in helpless despair.

When, then, this feeling of unreality or hypocrisy comes, do not be troubled by it. Only see to it that your will is in God's hands, that your inward self is abandoned to His working. Your surging emotions—like a tossing vessel at anchor, which by degrees yields to the steady pull of the cable—finding themselves attached to the mighty power of God by the choice of your will, must inevitably come into captivity and give their allegiance to Him; and you will sooner or later verify the truth of the saying that, "if any man will do his will, he shall know of the doctrine" (John 7:17). (*SEC*, 84–85)

APRIL 8
DECIDING AND PERSISTING

The important thing in your experience is not the verdict of your emotions but what your will decides. You are far more in danger of hypocrisy and untruth in yielding to the assertions of your feelings than in holding fast to the decision of your will. So if your will is on God's side, you are no hypocrite at this moment in claiming as your own the blessed reality of belonging altogether to Him, even though your emotions may declare the contrary.

I am convinced that throughout the Bible the expressions concerning the "heart" do not mean the emotions but the will, the personality of a person. The object of God's dealings with an individual is that this "I" may be yielded up to Him and this central life abandoned to His control. It is not one's feelings that God wants, but his person.

But let us not make a mistake here. I say we must "give up" our wills, but I do not mean we are to be left will-less. We are not to give up our wills and be left like limp nerveless creatures, without any will at all. We are simply to substitute for our misdirected wills of ignorance and immaturity, the higher, divine, mature will of God. (*SEC*, 86–87)

APRIL 9
SEEKING FOR LEADING

We must believe that divine guidance is promised to us, and our faith must therefore confidently look for and expect it. Settle this point first: Divine guidance has been promised, and if you seek it, you are sure to receive it.

Next, you must remember that our God has all knowledge and all wisdom, and that therefore it is very possible He may guide you into paths wherein He knows great blessings are awaiting you, but which, to the short-sighted human eyes around

you, seem sure to result in confusion and loss. You must recognize that God's thoughts are not as man's thoughts, nor His
ways as man's ways (cf. lsa. 55:8-9); and that He alone, who
knows the end of things from the beginning, can judge what the
results of any course of action may be. His love for you may
lead you to run counter to the loving wishes of even your dearest
friends. In order to be a disciple and follower of your Lord, you
may be called on to forsake inwardly all that you have, even
father or mother, or brother or sister, or husband or wife, or
even your own life (cf. Matt. 19:29).

Unless this possibility is clearly recognized, you will be very
likely to get into difficulty, because it often happens that the
child of God who enters on this life of obedience is sooner or
later led into paths which meet with the disapproval of those he
loves. Unless he is prepared for this and can trust the Lord
through it all, he will scarcely know what to do. (*SEC*, 91-92)

APRIL 10
DIRECTING AND LEADING

There are four ways God reveals His will to us—through the
Scriptures, through providential circumstances, through the
convictions of our own higher judgment, and through the inward
impressions of the Holy Spirit on our minds. Where these four
harmonize, God speaks. His voice will always be in harmony
with itself no matter how many different ways He may speak.
The voices may be many; the message can be but one. If God
tells me in one voice to do something or to leave it undone, He
cannot possibly tell me the opposite in another voice. If there is
a contradiction in the voices, the speakers cannot be the same.
Therefore, my rule for distinguishing the voice of God would
be to bring it to the test of harmony.

The Scriptures come first. If you are in doubt on any subject,
you must, first of all, consult the Bible to see whether there is
any law there revealed concerning the subject; you must not ask
nor expect a separate, direct, personal revelation. A great many
fatal mistakes are made in the matter of guidance by the over-
looking of this simple rule. Where our Father has written out
for us a plain direction about something, He will not make a

special revelation to us about that thing. If we fail to search out and obey the Scripture rule, where there is one, and look instead for an inward voice, we will open ourselves to delusions and will almost inevitably get into error. (*SEC*, 92–93)

APRIL 11
READING AND LEADING

It is essential to remember that the Bible is a book of principles and not a book of disjointed aphorisms. Isolated texts may often be used to sanction things to which the principles of Scripture are totally opposed. I believe all fanaticism comes in this way. An isolated text is so impressed on the mind that it seems a necessity to obey it, no matter what wrong thing it may lead into, and thus the principles of Scripture are violated under the very plea of obedience to the Scriptures.

If, however, on searching the Bible you do not find any principles that will settle your special point of difficulty, you must then seek guidance in the other ways (see devotion for April 10), and God will surely voice himself to you, either by a conviction of your judgment or by providential circumstances or by a clear inward impression. In all true guidance, the four voices will harmonize, for God cannot say in one voice that which He contradicts in another. Therefore, if you have an impression of duty, you must see whether it is in accordance with Scripture, whether it commands itself to your own higher judgment, and whether, as we Quakers say, the ''way opens'' for its carrying out.

If any one of these tests fails, it is not safe to proceed. You must wait in quiet trust until the Lord shows you the point of harmony, which He surely will, sooner or later, if it is His voice that is speaking. Anything that is out of this divine harmony must be rejected, therefore, as not coming from God. (*SEC*, 95–96)

APRIL 12
IMPRESSING BUT DELUDING

We must never forget that impressions can come from other sources as well as from the Holy Spirit. The strong personalities of those around us are the source of a great many of our impressions. Impressions also often arise from our wrong physical conditions, which color things far more than we dream. And finally, impressions come from those spiritual enemies who lie in wait for every traveler who seeks to enter the higher regions of the spiritual life. These spiritual enemies must necessarily communicate with us by means of our spiritual faculties. Their voices therefore will be, as the voice of God is, an inward impression made on our spirits. Consequently, just as the Holy Spirit may tell us by impressions what is the will of God concerning us, so also will these spiritual enemies tell us by impressions what is their will concerning us, disguising themselves, of course, as angels of light who have come to lead us closer to God.

Many earnest and honest-hearted children of God have been thus deluded into paths of extreme fanaticism, while all the while thinking they were closely following the Lord. God, who sees the sincerity of their hearts, can and does, I am sure, pity and forgive; but the consequences of this life are often very sad. It is not enough to have a "leading"; we must find out the source of that leading before we follow it. It is not enough, either, for the leading to be very remarkable or the coincidences to be very striking, to stamp it as being surely from God. It is essential, therefore, that our leadings all be tested by Scripture. (*SEC*, 96–97)

APRIL 13
GUIDING AND OBEYING

We must not be deterred from embracing the blessed privilege of divine guidance by a dread of the dangers that environ it. That God cares enough about us to desire to regulate the details of our lives, is the strongest proof of love He could give. That He should condescend to let us know how to live and walk to please Him, seems almost too good to be true. We never care about the little details of people's lives unless we love them. It is a matter of indifference to us what the majority of people we meet do, or how they spend their time. But as soon as we begin to love someone, we begin at once to care. God's law, therefore, is only another name for God's love. The more minutely that law descends into the details of our lives, the more sure we are of the depth and reality of God's love. We can never know the full joy and privileges of the life hid with Christ in God until we have learned the lesson of a daily and hourly guidance.

God's promise is that He will work in us to will as well as to do of His good pleasure (Phil. 2:13). This means, of course, that He will take possession of our will and work it for us. His suggestions will come to us not so much as commands from the outside as desires springing up within. They will originate in our will, and we will feel as though we desired to do so and so, not as though we must. This makes our service one of perfect liberty, let the accompanying circumstances be as difficult as they may. God writes His laws on our hearts and on our minds (cf. Heb. 10:16) so that our affection and our understanding embrace them, and we are drawn to obey, instead of being driven to it. (*SEC*, 99–100)

APRIL 14
SEARCHING AND WAITING

Sometimes, in spite of all our efforts to discover the truth, the divine sense of "oughtness" does not seem to come and our doubts and perplexities continue unenlightened. In addition, our friends differ from us and may oppose our course. In such a case there is nothing to do but to wait until the light comes. We must wait in faith and in an attitude of entire surrender, saying a continual yes to the will of our Lord. If the suggestion is from Him, it will continue and strengthen; if it is not from Him, it will disappear. If it continues, if it troubles us in our moments of prayer and disturbs our peace, and if it conforms to the test of the divine harmony of which I have spoken (see devotion for

April 10), we may feel sure it is from God. Then we must yield to it or suffer an unspeakable loss.

The apostle Paul says that "whatsoever is not of faith is sin" (Rom. 14:23). In all doubtful things, then, you must stand still and refrain from action until God gives you light to know more clearly His mind concerning them. Very often you will find that the doubt has been His voice calling you to come into more perfect conformity to His will; but sometimes these doubtful things are only temptations or morbid feelings, to which it would be most unwise for you to yield. The only safe way is to wait until you can act in faith. (*SEC*, 101–2)

APRIL 15
DEALING WITH SINNING

Misunderstanding on the point of conscious sin opens the way for great dangers in the life of faith. When a believer who has entered on the highway of holiness finds himself surprised into sin, he is tempted to be utterly discouraged and to give everything up as lost; or in order to preserve the doctrines untouched, he covers his sin up, calling it infirmity and refusing to be candid and above-board about it. Either of these courses is equally fatal to any real growth and progress in the life of holiness. The only way is to face the sad fact at once, call the thing by its right name, and discover, if possible, the reason and the remedy.

The life of union with God requires the utmost honesty with Him and with ourselves. The blessing that the sin itself would only momentarily disturb is sure to be lost by a dishonest dealing with it. A sudden failure is no reason for being discouraged and giving up all as lost. Neither is the integrity of our doctrine touched by it. We are not preaching a state but a walk. The highway of holiness is not a place but a way. Sanctification is not a thing to be picked up at a certain stage of our experience and forever after possessed; it is a life to be lived day by day and hour by hour. We may for a moment turn aside from a path, but the path is not obliterated by our wandering and can be instantly regained. (*SEC*, 129–30)

APRIL 16
FIGHTING DOUBTING

A great many Christians are slaves to an inveterate habit of doubting. I am not referring to doubts about the existence of God or the truths of the Bible, but doubts about their own personal relations with the God in whom they profess to believe, doubts about the forgiveness of their sins, doubts about their hope of heaven, and doubts about their own inward experience. No drunkard was ever more in bondage to his habit of drink than they are to their habit of doubting. Every step of their spiritual progress is taken against the fearful odds of an army of doubts. Their lives are made wretched, their usefulness is effectually hindered, and their communion with God is continually broken by their doubts.

It seems strange that people whose very name *believers* implies that their one chief characteristic is that they believe, should have to confess that they have doubts. Yet it is such a universal habit, that I feel if the name were to be given over again, the only fitting and descriptive name that could be given to many of God's children would be *doubters*. In fact, most Christians have settled down under their doubts as a people might lament over rheumatism, making themselves out as "interesting cases" of special and peculiar trial, requiring the tenderest sympathy and the utmost consideration.

Spiritual conflicts! Far better would they be named did we call them spiritual rebellions! Our fight is to be a fight of faith; and the moment we let in doubts, our fight ceases and our rebellion begins. (*SEC*, 105–7)

APRIL 17
GIVING UP DOUBTING

Doubting is, I am convinced, to many people a real luxury, and to deny themselves this luxury would be the hardest piece of self-denial they have ever known. It is a luxury which, like the indulgence in some other luxuries, brings very sorrowful results. Perhaps in looking at the sadness and misery doubting has brought into your own Christian experience, you may say, "Alas! It is no luxury to me, but only a fearful trial." But pause for a moment. Try giving it up, and you will soon find out whether it is a luxury or not. Do not your doubts come trooping to your door like a company of sympathizing friends who appreciate your hard case and have come to console you? Is it no luxury to sit down with them, entertain them, listen to their arguments, and join in with their condolences? Wouldn't it be real self-denial to turn from them and refuse to hear a word they have to say? Try it and see.

Have you never tasted the luxury of indulging in hard thoughts against those who have, as you think, injured you? Have you never known what a positive fascination it is to brood over their unkindnesses? It produces an interesting sort of wretchedness that you cannot easily give up. Such is the luxury of doubting. Things have gone wrong with you in your experience. What is more natural than to conclude that for some reason God has forsaken you, does not love you, and is indifferent to your welfare? How irresistible is the conviction that you are too wicked for Him to care for or too difficult for Him to manage! (*SEC*, 109–10)

APRIL 18
TURNING FROM DOUBTING

You cannot perhaps hinder the suggestions of doubt from coming to you any more than you can hinder someone in the street from swearing as you go by; consequently you are not sinning in the one case any more than in the other. Just as you can refuse to listen to them or join in their oaths, so can you also refuse to listen to the doubts or join in with them. They are not your doubts until you consent to them and adopt them as true. When they come you must at once turn from them.

Give up your liberty to doubt forever. Put your will in this matter over on the Lord's side and trust Him to keep you from falling. Tell Him all about your weakness and your long-encouraged habits of doubt and how helpless you are before them. Then commit the whole battle to Him. Tell Him you will not doubt again, putting forth all your will power on His side and against His Enemy and yours. Then keep your face steadfastly "looking unto Jesus," away from yourself and away from your doubts, holding fast the profession of your faith without wavering, because "he is faithful that promised" (Heb. 10:23). Rely on His faithfulness, not on your own. You have committed the keeping of your soul to Him as the faithful Creator, and you must never again admit the possibility of His being unfaithful.

Cultivate a continuous habit of believing, and sooner or later all of your doubts will vanish in the glory of the absolute faithfulness of God. (*SEC*, 115–17)

APRIL 19
OVERCOMING TESTING

Temptation is one of the instruments used by God to complete our perfection; and thus sin's own weapons are turned against itself, and we can see how it is that all things, even temptations, can work together for good to those who love God (cf. Rom. 8:28).

As to the way of victory over temptation, it seems hardly necessary to say that it is to be by faith; for this is, of course, the foundation on which the whole inner life rests. Our one great motto is, "We are nothing: Christ is all"; and always we have started out to stand and walk and overcome and live by faith. We have discovered our own helplessness and know that we cannot do anything for ourselves. We have learned that our only way, therefore, is to hand the temptation over to our Lord and trust Him to conquer it for us. When we put it into His hands, we must leave it there, which is, I think, the greatest difficulty of all. It seems impossible to believe that the Lord can or will manage our temptations without our help, especially if they do not immediately disappear. To go on patiently "enduring" the continuance of a temptation without yielding to it and also without snatching ourselves out of the Lord's hands in regard to it, is a wonderful victory for our impatient natures, a victory we will gain if we will do what pleases God.

We must then commit ourselves to the Lord for victory over our temptations just as we committed ourselves at first for forgiveness, and we must leave ourselves just as utterly in His hands for one as for the other. (*SEC*, 126)

APRIL 20
SINNING WHILE BELIEVING

"Failures," some will say; "we thought there were no failures in the life of faith!"

To this I would answer that there ought not to be and need not be, but, as a fact, sometimes are. We must deal with facts, not theories. No safe teacher of the life of faith ever says that it becomes impossible to sin; he only insists that sin ceases to be a necessity and, therefore, continual victory is available to us. Very few, if any, can say that they have not been overcome by at least a momentary temptation. *Victory is Available*

Of course, in speaking of sin here, I mean conscious, known sin. I do not touch on the subject of sins of ignorance, the inevitable sin of our nature, which is met by the provision of Christ and does not disturb our fellowship with God. I have no desire or ability to treat the doctrines concerning sin; these I will leave with the theologians to discuss and settle. I will speak only of the believer's experience in the matter.

Many things we do innocently until an increasing light shows them to be wrong, and these may all be classed under sins of ignorance. Because they are done in ignorance, they do not bring us under condemnation and do not come within the range of the present discussion. (*SEC*, 128–129)

APRIL 21
FAILING BUT NOT FALTERING

In this life and walk of faith, there may be momentary failures that, although very sad and greatly to be deplored, need not, if rightly met, disturb the attitude of the soul as to entire consecration and perfect trust, nor interrupt, for more than the passing moment, its happy communion with the Lord. Our sin is no reason for ceasing to trust, but only an unanswerable argument why we must trust more fully than ever. From whatever cause we have been betrayed into failure, it is certain that there is no remedy to be found in discouragement. Just as a child who is learning to walk might lie down in despair when he has fallen, so a believer who is learning to walk by faith might give up in despair when he has fallen into sin. The only thing to do in both cases is to get right up and try again.

"Up, sanctify the people," is always God's command. "Lie down and be discouraged," is always our temptation. Our feeling is that it is presumptuous and even almost impertinent to go at once to the Lord after having sinned against Him. It seems as if we ought to suffer the consequences of our sin first for a little while and endure the accusings of our conscience. We can hardly believe that the Lord can be willing at once to receive us back into loving fellowship.

In the same moment that we are conscious of sin, we ought to confess and believe that we are forgiven. This is especially essential to an unwavering walk in the "life . . . hid with Christ in God" (Col. 3:3), for no separation from Him can be tolerated here for an instant. (*SEC*, 130–33)

APRIL 22
COVERING SINNING

Anything cherished in the heart contrary to the will of God, let it seem ever so insignificant or be ever so deeply hidden, will cause us to fall before our enemies. Any conscious root of bitterness toward another, any self-seeking, any harsh judgments, any slackness in obeying the voice of the Lord, any doubtful habits or surroundings—these things or any one of them, consciously indulged, will effectually cripple and paralyze our spiritual life. We may have hidden the evil in the remotest corner of our hearts, refusing to recognize its existence and persisting in declaration of consecration and full trust. We may be more earnest than ever in our religious duties and have the eyes of our understanding opened more and more to the truth and beauty of the life and walk of faith. We may seem to ourselves and to others to have reached an almost impregnable position of victory, and yet we may find ourselves suffering bitter defeats. We may wonder and question and despair and pray. Nothing will do any good until the wrong thing is dug up from its hiding place, brought out to the light, and laid before God.

The moment, therefore, that we meet with a defeat, we must at once seek for the cause, some hidden want of consecration lying at the very center of our being. Just as a headache is not the disease itself but only a symptom of a disease situated in some other part of the body, so our failure is only the symptom of an evil probably hidden in a very different part of our nature. (*SEC*, 139–40)

APRIL 23
SEEING AND ABANDONING

One of the greatest obstacles to an unwavering experience in the life of faith is the difficulty of seeing God in everything. People say, "I can easily submit to things that come from God, but I cannot submit to people, and most of my trials and crosses come through human instrumentality." This is no imaginary trouble but is of vital importance. If it cannot be met, it makes the life of faith an impossible theory. Nearly everything in life comes to us through human instrumentalities, and most of our trials are the result of somebody's failure, ignorance, carelessness, or sin. We know God cannot be the author of these things, yet, unless He is the agent in the matter, how can we say to Him about it, "Thy will be done"?

Besides, what good is there in trusting our affairs to God if others are allowed to come in and rearrange them; and how is it possible to live by faith if human agencies are to have a prevailing influence in molding our lives?

Moreover, things in which we can see God's hand always have a sweetness in them that consoles while it wounds, but the trials inflicted by people are full of nothing but bitterness.

What is needed, then, is to see God in everything and to receive everything directly from His hands, with no intervention of second causes. It is to just this that we must be brought before we can know an abiding experience of entire abandonment and perfect trust. Our abandonment must be to God, not to others, and our trust must be in Him, not in any arm of flesh, or we will fail at the first trial. (*SEC*, 144–45)

APRIL 24
TRUSTING HIS CARING

Secondary causes must all be under the control of our Father, and not one of them can touch us except with His knowledge and permission. It may be the sin of man that originates the action, and therefore the thing itself cannot be said to be the will of God; but by the time it reaches us it has become God's will for us and must be accepted as directly from His hands. No person or group of persons, no power in earth or heaven, can touch the soul that is abiding in Christ without first passing through his encircling presence and receiving the seal of His permission. If God be for us, it matters not who may be against us; nothing can disturb or harm us.

An earthly parent's care for a helpless child is a feeble illustration of this. If the child is in its father's arms, nothing can touch it without that father's consent, unless he is too weak to prevent it. And even if this should be the case, he suffers the harm first in his own person before he allows it to reach his child.

If an earthly parent would care for his child like this, how much more will our heavenly Father, whose love is infinitely greater, and whose strength and wisdom can never be baffled, care for us! Some scarcely think that He is equal to themselves in tenderness and love, and they charge Him with an indifference of which they would feel themselves incapable. The truth is that His care is infinitely superior. He takes note of the minutest matters that can affect the lives of His children and regulates them all according to His own perfect will, let their origins be what they may. (*SEC*, 147–48)

APRIL 25
BINDING OR LIBERATING

There are two kinds of Christian experience: one is an experience of bondage and the other an experience of liberty.

In the first case, the soul is controlled by a stern sense of duty and obeys the law of God, either from fear of punishment or from expectation of wages. In the other case, the controlling power is an inward life principle that works out, by the force of its own motions or instincts, the will of the divine Lifegiver, without fear of punishment or hope of reward. In the first, the Christian is a servant and works for hire; in the second, he is a son and works for love.

There ought not to be this contrast in the experience of Christians, but as we have to deal with what is, rather than with what ought to be, we cannot shut our eyes to the bondage in which so many of God's children spend a large part of their Christian lives. The reason for this bondage and the remedy for it are not difficult to find: the reason is legality, and the remedy is Christ.

Nowhere do we find those two forms or stages of Christian life more fully developed and contrasted than in the Epistle to the Galatians. The Galatian Christians had begun in the right attitude; they had entered into the spiritual life by the "hearing of faith" (Gal. 3:5). But when it came to a question of how they were to live in this life, they had changed their ground. They had sought to substitute works for faith. Having "begun in the Spirit," they were now seeking to be "made perfect by the flesh" (Gal. 3:3). They had, in short, descended in their Christian living, from the plane of life to the plane of law. (*SEC*, 157–58)

APRIL 26
BEING NOT DOING

We are continually tempted to forget that it is not what people do that is the vital matter but rather what they are. In Christ Jesus neither our performance of or omission of legal observances avails anything: what counts is that we are "a new creature" (2 Cor. 5:17). God is a great deal more concerned about our really being "new creatures" than about anything else, because He knows that if we are right in our inner being, we will certainly do right outwardly. We may, in fact, sometimes even do right without being right at all, but no doing of this kind has any vitality in it or is of any real account. The essential thing,

87

therefore, is character; doing is valuable only as it is an indication of being.

Paul was grieved with the Galatian Christians because they seemed to have lost sight of the truth that the inward life, the "new creature," was the only thing that availed. They had begun on this plane, but they had "fallen from grace" (Gal. 5:4) to a lower plane, where the "oldness of the letter" was put in place of the "newness of the spirit" (Rom. 7:6). Paul wrote, "Christ is become of no effect unto you, whosoever of you are justified by the law; ye are fallen from grace" (Gal. 5:4).

This passage is the only one in which the expression "fallen from grace" is used in the New Testament. It means that the Galatians had made the mistake of thinking that something else beside Christ was necessary for their right Christian living. Paul warned them to remember that Christ alone was enough, and that nothing else must be added. (*SEC*, 159)

APRIL 27
WOOING NOT DEMANDING

The law says, This do and you will live.

The gospel says, Live, and then you will do.

The law says, Pay me what you owe me.

The gospel says, I freely forgive you everything.

The law says, Make yourself a new heart and a new spirit.

The gospel says, A new heart will I give you, and a new spirit will I put within you.

The law says, You shall love the Lord your God with all your heart, and with all your soul, and with all your mind.

The gospel says, Herein is love, not that we loved God, but that He loved us and sent His son to be the propitiation for our sins.

The law says, Cursed is every one who doesn't continue in all things written in the book of the law to do them.

The gospel says, Blessed is the man whose iniquities are forgiven, and whose sins are covered.

The law says, The wages of sin is death.

The gospel says, The gift of God is eternal life through Jesus Christ our Lord.

(*SEC*, 160–61)

APRIL 28
FREEING NOT RESTRICTING

The law demands holiness.
The gospel gives holiness.
The law says, Do.
The gospel says, Done.
The law extorts the unwilling service of a slave.
The gospel wins the loving service of a son and friend.
The law makes blessings the result of obedience.
The gospel makes obedience the result of blessings.
The law places the day of rest at the end of the week's work.
The gospel places it at its beginning.
The law says, If.
The gospel says, Therefore.
The law was given for the restraint of the old man.
The gospel was given to bring liberty to the new man.
Under the law, salvation was wages.
Under the gospel, salvation is a gift.

(*SEC*, 161)

APRIL 29
SERVING BY LOVING

Paul entreats us: "Stand fast . . . in the liberty wherewith Christ hath made us free, and be not entangled again with the yoke of bondage" (Gal. 5:1).

Our freedom from bondage to sin can be illustrated this way. It is as if a woman had a male employer; she is paid for her work in weekly wages, and under the rules of her employer, whom she had tried to please, but toward whom her service had been one of obligation only. Finally, however, the employer falls in love with her, and she becomes his bride and shares all his fortunes. At once the whole spirit of her service is changed. She may perhaps continue to do the same things that she did before, but she does them now from a different motive. The old sense of duty is lost in the new sense of love. The cold word "employer" is transformed into the loving word "husband." And it shall be at that day, saith the LORD, that thou shalt call me Ishi [my husband]; and shalt call me no more Baali [my Lord]" (Hos. 2:16).

But imagine this bride beginning after a while to look back on her low estate and to be so overwhelmed by the retrospect as to feel unworthy of union with her husband, and consequently to lose the inward sense of this union. Who can doubt that very soon the old sense of working for wages would drive out the new sense of working for love, and in spirit the old name, "my employer," would take the place of the new name, "my husband"?

We exclaim at the folly of such a course. But isn't this just what happens to many Christians? (*SEC*, 163)

APRIL 30
INHERITING, NOT WORKING

Legally minded Christians do not deny Christ; they only seek to add something to Him. Perhaps it is Christ and good works or Christ and earnest feelings or Christ and clear doctrines or Christ and certain religious performances. All these are good in themselves and good as the fruit of salvation, but to add anything to Christ, no matter how good it may be, as the procuring cause of salvation, is to deny His completeness and exalt self.

Men will undergo many painful self-sacrifices rather than take the place of helplessness and worthlessness. A man will gladly be a Saint Simon Stylites or even a fakir, if only it is self that does it, so that self may share the glory. A religion of bondage always exalts self. It is what I do—my efforts, my wrestlings, my faithfulness—that counts. But a religion of liberty leaves self nothing to glory in; it is all Christ and what He does, what He is, and how wonderfully He saves that is important. A child does not boast of himself but of his father and mother, and our souls can "make their boast in the LORD" (Ps. 34:2, para.)

when, in this life of liberty, we have learned to know that He and He alone is the sufficient supply for our every need.

We are the children of God and therefore His heirs; and our possessions come to us not by working for them but by inheritance from our Father. (*SEC*, 163–64)

MAY 1
LOVING AND SERVING

Christ says that except we "become as little children," we cannot enter into the kingdom of heaven (Matt. 18:3). It is impossible to get the child spirit until the servant spirit has disappeared. Notice that I do not say the "spirit of service," but the "servant spirit." Every good child is filled with the spirit of service but ought not have anything of the servant spirit. The child serves from love; the servant works for wages.

If a child of loving parents should get the idea that his parents would not give him food and clothing unless he earned them in some way, all the sweetness of the relationship between parent and child would be destroyed. As soon as we begin to "work for our living" in spiritual things, we have stepped out of the son's place into the servant's, and have "fallen from grace" (cf. Gal. 5:4).

One servant, of whom we read in the Bible, thought his lord was a hard master (cf. Matt. 25:24), and the spirit of bondage makes us think the same of Christ. Many Christians have bowed their necks to the yoke of Christ as to a yoke of bondage, reading His declaration that His yoke is easy (Matt 11:30) as though it were a fairy tale. So deeply ingrained in the church is the idea that the Christian life is a kind of bondage, that whenever a child of God finds himself walking at liberty, he begins to think there must be something wrong in his experience. (*SEC*, 165–67)

MAY 2
LOVING MEANS RECEIVING

The secret of the Christian life is revealed in the child/father relationship. Nothing more is needed than to believe that God is as good a father as the best ideal earthly father, and that the relationship of a Christian to Him is just the same as that of a child to his parent in this world. A child does not need to carry about in his own pocket the money for his support. If his father has plenty, that satisfies the child and is a great deal better than if it were in the child's own possession, since in that case it might get lost. In the same way it is not necessary for Christians to have all their spiritual possessions in their own keeping. It is far better that their riches should be stored up for them in Christ.

When people are comparative strangers to one another, they cannot with any comfort receive great gifts from each other. But when they are united in spirit, with a bond of true love between them, then no matter how great the gifts may be that pass from one to the other, they can be accepted without any feeling of embarrassment or obligation on either side.

This principle holds good in the spiritual life. When Christians are living far off from God, they cannot be brought to accept any great gifts from Him. But when Christians get near enough to the Lord to feel the true spirit of adoption, they are ready to accept with delight all the blessings He has in store for them. For then they discover that He is only eager, as parents are, to pour out every good gift on His children. They see that, in fact, all things are theirs, because they are Christ's, and Christ is God's (cf. 1 Cor. 3:21–23). (*SEC*, 167–68)

MAY 3
KNOWING MEANS POSSESSING

Sometimes a great mystery is made out of the life hid with Christ in God as though it is a strange mystical thing that ordinary people cannot understand. But the contrast between bondage and liberty makes it very plain: we are no longer servants but sons, and must enter into the privileges of this relationship. We all know what it is to be a child; there is no mystery about that. God did not use the figures of Father and children without knowing all that this relationship implies. Those, therefore, who know Him as their Father, know the whole secret. They are their Father's heirs and may now enter into possession of all that is necessary for their present needs. They will therefore be very simple in their prayers. "Lord," they will say, "I am your child, and I need such and such things." "My child," He will answer, "all things are yours in Christ; come and take just what you need."

Where the executors are honorable men, the heirs to an estate are not obliged to "struggle" for their inheritance. The executors are appointed not to keep them out of it but to help them into possession of it. I sometimes think Christians look on our Lord as someone appointed to keep them out of their possessions, rather than to bring them in to them. They little know how such an implication grieves and dishonors Christ. When they do recognize it, the spirit of bondage becomes impossible to them. (*SEC*, 168–69)

MAY 4
FULFILLING, NOT REBELLING

Our liberty must come from an understanding of the mind and thoughts of God toward us.

What are the facts of the case? If God has called us only to be servants, then the Christians who live lives of weary bondage are right. But if He has called us to be children and heirs, if we are His friends, His brethren, His bride, how sadly and grievously wrong we are in being entangled under any yoke of bondage, no matter how pious a yoke it may seem to be!

The thought of bondage is utterly abhorrent to any of earth's true relationships, and surely it must be more repugnant to a heavenly relationship. It will not hinder one's final entrance into heavenly rest, but it will put one in the company of those who are described as being saved as by fire but losing all else. "Against such there is no law" (Gal. 5:23) is the divine sentence concerning all who live and walk in the Spirit; and you will find it most blessedly true if you will lay aside all self-effort and self-dependence and consent to let Christ live and work in you.

The person who lives by the power of an inward righteous nature is not under bondage to the outward law of righteousness; but the one who is restrained by the outward law alone, without the inward restraint of a righteous nature, is a slave to the law. The one fulfills the law in his soul, and is therefore free. The other rebels against the law in his soul, and is therefore bound. (*SEC*, 169–70)

MAY 5
GROWING IN NOT GROWING INTO

Trouble comes when believers try to grow *into* grace rather than *in* it. The children of Israel, wandering in the wilderness, are a perfect picture of this sort of growing. They traveled about for forty years, finding little rest from their wanderings, yet at the end of it all, they were no nearer the Promised Land than they were at the beginning. When they started their wandering at Kadesh Barnea, they were at the borders of the land, and a few steps would have taken them into it. When they ended their wandering in the plains of Moab, they were also at its borders; only now there was a river to cross, which at first there would not have been.

All their wanderings and fightings in the wilderness had not put them in possession of one inch of the Promised Land. In order to get possession of this land, it was necessary for them first to be in it; and in order to grow in grace, it is necessary first to be planted in grace. When in the land, however, their conquest was rapid; and when planted in grace, the growth of the spiritual life becomes vigorous and rapid beyond all conceiving. For grace is a most fruitful soil, and the plants that grow therein are plants of a marvelous growth. They are tended by a divine Husbandman, warmed by the Sun of Righteousness, and watered by the dew from heaven. Surely it is no wonder that they bring forth fruit, "some an hundredfold, some sixty-fold, some thirty-fold" (Matt. 13:8). (*SEC*, 173–74)

MAY 6
UNBOUNDING LOVING

What is meant by growing in grace? It is difficult to answer this question because so few people have any conception of what the grace of God really is. To say that it is free unmerited favor, expresses only a little of its meaning. It is the unhindered, wondrous, boundless love of God, poured out on us in an infinite variety of ways, without stint or measure, not according to our deserving, but according to His measureless heart of love.

I sometimes think a different meaning is given to the word *love* when it is associated with God, from that which we so well understand in its human application. We seem to think that divine love is hard, self-seeking, and distant, concerned about its own glory, and indifferent to the fate of others. But if ever human love was tender, self-sacrificing, and devoted, if ever it could bear and forbear, if ever it could suffer gladly for its loved one, if ever it was willing to pour itself out in a lavish abandonment for the comfort or pleasure of its objects, then indefinitely more is divine love tender, self-sacrificing, and devoted, glad to bear and forbear, and eager to lavish its best gifts and blessings on the objects of its love.

Put together all the tenderest love you know of, dear reader, the deepest you have ever felt and the strongest that has ever been poured out on you; heap on it all the love of all the loving human hearts in the world; then multiply it by infinity, and you will have a faint glimpse of the love and grace of God! (*SEC*, 174–75)

MAY 7
GROWING AND TRUSTING

In order to grow in grace, the soul must be planted in the very heart of divine love, enveloped by it, steeped in it. The soul must grow in the apprehension of divine love day by day, entrust everything to its care, and have no shadow of doubt but that it will surely order all things well.

To grow in grace is to oppose all growth in self-dependence or self-effort, in fact to legality of every kind. It is to put our growing, as well as everything else, into the hands of the Lord and leave it with Him. It is to be so satisfied with our Husbandman and with His skill and wisdom that not a question will cross our minds as to His mode of treatment or His plan of cultivation.

To grow in grace is to grow as the lilies grow or as the babies grow, without care and without anxiety; to grow by the power of an inward life-principle that cannot help but grow; to grow because we live and therefore must grow; to grow because He who has planted us has planted a growing thing and has made us on purpose to grow.

The result of this kind of growing is sure. Even Solomon in all his glory was not arrayed like one of God's lilies. Though we may "toil and spin" to make ourselves beautiful clothes, and stretch and strain to add to our growing, we will accomplish nothing. No array of ours can equal the beautiful dress in which the great Husbandman clothes the plants that grow in His garden of grace under His fostering care (cf. Matt. 6:28–30). (*SEC*, 175–76)

MAY 8
GROWING, NOT HINDERING

We all need to "consider the lilies of the field" (Matt. 6:28) and learn their secret. Grow, dear Christians, in God's way, which is the only effectual way. See to it that you are planted in grace, and then let the divine Husbandman cultivate you in His own way and by His own means. Put yourself out in the sunshine of His presence and let the dew of heaven come down on you, and see what the result will be. Leaves and flowers and fruit must surely come in their season, for your Husbandman is skillful, and He never fails in His harvesting.

Only see to it that you do not oppose the shining of the Sun of Righteousness or the falling of the dew from heaven. The thinnest covering may serve to keep off the sunshine and the dew, and the plant may wither, even where these are most abundant. And so also the slightest barrier between your soul and

Christ may cause you to dwindle and fade, as a plant in a cellar or under a bushel.

Keep the sky clear. Open wide every avenue of your being to receive the blessed influences your divine Husbandman may bring to bear on you. Bask in the sunshine of His love. Drink of the waters of His goodness. Keep your face upturned to Him, as the flowers do to the sun. Look, and your soul will live and grow. (*SEC*, 178).

MAY 9
ABANDONING AND ABIDING

It may be objected that we are not inanimate flowers but intelligent human beings with personal powers and personal responsibilities. This is true, and it makes this important difference: what the flower is by nature, we must be by an intelligent and free surrender. To be one of God's lilies means an inner abandonment of the rarest kind. It means that we are to be infinitely passive and yet infinitely active also; passive as regards self and its workings, active as regards attention and response to God. We must lay down all the activity of the creature and must let only the activities of God work in us, through us, and by us. Self must step aside to let God work.

You need make no effort to grow, therefore; but let your efforts instead be concentrated on abiding in the Vine. The divine Husbandman who has the care of the Vine, will care also for you who are His branches. He will so prune and purge and water and tend you, that you will grow and bring forth fruit, and your fruit will remain (cf. John 15:5, 16). Like the lily, you will find yourself arrayed in apparel so glorious that that of Solomon will be as nothing to it (see Matt. 6:28–29). (*SEC*, 178–79)

MAY 10
ABANDONING AND BLOSSOMING

Do you seem to be planted in a desert soil where nothing can grow? Put yourself into the hands of the good Husbandman, and He will at once begin to make that very desert blossom as the rose, and will cause springs and fountains of water to start up out of its sandy wastes. For the promise is sure: The person who trusts in the Lord "shall be as a tree planted by the waters, and that spreadeth out her roots by the river, and shall not see when heat cometh, but her leaf shall be green; and shall not be careful in the year of drought, neither shall cease from yielding fruit" (Jer. 17:8).

It is the great prerogative of our divine Husbandman that He is able to turn any soil, whatever it may be like, into the soil of grace the moment we put our growing into His hands. He does not need to transplant us into a different field, but right where we are, with just the circumstances that surround us, He makes His sun to shine and His dew to fall on us, and transforms the very things that were our greatest hindrances into the chiefest and most blessed means of our growth.

No matter what the circumstances, God's wonder-working power can accomplish our growth; and we must trust Him. Surely He is a Husbandman we can trust. Storms, winds, rains, or sunshine, must all be accepted at His hands, with the most unwavering confidence that He who has undertaken to cultivate us and bring us to maturity, knows the best way to accomplish His end and will regulate the elements expressly with a view to our most rapid growth. (*SEC*, 179–80)

MAY 11
NURTURING OUR GROWING

Give up all your efforts to grow and simply let yourself grow. Leave it all to the Husbandman whose care it is, and who alone is able to manage it. If you will only put yourself into His hands and let Him have His own way with you, no dwarfing of your growth in the years that are past, no apparent dryness of your inward springs of life, no crookedness or deformity in your development, can in the least mar the perfect work that He will accomplish.

God's gracious promise to His backsliding children assures you of this. "I will heal their backsliding," He says, "I will love them freely: for mine anger is turned away from him. I will be as the dew unto Israel: he shall grow as the lily, and cast forth his roots as Lebanon. His branches shall spread, and his beauty shall be as the olive tree, and his smell as Lebanon. They that dwell under his shadow shall return; they shall revive as the corn, and grow as the vine: the scent thereof shall be as the wine of Lebanon'' (Hos. 14:4–7). And again He says, ''Be not afraid . . . : for the pastures of the wilderness do spring, for the tree beareth her fruit, the fig tree and the vine do yield their strength. . . . And the floors shall be full of wheat, and the vats shall overflow with wine and oil. And I will restore to you the years that the locust hath eaten'' (Joel 2:22–25).

Surely these words give us the picture of a life and growth far different from the ordinary life and growth of Christians—a life of rest and a growth without effort, yet crowned with glorious results. (*SEC*, 180–81)

MAY 12
GROWING, NOT WORRYING

All the resources of God's infinite grace will be brought to bear on the growing of the tiniest flower in His spiritual garden as certainly as they are in His earthly creation. As the violet abides peacefully in its place, content to receive its daily portion without concerning itself about the wandering of the winds or the falling of the rain, so must we repose in the present moment as it comes to us from God, content with our daily portion and without anxious thoughts, sure that all things will be made to prosper for us.

This is the kind of growth in grace in which we who have entered into the life of full trust believe. We can have a growth without care or anxiety on our part. We can blossom out into flower and fruit and become like a ''tree planted by the rivers of water, that bringeth forth his fruit in his season; his leaf also shall not wither; and whatsoever he doeth shall prosper'' (Ps. 1:3).

We rejoice to know that there are growing up now in the Lord's vineyard many such plants, who, as the lilies behold the face of the sun and grow thereby, are, by ''beholding as in a glass the glory of the Lord,'' being changed into the same image from glory to glory, even as by the Spirit of the Lord (2 Cor. 3:18). (*SEC*, 182)

MAY 13
GROWING AND ABIDING

Should you ask a believer who is blossoming beautifully under God's care how it is that he grows so rapidly and with such success, his answer would be that he is not concerned about his growing and is hardly conscious that he does grow. The Lord has told him to abide in Him and has promised that if he does thus abide, he will certainly bring forth much fruit. He is concerned, therefore, only about the abiding, which is his part, and is content to leave the cultivating, growing, training, and pruning, to the good Husbandman, who alone is able to manage these things.

Such souls are not engaged in watching self but in looking to Jesus. They do not toil and spin for their spiritual garments but leave themselves in the hands of the Lord to be arrayed as it may please Him. Self-effort and self-dependence are at an end with them. Formerly they tried to be not only the garden but the gardener as well and undertook to fulfill the duties of both. Now they are content to be what they are—the garden only. They are willing to leave the gardener's duties to the divine Husbandman, who alone is responsible for their rightful performance.

Their interest in self is gone, transferred into the hands of God. Christ alone is their all in all. The blessed result is that not even Solomon in all his glory was arrayed as these will be (cf. Matt. 6:28–29). (*SEC*, 182–83)

MAY 14
TRUSTING, NOT MANAGING

Growing is not a thing of effort but is the result of an inward life-principle of growth. All the stretching and pulling in the world could not make a dead oak grow; but a live oak grows without stretching. The essential thing, therefore, is to get within you that growing life, and then you cannot help but grow. This life is the life "hid with Christ in God" (Col. 3:3), the wonderful divine life of the indwelling Holy Spirit. Be filled and, whether you are conscious of it or not, you must grow; you cannot help growing.

Do not be troubled about your growing, but see to it that you have the growing life. Abide in the Vine. Let the life from Him flow through all your spiritual veins. Interpose no barrier to His mighty life-giving power. Yield yourself up to His lovely control. Put your growing into His hands as completely as you have put all your other affairs. Allow Him to manage it as He will. Do not concern yourself about it, nor even think of it.

Do not, as children do, keep digging up your plants to see if they are growing. Trust the divine Husbandman absolutely and always. Accept each moment's dispensation as it comes to you from His hands. Say a continual yes to your Father's will. Finally, in this, as in all the other cares of your life, "Be careful for nothing; but in every thing by prayer and supplication with thanksgiving let your requests be made known unto God. And the peace of God, which passeth all understanding, shall keep your hearts and minds through Christ Jesus" (Phil. 4:6–7). (*SEC*, 183–84)

MAY 15
WILLING AND WANTING

If a man's will is really set on a thing, he regards with a sublime indifference the obstacles that lie in the way of his reaching it. He laughs at the idea of any difficulties hindering him. How many men have gone gladly and thankfully to the ends of the world in search of worldly fortunes or to fulfill worldly ambitions, and have scorned the thought of any "cross" connected with it!

How many mothers have congratulated themselves and rejoiced over the honor done their sons in being promoted to some place of power and usefulness in their country's service, even though it involved perhaps years of separation and a life of hardship for their dear ones! Yet these same men and these very mothers would have felt and said that they were taking up crosses

101

almost too heavy to be borne, had the service of Christ required the same sacrifice of home, friends, and worldly ease.

How we look at things determines whether we think they are crosses or not. I am ashamed to think that any Christian should ever shed tears over doing a thing for Christ that a worldly man would be only too glad to do for money.

We need believers who want to do God's will as much as other people want to do their own will. It is what God intended for us, and it is what he has promised. In describing the new covenant, He says it will no more be the old covenant made on Sinai—that is, a law given from the outside, controlling a man by force—but it will be a law written within, constraining a man by love (Jer. 31:33; Heb. 10:16). (*SEC*, 188–89)

MAY 16
SURRENDERING AND SERVING

If you are in bondage in the matter of service, surrender control of your will to the Lord. Say, "Yes, Lord, yes!" to everything, and trust Him to work in you to bring your wishes and affections into conformity with His own acceptable and perfect will.

God works wonderful miracles in wills that are surrendered to Him. He makes hard things easy and bitter things sweet. He doesn't actually put easy things in the place of the hard, but He changes the hard thing into an easy one, and makes us love to do the thing we formerly hated. While we rebel against the yoke and try to avoid it, we find it hard and galling. But when we take His yoke on us with a consenting will, we find it easy and comfortable.

Many Christians love God's will in the abstract but have great problems in connection with doing it. From this there is deliverance in the wonderful life of faith. For in this life we need not carry our own burdens; the Lord is our burden-bearer, and on Him we can lay every care. He says, in effect, "Be careful for nothing, but make your requests known, and I will take care of them all" (Phil. 4:6, para.). (*SEC*, 190–92)

YIELDING AND RESTING

Paul could say, "Most gladly . . . will I . . . glory in my infirmities, that the power of Christ may rest upon me" (2 Cor. 12:9). Who would not glory in being so weak and helpless that the Lord Jesus Christ should find no hindrance to the perfect working of His mighty power through us and in us?

If the work is Christ's, the responsibility is His also, and we have no need to worry about results. Everything in reference to His work in us is known to Him, and He can manage it all. Why not leave it all with Him, then, and consent to be treated like a child and guided where to go? The most effectual workers I know are those who do not feel the least anxiety about their work, but who commit it all to their Master. They ask Him to guide them moment by moment and trust Him implicitly for each moment's supply of wisdom and strength.

To look at them you would perhaps think they were too free from care. But when you have learned God's secret of trusting and see the beauty and power of the life that is yielded up to His working, you will cease to condemn and will begin to wonder how any of God's workers can dare to carry the burdens or assume the responsibilities that He alone is able to bear. (*SEC*, 193–94)

MAY 18
BLOOMING, NOT TOILING

"Consider the lilies of the field, how they grow; they toil not, neither do they spin: and I say unto you, That even Solomon in all his glory was not arrayed like one of these" (Matt. 6:28). The lily does not toil or spin, it does not stretch or strain, it does not make any effort of any kind to grow, it is not even conscious that it is growing; but by an inward life-principle, and through the nurturing care of God's providence and the fostering of a gardener, by the heat of the sun and the falling of the rain, it grows and buds and blossoms into the beautiful plant God meant it to be.

The result of this sort of growing in the Christian life is sure. Even Solomon in all his glory, our Lord says, was not arrayed like one of God's lilies. Solomon's array cost much toiling and spinning and gold and silver in abundance; but the lily's array costs none of these. Though we may toil and spin to make for ourselves beautiful spiritual garments and may strain and stretch in our efforts after spiritual growth, we will accomplish nothing; for no man by taking thought can add one cubit to his stature (Matt. 6:27), and no array of ours can ever equal the beautiful dress with which the great Gardener clothes the plants that grow in His garden of grace under His fostering care. (*SEC*, 176)

MAY 19
WANTING HIS WILLING

No one person is responsible for all the work in the world but only for a small share. Our duty is personal and individual. The Master does not say to us, "Go and do everything"; rather He marks out a special path for each of us and gives to each a special duty.

There are "diversities of gifts" (1 Cor. 12:4) in the kingdom of God, and these gifts are given to "every man according to his . . . ability" (Matt. 25:15). I may have five talents or two or only one. I may be called to do twenty things or only one. My responsibility is simply to do that which I am called to do and nothing more. "The steps of a good man are ordered by the LORD" (Ps. 37:23)—not his way only, but each separate step in that way.

Thus the Christian life, when it is the development of the divine life working within, becomes an easy and natural life. Most Christians live on a strain because their wills are not fully in harmony with the will of God. The connection is not perfectly made at every point, and it requires an effort to move the machinery. But when once the connection is fully made and the "law of the Spirit of life in Christ Jesus" can work in us with all its mighty power, we are then indeed made "free from the law of sin and death'' (Rom. 8:2) and will know the glorious liberty of the children of God. (*SEC*, 194–96)

MAY 20
INDULGING IN REFLECTING

One form of bondage from which the life of faith delivers the soul, is in reference to the afterthoughts which always follow any Christian work. These afterthoughts are of two sorts: either the soul congratulates itself on its success and is lifted up; or it is distressed over its failure and is utterly cast down. One of these is sure to come. Of the two, I think the former is the more to be dreaded, although the latter causes at the time greater suffering. In the life of trust neither will trouble us; for, having committed ourselves in our work to the Lord, we will be satisfied to leave it to Him and will not think about ourselves in the matter.

Years ago I came across this sentence in an old book: ''Never indulge, at the close of an action, in any self-reflective acts of any kind, whether of self-congratulation or of self-despair. Forget the things that are behind, the moment they are past, leaving them with God.'' This has been of unspeakable value to me. When the temptation comes—as it does to almost every worker after the performance of any service—to indulge in these reflections of one sort or the other, I turn from them at once and refuse to think about my work at all, leaving it with the Lord to overrule the mistakes and to bless it as He chooses. I believe there would be far fewer blue Mondays for ministers of the gospel than there are now if they would adopt this plan; and I am sure all workers would find their work far less wearing. (*SEC*, 196–97)

MAY 21
CONSECRATING AND WALKING

The standard of practical holy living has been so low among Christians that the least degree of real commitment of life and walk is looked on with surprise and often even with disapprobation by a large portion of the church. For the most part, the followers of the Lord Jesus Christ are satisfied with a life so conformed to the world, that to a casual observer, no difference is discernible.

We who have heard the call of our God to a life of entire consecration and perfect trust must do differently. We must come out from the world and be separate. We must set our affections on heavenly things, not on earthly ones. We must seek first the kingdom of God and His righteousness, surrendering every thing that would interfere with this. We must walk through the world as Christ walked. We must have the mind that was in Him. We must be kind to one another, tender-hearted, forgiving one another, even as God, for Christ's sake, has forgiven us. We must not resent injuries or unkindness but must return good for evil and turn the other cheek to the hand that smites us. We must seek not our own honor but the honor of others. We must be gentle, meek, and yielding, not standing up for our own rights but for the rights of others. We must do everything not for our own glory but for the glory of God.

To sum it all up, since He who has called us is holy, so we must be holy in all manner of conversation, because it is written, "Be ye holy; for I am holy" (1 Peter 1:16). (*SEC*, 200–201)

MAY 22
LIVING IS WITNESSING

Some Christians seem to think that all the requirements of a holy life are met when they are very active and successful in Christian work. Because they do so much for the Lord in public, they feel a liberty to be disagreeable and unchristlike in private. But this is not the sort of Christian life I am depicting. If we are to walk as Christ walked, it must be in private as well as in public, at home as well as abroad; and it must be every hour all day long, not only at stated periods or on certain fixed occasions. We must be just as Christlike to our employees as we are to our minister, and just as "good" in our place of work as we are in our prayer meeting. It is in daily living, indeed, that practical piety can best show itself; and we may well question any "professions" that fail under this test of daily life.

A cross Christian; an anxious Christian; a discouraged, gloomy Christian; a doubting Christian; a complaining Christian; an exacting Christian; a selfish Christian; a cruel, hardhearted Christian; a self-indulgent Christian; a Christian with a sharp tongue or bitter spirit—all these may be very earnest in their work and have honorable places in the church, but they are not Christlike Christians. (*SEC*, 201–2)

MAY 23
SEEING IS BELIEVING

The life hid with Christ in God is a hidden life as to its source, but it must not be hidden as to its practical results. People must see that we walk as Christ walked if we say that we are abiding in Him. We must prove that we *possess* what we *profess*.

This means a great deal. It means that we must turn our backs on everything that is contrary to the perfect will of God. It means that we are to be a "peculiar people" (cf. Titus 2:14) not only in the eyes of God but in the eyes of the world around us. Wherever we go, it will be known from our habits, tempers, conversation, and pursuits, that we are followers of the Lord Jesus Christ. We must no longer look on our money as our own but as belonging to the Lord, to be used in His service. We must not feel at liberty to use our energies exclusively in the pursuit of worldly means, but must recognize that if we seek first the kingdom of God and His righteousness, all needful things will be added unto us (cf. Matt. 6:33). We will find ourselves forbidden to seek the highest places or to strain after worldly advantages. We will not be permitted to make self, as heretofore, the center of all our thoughts and aims. Our days will have to be spent not in serving ourselves but in serving the Lord. We will find ourselves called on to bear one another's burdens and so fulfill the law of Christ. All our daily duties will be more perfectly performed than ever, because whatever we do will be done, "not with eyeservice, as menpleasers; but as the servants of Christ, doing the will of God from the heart" (Eph. 6:6). (*SEC*, 202–3)

MAY 24
GIVING UP AND GROWING UP

We will undoubtedly be led by the Spirit of God if we give ourselves up to His guidance. But unless we have the right standard of Christian life set before us, we may be hindered by our ignorance from recognizing His voice. I have noticed that wherever there has been a faithful following of the Lord in a consecrated soul, several things have, sooner or later, inevitably followed.

Meekness and quietness of spirit become in time the characteristics of the daily life. A submissive acceptance of the will of God as it comes in the hourly events of each day is manifested. Pliability in the hands of God to do or to suffer all the good pleasure of His will; sweetness under provocation; calmness in the midst of turmoil and bustle; a listening to the wishes of others, an insensibility to slights and affronts; absence of worry or anxiety; deliverance from care and fear—all these and many other similar graces are invariably found to be the natural outward development of that inward life which is hid with Christ in God.

Year after year such Christians are seen to grow more unworldly, more serene, more heavenly minded, more transformed, more like Christ, until even their faces express so much of the beautiful inward divine life that all who look at them cannot but notice that they are abiding in Jesus. (*SEC*, 203–4)

MAY 25
LEARNING LIVING

Let everything else go that you may live out, in a practical daily walk and conversation, the Christ-life you have dwelling within you. You are united to your Lord by a wonderful tie; walk, then, as He walked, and show to the unbelieving world the blessed reality of His mighty power to save. You need not fear to consent to this, for He is your Savior and has power to do it all. He is not asking you, in your weakness, to do it yourself. He only asks you to yield yourself to Him that He may work in you and through you by His own mighty power. Your part is to yield yourself. His part is to work; and never, never will He give you any command that is not accompanied by ample power to obey it.

Take no thought for the morrow in this matter, but abandon yourself with a generous trust to the Good Shepherd, who has promised never to call His sheep out into any path without himself going before them. Take each little step as He makes it plain to you. Bring all your life, in each of its details, to Him to regulate and guide. Follow gladly and quickly the suggestions of His Spirit in your soul. Day by day He will bring you more and more into conformity with His will in all things, molding you and fashioning you into a "vessel" for His honor, sanctified and meet for His use. He will give to you the joy of being an "epistle of Christ" (2 Cor. 3:3), "known and read of all" (v. 2). Your light will shine so brightly that people seeing not you but your good works will glorify not you but your Father in heaven. (*SEC*, 207–8)

MAY 26
LOVING IS TRANSFORMING

Do not be afraid to let yourself go in a wholehearted devotedness to your Lord. Others may not approve, but He will; and that is enough. Do not limit or measure your obedience or your service. Let your heart and your hand be as free to serve Him as His heart and hand were to serve you. Let Him have all there is of you—body, soul, mind, spirit, time, talents, voice—everything. Lay your whole life open before Him that He may control it. Say to Him each day, "Lord, enable me to regulate this day so as to please you. Give me spirit and insight to discover what your will is in all the relations of my life. Guide me in my pursuits, my friendships, my reading, my dress, my Christian work." Do not let there be a day or an hour in which you are not consciously doing His will and wholly following Him. A personal service to your Lord such as this will give a halo to the poorest life and gild the most monotonous existence with a heavenly glow. Have you ever grieved that the romance of youth is so soon lost in the hard realities of the world? Bring Christ into your life and into all its details in this way, and a romance far grander than the brightest days of youth could ever know will thrill your soul and nothing will seem hard or stern again.

May our surrendered hearts reach out with an eager delight to discover and embrace the lovely will of our loving God! (*SEC*, 217–18)

MAY 27
LOVING IS SURRENDERING

If you have ever loved anyone enough to find sacrifice and service on his or her behalf a joy; if a whole-souled abandonment of your will to the will of another has ever gleamed across you as a blessed and longed-for privilege or as a precious reality, then, by all the tender, longing love of Christ, I entreat you to let it be so toward Him.

Jesus Christ loves you with more than the love of friendship. As a bridegroom rejoices over his bride, so He rejoices over you, and nothing but the bride's surrender will satisfy Him. He has given you all, and he asks for all in return. The slightest reserve will grieve Him to the heart. He spared not himself, and how can you spare yourself? For your sake He poured out in a lavish abandonment all that He had, and for His sake you must pour out all that you have without limit.

Be generous in your self-surrender! Meet His measureless devotion to you with a measureless devotion to Him. Be glad and eager to throw yourself unreservedly into His loving arms and to hand over the control of your life to Him. Whatever there is of you, let Him have it all. Give up forever everything that is separate from Him. Consent to resign, from this time forward, all liberty of choice, and glory in the blessed nearness of union which makes this enthusiasm of devotion not only possible but necessary. (*SEC*, 213)

MAY 28
LOVING IS DELIGHTING

Have you never longed to lavish your love and attentions on someone separated from you by position or circumstances? Have you never felt a capacity for self-surrender and devotion that has seemed to burn within you like a fire, yet you had no object on which to lavish it? Have not your hands been full of alabaster boxes of precious ointment, which you have never been near enough to any person to pour out? If, then, you are hearing the voice of your Lord calling you to a place near Him that will require a separation from everything else that will make an enthusiasm of devotion not only possible but necessary, will you shrink or hesitate? Will you think it hard that He reveals to you more of His mind than He does to others and that He will not allow you to be happy in anything that separates you from Him?

Do you want to go where Christ cannot go with you or have pursuits He cannot share? No, no, a thousand times no! You will spring out to meet His inviting will with an eager joy. His slightest wish will become such a binding law to you that it would fairly break your heart to disobey. You will glory in the very narrowness of the path He lays out for you. The obligations of love will become its greatest privileges. The right you have acquired to lavish the uttermost wealth of abandonment of all that you have on your Lord will seem to lift you into a region of unspeakable glory. The perfect happiness of perfect obedience will dawn on your soul, and you will begin to know something of what David meant when He said, "I delight to do thy will, O my God" (Ps. 40:8). (*SEC*, 213–14)

MAY 29
NEEDING HIM, NEEDING US

Has the Lord no joy in those who have surrendered themselves to Him and love to obey Him? That we should need Him, is easy to comprehend; that He should need us, seems incomprehensible. That our desire should be toward Him, is a matter of course; but that His desire should be toward us, passes the bounds of human belief. Yet He says it, and what can we do but believe Him?

Christ has made our hearts capable of this supreme overwhelming affection and has offered himself as the object of it. It is infinitely precious to Him. So much does He value it, that He has made it the first and chiefest of all His commandments that we should love Him with all our might and with all our strength. Continually at every heart He is knocking, asking to be taken in as the supreme object of love. "Will you have me," He says to the believer, "to be yours? Will you follow me into suffering and loneliness and ask for no reward but my smile of approval and my word of praise? Will you be content with pleasing me, and me only? May I have my way with you in all things? Will you come into so close a union with me as to make a separation from the world necessary? Will you accept me for your heavenly Bridegroom and leave all others to cleave only to me?"

In a thousand ways He makes this offer of union with himself to every believer. (*SEC*, 215–16)

MAY 30
ASSENTING AND DELIGHTING

Not everyone says yes to Christ. Other loves and other interests seem to some too precious to be cast aside. They will not miss heaven because of this, but they will miss an unspeakable present joy.

You, however, are not one of these. From the very first your soul has cried out eagerly and gladly to all His offers, "Yes, Lord, yes!" You are more than ready to pour out on Him all your richest treasures of love and devotedness. You have brought to Him an enthusiasm of self-surrender that perhaps may disturb and distress the so-called prudent and moderate Christians around you. Your love makes necessary a separation from the world, of which a lower love cannot even conceive. Sacrifices and services are possible and sweet to you. The life of love, on which you have entered, gives you the right to a lavish outpouring of your all on your beloved One. An intimacy and friendship that more distant souls cannot enter on, become now, not only your privilege but your duty. To you He can make known His secrets, and to you He looks for an instant response to every requirement of His love.

Oh, how wonderful is the glorious unspeakable privilege on which you have entered! How little it will matter to you if men will hate you, separate you from their company, and reproach you and cast out your name as evil for His dear sake! You may well "rejoice . . . in that day, and leap for joy, for behold, your reward is great in heaven" (Luke 6:23). If you are a partaker of His suffering, you will also be of His glory. (*SEC*, 216–17)

MAY 31
LOVING IS INDWELLING

All the dealings of God with the soul of the believer are in order to bring it into oneness with himself that the prayer of our Lord may be fulfilled: "That they all may be one; as thou, Father, art in me, and I in thee, that they also may be one in us . . . I in them, and thou in me, and that they may be made perfect in one; and that the world may know that thou hast sent me, and hast loved them, as thou hast loved me" (John 17:21–23).

This divine union was the glorious purpose in the heart of God for His people from before the foundation of the world. A mystery hid from ages and generations, it was accomplished in the death of Christ. It has been made known by the Scriptures and is realized as an actual experience by many of God's dear children.

But not by all. God desires this union with all, and He has not hidden it or made it hard, but the eyes of many are too dim and their hearts too unbelieving for them to grasp it. It is therefore for the purpose of bringing His people into the personal and actual realization of this, that the Lord calls on them so earnestly and so repeatedly to abandon themselves to Him that He may work in them all the good pleasure of His will.

Everything in the Christian life leads up to this perfect union. The Lord has made us for it, and until we have intelligently apprehended it and voluntarily consented to embrace it, the travail of His soul for us is not satisfied, nor have our hearts found their destined and real rest. (*SEC*, 219–20)

JUNE 1
LOVING IS UNITING

The usual course of Christian experience is pictured in the history of the disciples. First they were awakened to see their condition and their need, and they came to Christ and gave allegiance to Him. Then they followed Him, worked for Him, and believed in Him; and yet how unlike Him they were! Seeking to be set up one above the other; running away from the cross; misunderstanding His mission and His words; forsaking Him in time of danger—these were just a few of their weaknesses. But Christ still sent them out to preach, recognized them as His disciples, and gave them power to work for Him. They knew Christ only after the flesh, as outside of them, their Lord and Master, but not yet their life.

Then came Pentecost, and these same disciples came to know Christ as inwardly revealed, as one in union with them, their very indwelling life. Henceforth He was to them Christ within, working in them to will and to do of His good pleasure, delivering them by the law of the Spirit of His life from the bondage to the law of sin and death under which they had been held. No longer was there a war of wills and a clashing of interests between Christ and His disciples. One will alone animated them, and that was His will. One interest alone was dear to them, and that was His. They were made one with Him. (*SEC*, 220)

JUNE 2
LOVING IS BINDING

The Scriptures teach about the marvelous union of Christ with His believers. Paul told the Corinthian Christians that they were to be the temple of God and that the Spirit of God lived in them. Then we learn that those to whom these wonderful words were spoken were "babes in Christ" who were "yet carnal" and walked according to men (1 Cor. 3:1-3). In light of this, can you not see that this soul-union of which I speak, this glorious mystery of an indwelling God, is the possession of even the weakest and most failing believer in Christ? It is not a new thing you are to ask for; you need only realize that you already have it. Of every believer in the Lord Jesus it is absolutely true that his "body is the temple of the Holy Ghost which is in him, which he has to God" (1 Cor. 6:19, para.).

Although it is true that the Holy Spirit indwells the believer, it is equally true that unless the believer knows it and lives in the power of it, it is to him as though it were not. Like the treasures under a man's field, which existed there before they were known or used by him, so the life of Christ dwells in each believer as really before he knows it and lives in it as it does afterward. Its power, however, is not manifested until, intelligently and voluntarily, the believer ceases from his own life and accepts Christ's life in its place. (*SEC*, 221–22)

JUNE 3
UNITING AND BEING

Union with Christ is not a matter of emotions but of character. It is not something we are to feel but something we are to be. We may feel it very blessedly, but the vital thing is not the feeling but the reality.

No one can be one with Christ who is not Christlike. This is a manifest truth, yet I fear it is often overlooked. Strong emotions of love and joy are taken as proofs of divine union in cases where the absolutely essential proofs of a Christlike life and character are conspicuously wanting. This is contrary to the Scripture declaration that "He that saith he abideth in him ought himself also so to walk, even as he walked" (1 John 2:6). There is no escape from this, for it is not only a divine declaration but is in the very nature of things as well.

We speak of being one with a friend, and we mean that we have a union of purposes and thoughts and desires. No matter how enthusiastic our friends may be in their expressions of love and unity, there can be no real oneness between us unless there are, at least in some degree, the same likes and dislikes, the same thoughts, purposes, and ideals. Oneness with Christ means

115

being made a partaker of His nature as well as of His life; for nature and life are, of course, one.

Sweetness, gentleness, meekness, patience, long-suffering, charity, and kindness will all be natural to the Christian who is a partaker of the nature of Christ. (*SEC*, 222–23)

JUNE 4
UNITING IS SANCTIFYING

People who live in their emotions feel so at one with Christ that they look no farther than this feeling. They often delude themselves with thinking they have come into the divine union, when all the while their nature and dispositions are still under the sway of self-love.

We all know that our emotions are most untrustworthy and are largely the result of our physical condition or our natural temperaments. It is a fatal mistake, therefore, to make them the test of our oneness with Christ. This mistake works both ways. If I have very joyous emotions, I may be deluded into thinking I have entered the divine union when I have not. If I have no emotions, I may grieve over my failure to enter when I really have entered.

Character is the only real test. God is holy, and those who are one with Him will be holy also. Our Lord himself expressed His oneness with the Father in such words as these: "The Son can do nothing of himself, but what he seeth the Father do: for what things soever he doeth, these also doeth the Son likewise" (John 5:19). "If I do not the works of my Father, believe me not. But if I do, though ye believe not me, believe the works; that ye may know, and believe, that the Father is in me, and I in him" (John 10:37–38). (*SEC*, 223–24)

JUNE 5
REJOICING AND REALIZING

The test Christ gave by which the reality of His oneness with the Father was to be known, was that He did the works of the Father; and I know no other test for us now.

As a tree is known by its fruit, if we have entered into the divine union, we will bear the divine fruit of a Christlike life and conversation. Our Lord said, "He that saith, I know him, and keepeth not his commandments, is a liar, and the truth is not in him. But whoso keepeth his word, in him verily is the love of God perfected: hereby know we that we are in him" (1 John 2:5).

We know that we are in Christ if we keep His Word, so pay no regard to your feelings in this matter of oneness with Christ, but see to it that you have the fruit of a oneness in character, walk, and mind. Your emotions may be very delightful, or they may be very depressing. In neither case are they any real indication of your spiritual state. Your joy in the Lord is to be a far deeper thing than a mere emotion. It is to be the joy of knowledge, of perception, of actual existence. It is far better to be a bird, with all the actual realities of flying, than only to feel as if you are a bird, with no actual power of flying at all. Reality is always the vital thing. (*SEC*, 224–25)

JUNE 6
CONSENTING AND UNITING

Far more glorious than it is to have Christ as a dweller in the house or in the heart, is it to be brought into such a real and actual union with Him as to be one with Him—one will, one purpose, one interest, one life. Human words cannot express such a glory as this. Yet it ought to be expressed, and our souls ought to be made so unutterably hungry to realize it, that day or night we will not be able to rest without it.

Do you understand the words "one with Christ"? Do you catch the slightest glimpse of their marvelous meaning? Does not your whole soul begin to exult over such a wondrous destiny? It seems too wonderful to be true that such poor, weak, foolish beings as we are should be created for such an end as this; yet it is a blessed reality.

We are even commanded to enter into oneness with Christ. We are exhorted to lay down our own lives that His life may be lived in us. We are asked to have no interests but His interests, to share His riches, to enter into His joys, to partake of His sorrows, to manifest His likeness, to have the same mind as He had, to think and feel and act and walk as He did.

Will we consent to all this? The Lord will not force it on us, for He wants us as His companions and friends. We must do it voluntarily. The bride must say a willing yes to the Bridegroom, or the joy of their union is lacking. (*SEC*, 226–27)

JUNE 7
WILLING, DYING, LIVING

Can we not say a willing yes to our Lord? It is a very simple transaction, yet very real. There are three steps: first, we must be convinced that the Scriptures teach this glorious indwelling of God; then we must surrender our whole self to Him to be possessed by Him; and finally, we must believe that He has taken possession and is dwelling in us. We must begin to reckon ourselves dead and to reckon Christ as our only life. We must maintain this attitude of soul unwaveringly. It will help us to say, "I am crucified with Christ: nevertheless I live; yet not I but Christ liveth in me" (Gal. 2:20), over and over day and night until it becomes the habitual breathing of our souls.

We must continually put off our self-life by faith and put on the life of Christ practically as well as by faith. We must put self to death in all the details of daily life and let Christ live and work in us instead. We must never do the selfish thing but always the Christlike thing. Through constant repetition this will become the attitude of our whole being and we will come at last to understand something of what it means to be made one with Christ as He and the Father are one. Christ left all to be joined to us; will we not also leave all to be joined to Him? Our Lord prayed for this divine union, saying, "Neither pray I for these alone but for them also which shall believe on me through their word; that they all may be one; as thou, Father, art in me, and I in thee, that they also may be one in us" (John 17:20–21). (*SEC*, 227–28)

JUNE 8
KNOWING AND ACTING

"The adoption of sons" (Gal. 4:5) is surely an adoption about which there can be no uncertainty. One would think that we for whom Christ died could not question a fact so plainly stated or refuse to call God our Father. Yet many do refuse and think it presumptuous to call God their Father or to take their places boldly as His sons and heirs.

If you will look at the opening verses of each epistle in the New Testament, you will see that they are all addressed to people who knew beyond doubt that they were reconciled and forgiven children of God.

Again notice how invariably all the exhortations to holiness in the Epistles are based on an assured knowledge of our position as children of God.

We are not called on to forgive one another in order to induce Christ to forgive us; we are to forgive others because we know that He has already forgiven us. We are not commanded to be followers of God in order to become His children but because we know we are His children.

A man cannot act like a king unless he knows that he is a king; and similarly we cannot act like the sons of God unless we know that we are His sons. In fact, the knowledge of our position and standing is the essential foundation of everything else in the Christian life. (*EDR*, 7–9)

JUNE 9
BELIEVING, KNOWING, FEELING

The divine order is always: first, get your facts; second, put faith in those facts; and finally, acknowledge the feelings that come as a result of believing the facts. This order is always followed in earthly matters; but curiously enough in religious matters a great many people, otherwise very sensible, reverse this order. They put feelings first, then faith in those feelings, and come to the facts last, looking on them, one would suppose, as the result of their feelings.

Many, however, will say, "Ah, yes, I could easily believe it, if only I had the witness in myself, as the Bible says I am to have." But when is a person to have that inner witness—before he believes, or after? Does Scripture say, "he that hath the witness in himself shall believe," or "he that believeth . . . hath the witness in himself" (1 John 5:10)? Whether you put the believing or the witness first makes all the difference. The Bible puts the believing first.

The day of knowledge will dawn for us when we come to the point of implicitly believing God! It must be understood, however, that this knowledge will come to us not as a feeling but as a perception.

Feelings may do for Sundays or for exceptional occasions of special religious experience, but knowledge is the only thing that will avail us in our everyday life. (*EDR*, 11–13)

JUNE 10
FEEDING AND GROWING

Just as we must eat to live in our physical lives, so must we in our spiritual lives. "Give us this day our daily bread" (Matt. 6:11) is a prayer that includes the soul as well as the body, and unless the religion of Christ contains this necessary food for our weekday lives as well as for our Sunday lives, it is a grievous failure. But this it does. It is full of principles that apply to commonplace aspects of our lives. The soul that would grow strong must feed itself on these as well as on the more dainty fare of sermons and services and weekly celebrations.

It is of vital importance that we choose the right sort of spiritual food on which to feed. If unwholesome physical food injures physical health, so also must unwholesome mental food injure spiritual health. There is such a thing as spiritual indigestion, just as there is physical indigestion. More and more, physicians are urging that the state of our health is largely dependent on the food we eat; and gradually people are learning the importance of eating health-giving food. This is equally true on the spiritual plane, although it is not so generally recognized.

The laws of spiritual hygiene are as real and as inexorable as the laws of physical hygiene, and it is of vital importance to our soul's health that we realize this. (*EDR*, 14–15)

JUNE 11
EATING AND AILING

Perhaps we do not like our providential surroundings or our church or our preacher or our work or our family associations, and we are always thinking we could be better Christians if only our circumstances were different—if we could attend a different church, move into a different neighborhood, or engage in a different sort of work. Our souls "loathe the light food" (cf. Num. 21:5) of God's providing; and we question, as the Israelites did, whether God is really able to provide the spiritual food necessary for us in the "wilderness" where He has placed us.

The "wrath of God" is only another name for the inevitable results of our own bad actions. God's wrath is never, as human wrath generally is, an arbitrary condition of His mind, resulting from His displeasure at being crossed. It is simply the necessary result of a broken law, the inevitable reaping of that which has been sown. If a man eats unsuitable food, he will have indigestion. An ignorant person may say that it was the wrath of God that brought on his indigestion, but we who understand the laws of health know that his indigestion is simply the result of the unsuitable food he has eaten. Similarly the sickly spiritual condition of so many Christians is not, as they sometimes think, a direct infliction of God's displeasure but is simply and only the necessary consequence of the unsuitable and indigestible spiritual food on which they have been feeding. (*EDR*, 16–17)

JUNE 12
THINKING AND GROWING

Very few persons realize the effect of thought on the condition of the soul. It is, in fact, its food, the substance from which it gets its strength, health, and beauty, or on which it may become weak, unhealthy, and deformed. The things we think about are the things we feed on. If we think low and corrupt thoughts, we bring diseases on our soul, just as we bring diseases on our body by eating spoiled or unnutritious food.

Christ told His disciples that He was the "bread of life" (John 6:35). He meant that to feed on Him was to receive and believe the truths He taught them.

The things we think on are the things that feed our souls. If we think on pure and lovely things, we will grow pure and lovely like them; and the converse is equally true. Very few people realize this, and consequently there is a great deal of carelessness, even with careful people, in regard to their thoughts. They guard their words and actions with the utmost care, but their thoughts, which are the very root of everything in character and life, they neglect entirely. So long as it is not put into spoken words, what goes on in the mind seems of no consequence. No one hears or knows, and therefore they imagine that the vagrant thoughts that come and go do no harm. Such persons are careless about the food offered to their thoughts and accept without discrimination anything that comes. (*EDR*, 17–19)

JUNE 13
THINKING IS FEEDING

The apostle Paul says that we are to bring all our thoughts into captivity to the obedience of Christ (2 Cor. 10:5). This cannot mean, of course, that we are to be thinking of Christ every minute. Common sense shows us that that is neither possible nor desirable. It means that we are to have Christ's thoughts about things instead of our own, that we are to look at things as He does, and that we are to judge as He judges. This we are to do with "every thought," not with our Sunday thoughts only but with our weekday thoughts as well. It would never do for the health of our bodies to be careful of our food on Sundays only, paying no regard to what we eat the rest of the week. Similarly, it is idiotic to expect our souls to thrive if they are provided with suitable food on Sundays alone and are left to feed on ashes throughout the other days of the week.

Neither will little doses of suitable food now and then do. One hour of a Christlike way of looking at things will not make much headway in the matter of the soul's health against ten hours of unchristlike ways. Every thought we think, in every hour we live, must be not necessarily about Christ, but it must be the thought Christ would think were He placed in our circumstances. This is what it means to feed on Him and be nourished by the true Bread of Life that comes from heaven. (*EDR*, 21–22)

JUNE 14
KNOWING HIM PERSONALLY
what it life

The crucial question for each of us in our everyday life is: What do I think about Christ? To some the question may seem to require a doctrinal answer, and I do not at all say that there is no idea of doctrines involved in it. But the doctrinal answer, valuable as it may be, is not the one of most importance for every day. Our salvation does not depend on the doctrines concerning Christ but on the person of Christ himself, on what He is and on what He does.

If it were doctrines only that were in question, we might find it necessary to appeal to the creeds and dogmas of our own particular sect or denomination in order to find out just what we do believe or at least ought to believe. But it is our personal estimate of our Lord and Master that is in question. What is our own opinion of His character and His ways? What sort of person do we really think Him to be? Is He kind and loving, or is He harsh and severe? Is He trustworthy? Is He sympathizing? Is He true to His promises? Is He faithful? Is He self-sacrificing? Is He full of compassion, or is He full of condemnation? Is He our tender Brother, or is He our hard Taskmaster? Does He care most about himself or about us? Is He on our side or against us?

It is by our answers to questions like these that we will reveal what our real estimate of Christ is. We may have all the Christian doctrines at our fingers' ends yet not have the faintest conception of the real character of Christ himself.

What do you think about Christ? (*EDR*, 24–27)

out thoughts control our action

JUNE 15
NAMING IS KNOWING

To know Christ's "name" does not mean to know that He was called Christ or Jesus; it means to know His character. God's namings always mean character. They are never arbitrary as our namings are, having no connection with the work or character of the one named. They are always revelations. They tell us what the person is or what he does. The angel announced to Joseph concerning the child Mary was carrying, "Thou shalt call His name Jesus: for he shall save His people from their sins" (Matt. 1:21), Jesus meaning a Savior.

The question, "What do you think about Christ?" may equally be rendered, "By what name do you call Christ?" for name and character are one. What, then, are the names we individually are bestowing on our Lord? In words and on Sundays we are calling Him our "Lord and Savior Jesus Christ," but in thought and act in our everyday life we are unconsciously calling Him by many other names, and some of them may be names that would shock us to hear spoken or to see in print. So few of us, I fear, really know Him!

It is of no use for us to call Jesus "Master" or "Lord," while we are refusing to do the things He commands. Our words may hide our thoughts, but our actions reveal them. If we really think He is our Lord, we will not fail to obey Him. Thoughts, not words, control a person's actions. (*EDR*, 27–28)

JUNE 16
NAMING IS TRUSTING

The LORD is my Shepherd —

if I follow, think I have to trust + to bey. to say + Feel

In the Bible, Christ is called the Good Shepherd. "I am the good shepherd" (John 10:14), He says. We have said countless times since our early childhood, "The LORD is my shepherd" (Ps. 23:1). But how about our thoughts? Do they correspond with our words? What do we think of Christ? Do we think of Him as being our Shepherd, who cares for us as a good shepherd cares for his sheep? Or do we feel as if we ourselves are the

124

No fear of evil

He Loves — He Care — He provides + comfort

shepherds, who must keep a strict watch over Christ in order to make Him faithful to us?

There are certain characteristics that every good shepherd must have. He must devote himself with all his strength and wisdom to the care of his flock. He must forget his own ease and comfort in promoting their well-being. He must protect them from every danger and must stand between them and all their enemies. He must never forget them nor neglect them, and he must be willing to lay down his life for their sakes. Is this what we think of Christ when we call Him by the name of Shepherd? I am afraid we look on Him in regard to our daily life as an unfaithful shepherd who forgets and neglects his flock; or as a hireling who, when he sees the wolf coming, "leaveth the sheep, and fleeth" (John 10:12); or as the selfish shepherds of Ezekiel's prophecy who "fed themselves, and fed not [God's] flock" (Ezek. 34:8). We honor Christ on Sundays with our lips, but the hearts of too many, on weekdays, are far from Him. (*EDR*, 29)

Not unfaithful — will not neglect us

JUNE 17
NAMING IS BELIEVING

— He understands it — is tender + is careful

Christ is called our Comforter, but how many of us take a common-sense view of this name and really believe that He will not and does not leave us comfortless? A comforter must be one who understands our sorrow and need and who sympathizes with our sufferings. A comforter must not criticize or judge harshly. He must be tender and considerate and full of the charity that covers a multitude of faults. A comforter must put arms of love about us and whisper in our ears words of infinite kindness. A comforter is for dark times not for bright times. If anyone should call himself our comforter and then run away and hide himself when storms and trials come, we would think that his name of comforter was merely an empty title, and all his promises of comfort would be like idle tales.

His Love is kind at all times

Christ is also called Savior. If He is called by any one name more than another, it is this. He is called over and over the Savior of the world. Now, what is the common-sense view of a Savior? Manifestly, He is one who saves. He is not one who

SAVIOR

125

He SAVES us — NOW not Later

merely offers to save, but He must of necessity, from the very nature of the name, be one who actually does it. The only claim to the name lies in the fact behind the name. Do we think of Christ as actually saving us now? Or do we think of Him as offering to save us at some future time and accompanying that offer with such well-nigh impossible conditions that the salvation is practically not available for us at all? Everything in our Christian lives depends not on what we say of Christ but on what we think of Him when we call Him our Savior. (*EDR*, 30–32)

the

Not what we know & Believe is FAITH
But what we think + act on that SAVES

JUNE 18
KNOWING IS RESTING

The one absolutely essential thing is to know the Lord. I do not mean know about Him; that avails but little. I do mean to become acquainted with Him, to know what sort of a being He is.

Do I Know Him personally — Really

I can well understand how Paul could say so confidently that he counted all things but loss for the excellency of the knowledge of Christ (Phil. 3:8). When once the soul has come to this knowledge, all fear and doubt, and even perplexity are at an end, and perfect peace must of necessity reign undisturbed.

Know Him

No one can possibly have come to know Christ as He really is without entering into absolute rest. It is like the rest and peace of a young child in the presence of his mother. The child knows instinctively that his mother will not let anything harm him; therefore he has no fears. Christians who know the Lord, know intelligently that He will not let harm come to them; therefore they can have no fear. Where there is an invincible protector there can be no anxieties. What is needed then is for Christians to find out that they have just such a caretaker and protector in Christ. This is why Paul could say, and we can all unite with him, that all things are to be counted as loss for the excellency of the knowledge of Christ.

But some may ask, "How can I acquire this knowledge? It seems all so vague and mystical to me that I do not know where to begin." I would reply that there is nothing mystical about it. Begin by making yourself acquainted with Him in the way you

Knowing Him
in His presence is No Fear - doubt - but perfect peace & Rest

126

would any historical character you wanted to know: study His life and ponder His words. (*EDR*, 33–35)

[handwritten: Study His Life - His word - visit with Him!]

JUNE 19
YIELDING, TRUSTING, OBEYING

In everyday religion there are three things that are always absolutely necessary in the attitude of the soul toward the Lord: to yield, trust, and obey. No peace, no victory, no communion are possible where these are absent; and no difficulty is insurmountable where they are present. It is a sort of universal recipe for the cure of all spiritual diseases and difficulties.

To yield something means to give that thing to the care and keeping of another. To yield ourselves to the Lord, therefore, is to give entire possession and control of our being to Him. It means to abandon ourselves; to take hands off of ourselves. The word consecration is often used to express this yielding, but I hardly think it is a good substitute. For many people, consecrating themselves seems to convey the idea of doing something very self-sacrificing and good and grand. It therefore admits of a subtle form of self-glorification. But "yielding" conveys a far more humbling idea; it implies helplessness and weakness and the glorification of another rather than of ourselves. *[handwritten: not]* *[handwritten: work]*

To illustrate the difference between the two ideas, let us notice the difference between consecrating one's powers or one's money to some great work and the yielding of oneself in illness to the care of a skillful physician. In the one case we confer a favor, in the other we receive a favor. In the one case, self can glory; in the other, self is abased. (*EDR*, 36–37)

[handwritten: yield, trust & obey - A must - give - All Humble self - weakness - helplessness - Glory to Him]

JUNE 20
YIELDING, NOT CONSECRATING

If I were lost in a wild and lonely forest and a skillful guide came to my rescue, I could not be said to consecrate myself to that guide, but I would be said to yield myself to his care and guidance. To consecrate is an Old Testament idea and belongs

[handwritten: yield to His care + guidance]

to the old covenant of works; to yield is a New Testament idea and belongs to the new covenant of grace.

We are to "present" ourselves (Rom. 12:1), to hand ourselves over, to do with ourselves something similar to what we do with the money we entrust to the bank—give ourselves over to the care and keeping and use of God. It is not the idea of sacrifice in the sense we usually give that word, namely, as of a great cross taken up; it is the sense of surrender, of abandonment, of giving up the control and keeping and use of ourselves to the Lord. This is our "reasonable service," or, as I would express it, our common-sense service.

To yield to God means to belong to God, and to belong to God means to have all His infinite power and infinite love on our side. A man is bound to take care of anything that belongs to him, and so is God. Therefore, when I invite you to yield yourselves to Him, I am inviting you to avail yourselves of an inexpressible and most amazing privilege.

God always delivers those, regardless of circumstances or seemings, yield themselves up to His keeping. (*EDR*, 37–39)

JUNE 21
YIELDING AND TRUSTING

In the Bible the word "believe" is often used instead of the word "trust," but the idea is the same. In the New Testament especially, "believe" is the word generally used, but it does not refer to believing in doctrines or in history but rather believing in a person or, in other words, trusting that person. Christ always said, "Believe in me" not "Believe this or that about me" but "Believe in me, in me as a Savior who can save." You cannot very well trust in doctrines or plans no matter how much you may believe in them, but you can always trust in the Lord, whether or not you understand His plans or the doctrines concerning Him.

Trusting can hardly be said to be distinct from yielding. It is, in fact, the necessary correlation to it.

Trusting, therefore, simply means that when we have yielded, or given, ourselves to the Lord, we then have perfect confidence that He will manage us and everything concerning us exactly

128

right, and we consequently leave the whole care and managing in His hands. It is what we do a hundred times a day with other people. We are continually yielding ourselves or our affairs to the care and management of someone else and feel the least concern in so doing. We never pass a day that we do not take the steps of yielding and trusting. If we find it an easy and natural thing to do toward other human beings, how much easier it must be to do it toward God. (*EDR*, 39–40)

JUNE 22
YIELDING AND OBEYING

Obedience is the logical outcome of yielding and trusting.

If we want the Lord to care for us, protect us from our enemies, and provide for our needs, it stands to reason that we must obey His voice and walk in the paths He marks out for us.

Whatever difficulty we are in, therefore, we must take these steps. First, we must yield our circumstances absolutely to the Lord; second, we must trust Him without anxiety to manage it; and third, we must simply and quietly obey His will in regard to it. A parallel case would be for one to put a difficult matter into the hands of a lawyer and be required by that lawyer to do certain things or follow certain courses in order to insure the success of the case. Obviously, the only common-sense course to take would be to follow his advice and comply with his suggestions as completely as possible. To refuse to do so would be to make it impossible for the most skillful lawyer to carry the case to a successful issue.

Obedience, therefore, may be said to be simply a matter of self-interest. It is not a demand made of us but a privilege offered. Like yielding and trusting, it is simply a way of bringing divine wisdom and power to bear upon our affairs. If we would only learn to look at it this way, we would find that it had lost half of its terrors. We then would be able to say with our divine Master, "I delight to do thy will" (cf. Ps. 40:8), and not merely, "I consent to do it." (*EDR*, 41–42)

JUNE 23
YIELDING AND APPLYING

It remains for us to learn how to apply the remedy—yield, trust, obey—to the disease. Physicians will tell us that a remedy, to be effectual, must be faithfully taken as long as the need continues. In order, therefore, to make this cure-all effectual, we must faithfully take it. That is, we must yield ourselves and all our interests, weekday interests as well as Sunday ones, to God in a continual surrender. We must take our hands off ourselves and off our affairs of every kind, and then leave them all in perfect trust to the Lord to manage. Finally, we must simply, day by day and hour by hour, obey His will as far as we know it. This is to be done about everything, literally everything. We are to keep nothing back. Who would want to keep anything in his own care, when he has the privilege of putting it in God's care?

About the next thing that troubles you, take the three steps I have pointed out. Yield it entirely to the Lord, trust Him about it perfectly, and obey Him implicitly. Persist in this unwaveringly; and then see if, sooner or later, peace and deliverance do not surely come. I have never known it to fail. The deliverance may not always come in your own way, but it will surely come in God's way; and God's way is always the best way, the way we ourselves would choose if we knew all that He knows. (*EDR*, 43–44)

JUNE 24
EVERYTHING SERVING

The psalmist David declared that all things are God's servants (Ps. 119:91), and the apostle Paul declared that all things are ours (1 Cor. 3:21–22)—not just a few things but all things, not things on Sundays only but things on weekdays as well. We generally think that only the good people or the good things of life can serve God, but the psalmist tells us that all things, whether good or bad, are God's servants. That is, all things, no matter what their origin may be, are used by the Lord to accomplish His purposes, and all are made to work together for His ends.

Both the psalmist and the apostle spoke out of the midst of some of the darkest problems and mysteries of life. The psalmist told of how the proud had "digged pits" for him (Ps. 119:85), and of how his enemies had persecuted him; yet in the very face of things, which must have seemed mysterious to him, he could still declare that God's faithfulness was to all generations, and that all things were His servants. The "wrath of man" (cf. Ps. 76:10) is certainly a wrong thing, and yet even this becomes God's servant and is forced to accomplish His purposes and bring Him praise.

While the Lord does not inaugurate the evil, when that evil is directed against His children, He makes it His "servant" to carry them a blessing. All things are yours not to trouble you and do you harm but to bless you and do you good. (*EDR*, 46–51)

JUNE 25
THANKSGIVING IN TESTING

No one can possibly obey the command to give thanks in everything (1 Thess. 5:18), who fails to see that all things are God's servants (Ps. 119:91). But to those who do see this, every event of life, even the most disagreeable, is only a bearer of blessing; and as a consequence, all their days are filled with continual thanksgiving.

Perhaps some may ask why it is, if all things are indeed God's servants, sent to bring us some message or gift, that they themselves never seem to get these gifts or messages. The answer is simply that because these gifts and messages have come to them wrapped in coarse and ugly packages, and by the hands of rough-looking messengers, they have refused to receive and open them. Their ears have been so filled with their own complainings that they could not hear God's message, and their eyes have been so absorbed in looking at the visible suffering and hardness that they failed to look for the unseen blessing.

It is the truest common sense, therefore, to welcome every

event of life as God's servant bringing us something from Him, to overlook the disagreeableness of the messenger in the joy of the message, and to forget the hurt of the trial in the sweetness of the blessing it brings.

Paul had learned this lesson and came at last even to "take pleasure" (2 Cor. 12:10) in the "messenger of Satan" that was sent to "buffet" him (v. 7). This "thorn in the flesh" (v. 7) was the blessed revelation to his soul of the power of Christ resting on him. For the sake of a similar revelation, who would not welcome a similar thorn? (*EDR*, 55–57)

JUNE 26
TESTINGS BECOME BLESSINGS

There are no second causes to the children of God. There cannot be, because all the so-called "second causes" are God's "servants," and He could never allow any of them to interfere with His purposes or frustrate His will. Nothing can touch us without God's permission; and when that permission is granted, it can only be because He, in His love and wisdom, sees that the event He permits contains for us some blessing or some medicine that our souls need. If He withholds that permission, men and devils may rage in vain.

One of the greatest difficulties in the Christian life arises from the failure to see this fact. The child of God says, "It would be easy to say, 'Thy will be done,' to my trials if I could only see that they come from God. But my trials and crosses come almost always from some human hand, and I cannot say, 'Thy will be done,' to human beings." This is all true; but what if we should see in every human instrumentality one of God's "servants" coming to us with hands full of messages and blessings from Him? Could we not then receive them with submission and even with thankfulness? The trial itself may be very hard for flesh and blood to bear, and I do not mean that we can be thankful for that, but the blessing it brings is surely always cause for the deepest thankfulness. I may not be able to give thanks for an unkind friend, but I can give thanks for the patience and meekness brought to me through the instrumentality of this friend's unkindness. (*EDR*, 54–55)

132

JUNE 27
CONCENTRATING OR CONSECRATING

There is no subject more vital to an everyday religion than a clear understanding of the right relations of our own individuality to the rest of the world. To most people the greatest persons in the universe are themselves. Their lives are made up of endless variations on the word "me." What do people think of ME? How will things affect ME? Will this make ME happy? Do people value ME as they should? Look at MY great estate. Behold MY remarkable experiences. Listen to MY wisdom. Adopt MY views. Follow MY methods. And so on and so on through the varied range of daily life. Always and everywhere this giant ME intrudes himself, demanding attention and insisting on his rights.

The "preacher," as the author of Ecclesiastes calls himself, tried to solve the problem of earthly happiness. "I sought in my heart," he says, "till I might see what was that good for the sons of men, which they should do under the heaven all the days of their life" (2:3). He secured for himself everything that he thought would in any way add to the welfare and happiness of ME. At the end, in reviewing it all, he was forced to declare that "all was vanity and vexation of spirit, and there was no profit under the sun" (2:11).

A little exercise of common sense would show us that this must be the inevitable result of everything that has ME, and ME only, as its center. There is never any "profit" in it but always a grievous loss. (*EDR*, 58–59)

JUNE 28
GRASPING IS LOSING

Have we not all, in our own experience, discovered that every endeavor that has ME as its center has no profit in it? You have set your heart, perhaps, on procuring something for the benefit or pleasure of your own great big ME, but when you have secured it, this ungrateful ME has refused to be satisfied and has turned away in weariness and disgust from what it has cost you so much to procure. Or you have labored to have the claims of this ME recognized by those around you and have reared with great pains and effort a high pinnacle on which you have seated yourself to be admired by all beholders. And right at the critical moment, the pinnacle has tottered over, and your glorious ME has fallen into the dust, and contempt instead of honor, has become its portion. Never, under any circumstances, has it in the end paid you to try and exalt your great exacting ME, for always, sooner or later, it has all proved to be nothing but "vanity and vexation of spirit" (Eccl. 2:11).

One of the worst effects of self-praise is that our fancied good grows and swells as we look at it and talk about it; and hence a man whose eyes and thoughts are centered on self, comes to have for the most part a strangely exaggerated notion of the goodness and worthiness of his ME. It is like a sort of spiritual dropsy that swells the soul up to twice its natural size, and which looks, perhaps, on the surface like an increase of health and strength but is in reality only a symptom of a sore disease. Such a one is suffering from what the French call *La maladie du moi*, and it is one of the most fatal maladies there is. (*EDR*, 59–61)

JUNE 29
SERVING IS SUCCEEDING

It is an inevitable law that whoever exalts himself will be abased—perhaps not outwardly, so that he himself knows it, but secretly, in the estimation of those around who are always unfavorably impressed in exact proportion to the efforts self makes to create a favorable impression.

ME is a most exacting personage, requiring the best seats and the highest places for himself. He feels grievously wounded if his claims are not recognized and his rights not considered. Most of the quarrels among Christians arise from the clamorings of this gigantic ME. "So and so was exalted above ME; MY rights have been trampled on; no one considers ME." How much there is of this sort of thing, expressed or unexpressed, in every heart where ME is king! Few of us understand the true glory of taking our seats in the lowest rooms! Yet if we are to have real honor "in the presence of them that sit at meat" with us (Luke 14:10), this is what we must do.

To be the servant of all is not a gratifying position to ME. It is much more suitable to this mighty ME that others should bow to him and that he should exercise lordship and authority over them. It is, therefore, only when this tyrannical ME is cast out of our inner kingdom that we can understand the blessedness and glory of serving all and can realize the greatness that comes by this road. Humiliations are the medicine that the Great Physician generally administers to cure the spiritual illnesses that are caused by the soul's continual feeding on thoughts of ME. (*EDR*, 62–64)

JUNE 30
SELF-DENYING, NOT SELF-DISPARAGING

Our Lord tells us we do well to beware of people who "love salutations in the marketplaces" (Mark 12:38), and our own instincts tell us the same.

Some people think they are humble and lowly in heart when they say bitter and disparaging things about themselves, but I am convinced that the giant ME is often quite as much exalted and puffed up by self-blame as by self-praise. Self is so greedy of notice, that, if it cannot be praised, it would rather be blamed than not noticed at all. It is content to say all manner of ugly things about itself, if only it can by this means attract attention to itself. If it feels a delicacy about saying, "I am so good," it finds almost as much delight in saying, "I am so bad," which proves that it is not so very bad after all, since it can be so humble!

It is, however, a very different thing to say disparaging things about ourselves than having anyone else say them about us. If we are in the habit of making these self-disparaging remarks, let us think for a moment how we should feel if our friends were to agree with our remarks and were to repeat them to others as their own opinions. Suppose the next time you should say of yourself, "Oh, I am such a poor good-for-nothing creature," some one of your friends should reply, "Yes, that is exactly what I have always thought about you." How would your ME like that? What can be more delicious to a delicate self-love than to hear itself applauded for seeming humble? The truly meek and lowly heart does not want to talk about its ME at all, either for good or evil. (*EDR*, 64-65)

JULY 1
WILLING, NOT FEELING

In ordinary life everything depends on the will, which is, as we all know, the governing power in a person's nature. By the will, I do not mean our wishes, feelings, or longings, but our choice, our deciding power, the king within us to which all the rest of our nature must yield obedience. I mean, in short, the person himself, the ego—that personality in the depths of the being which is felt to be the real self. A great deal of trouble arises from the fact that so few seem to understand this secret of the will.

The common thought is that religion resides not in the will but in the emotions, and the emotions are looked on as the governing power in our nature. Consequently, all the attention of the soul is directed toward our feelings, and as these are satisfactory or otherwise, the soul rests or is troubled. The moment we discover that true religion resides in the will alone, we are raised above the domination of our feelings and realize that, so long as our will is steadfast toward God, the varying states of our emotions do not in the least affect the reality of the divine life in the soul. It is a great emancipation to make this discovery; and a little common sense applied to religion would soon, I think, reveal it to us all. (*EDR*, 68-69)

JULY 2
WILLING IS LIVING

The will is the stronghold of our being. If God is to get complete possession of us, He must possess our will. When He says to us, "My son, give me your heart," it is equivalent to saying, "Surrender your will to my control, that I may work in it to will and to do of my good pleasure." It is not the feelings of a man that God wants but his will.

The "hidden man of the heart" (1 Peter 3:4) is the Bible description of the will. Our feelings are not ourselves. What God desires is not fervent emotions but a pure intention of the will. The whole of His scrutiny falls on this "hidden man of the heart." Where He finds this honestly devoted to himself, He disregards all the clamor of our feelings and is satisfied.

It is very possible to pour out our emotions on a matter without really giving our hearts at all. We sometimes see people who are very lavish with their feelings but whose wills remain untouched. We call this sentimentality, and we mean that there is no reality in it. To get at reality, the heart, or in other words, the will, must be reached. What the will does is real, and nothing else is. (*EDR*, 72–73)

JULY 3
JUSTIFYING AND LOVING

"[Christ] through the eternal Spirit offered himself without spot to God" (Heb. 9:14).

We find unspeakable comfort in the study of the Old Testament type of Christ's offering for our sins. The Israelites' offerings were given according to God's instructions. He was a loving God who longed to deliver His people and who therefore himself provided the way by which it could be accomplished. And in the New Testament we read that "God was in Christ, reconciling the world unto himself, not imputing their trespasses unto them" (2 Cor. 5:19).

Many people seem to look at God as an angry judge whose wrath needs to be appeased and who can only be satisfied with the blood of His Son. The truth is that God is a loving and just creator whose very justice toward His helpless creatures has joined with His love to save us. We read in 1 John 3:16, "Hereby perceive we the love of God, because he laid down his life for us." And again, in John 3:16, "For God so loved the world, that he gave his only begotten Son, that whosoever believeth in him should not perish but have everlasting life."

It would require a volume to quote all the passages where this truth is set forth. The fact is, God's justice and love ought never to have been separated, for love always includes justice, and true justice cannot exist without love. It is indeed true, if we can only understand it, that, as Faber says, God's justice is a bed where we may lay our anxious hearts and be at perfect rest. (*OTT*, 48–49)

JULY 4
BEING LOVING

"He that loveth not knoweth not God; for God is love" (1 John 4:8).

Notice that this verse does not say merely that God is loving but that God is love. That is, it is His very nature, or essence, not merely one of His attributes but God himself. Therefore, all that He does is from the root of love; and we are compelled to believe this no matter how it may look, because it could not, in the very nature of things, be otherwise.

What kind of love is this? When did God begin to love us?

He was always love and, therefore, has always loved us. His love has no beginning, because it is from everlasting; and it has no ending, because it is to everlasting.

Some people think God loves us because we love Him and that He does not begin to love us until we first love Him. But in the very nature of things, it must be exactly the other way.

Our great need, therefore, is to find out this fact of His abiding love. Our question of one another, or of our own hearts, ought to be not, "Do you love God?" but, "Have you found out that God loves you?"

Why does God love us? God loves us because He is love and cannot help loving, just as the sun is light and cannot help shining. God does not wait for us to become good to love us. He loves us while we are still sinners just as mothers love their children even when they are naughty. (*VU*, 20–21)

JULY 5
LOVING IS UNFAILING

God is love; therefore love is the key to the mystery of God. He is not only loving, but He is infinitely more than that: He is love itself. The sun not only gives light, it is light—the source, center, and very being of light itself. This it always is, although it may be hidden from our eyes by clouds or misrepresented by colored or smoked glass.

We have all used the expression "God is love" hundreds of times, no doubt; but I am afraid it has conveyed to our minds no more real idea of the facts of the case than if we had said, "God is wood."

If we would know God, we must know what love is; and then we must apply to God all the best and highest that we know of love. For God is absolutely under the law of love; that is, He is under an inevitable constraint to obey it. He alone of all the universe, because His very essence or nature is love, cannot help loving. We whose natures are not altogether composed of love but are mixed up with a great many other things, do not always love. Because this is the case with ourselves, we think it must also be the case with God; and we torment ourselves with imagining that because of our own special unworthiness He will surely fail to love us. What a useless torment that is! (*EDR*, 175)

JULY 6
LOVING, NOT WAVERING

"We love him, because he first loved us," is what the Bible says (1 John 4:19). But we are continually tempted to reverse this order and say, "He loves us because we first loved Him"; and then, finding our own love so weak and poor, we naturally begin to doubt whether He loves us at all. We can never do anything but doubt so long as we think God's love for us is dependent on the amount of our love for Him. To think this, is to fly in the face of every word He has said about it. Our duty, therefore, is to throw aside every doubt and believe unwaveringly in the unmerited but unfailing love of God.

To keep ourselves in the love of God, or, in other words, to keep ourselves in God's love, does not mean, as so many think, to keep ourselves loving Him. It means to settle ourselves down, as it were, into His love as an absolute and unalterable fact, to take up our abode in it, and to stay in it forever. It means never to doubt His love or fear losing it, but to believe in it and trust it, despite all seemings to the contrary, utterly and steadfastly and forever.

The soul that is "rooted and grounded" in the love of God (Eph. 3:17) and keeps itself there unwaveringly, has got into a region where doubt is impossible. For who could doubt love? It is in the very nature of love to do the very best it possibly can for those it loves. This is its law. If we fear, we have never yet fully believed in the great tenderness of the love of God! (*EDR*, 221–22)

JULY 7
LOVING IS EVERLASTING

The law of divine love is that it is everlasting. It has had no beginning and can have no end. So little is this understood, that many people have a rooted conviction that God only begins to love them after they have shown Him that they love Him and that He ceases to love them the moment they in any way displease Him. They look at His love as a fickle thing not to be depended on.

Could we "perceive the love of God" (see 1 John 3:16), we would never again know a moment of "fear," let the outlook be as dark or dangerous as it might.

Love suffereth long.

Love is kind.

Love envieth not.

Love vaunteth not itself.

Love is not puffed up.

Love doth not behave itself unseemly.

Love seeketh not her own.

Love is not easily provoked.

140

Love thinketh no evil.
Love rejoiceth not in iniquity.
Love rejoiceth in the truth.
Love beareth all things.
Love believeth all things.
Love hopeth all things.
Love endureth all things.
Love never faileth (1 Cor. 13:4–8, para.).
This sort of love cannot be spelled s-e-l-f-i-s-h-n-e-s-s! (*EDR*, 178–79)

JULY 8
LOVING IS FREEING

The most essential law of love is that characteristic of it which makes it inclusive of all other laws, namely, ''Love worketh no ill to his neighbor'' (Rom. 13:10). It is the very nature of love that it cannot by any possibility work ill to its neighbor. It is as impossible as it would be for the sun to give darkness instead of light. Love loves and cannot, therefore, do anything contrary to love. It is not that it *will not* or *should not* but simply and only that it *cannot*.

We must remember, however, that a great deal of what is called love should really be spelled s-e-l-f-i-s-h-n-e-s-s. Some people love their own enjoyment of their friends more than they love the friends themselves, and they consider their own welfare in their intercourse with those they profess to love far more than the welfare of the so-called loved ones. It has been said that we never really love anyone until we can do without them for their good. Measured by this test, how few there are who really love. Many lives are marred and made miserable by the selfishness of some relative or friend (too often a parent), who, under the plea of exceeding love, will not allow the least liberty of action in the loved one and will do everything possible to hinder development in every area that does not add to their own personal pleasure or is not agreeable to them. Surely such a course, however it may be disguised, can spring from nothing but selfishness. (*EDR*, 173–74)

JULY 9
LOVING IS DEMANDING

"A new commandment I give unto you, That ye love one another; as I have loved you, that ye also love one another. By this shall all men know that ye are my disciples, if ye have love one to another" (John 13:34–35).

Let us apply this law in two ways: first, to define God's relationship to us, and, second, to teach us what ought to be our relationship to one another.

We all have an ideal as to what love between human beings should be, and we realize a sense of condemnation whenever we fail to come up to our standard. If it is true that we are to love one another as Christ loves us, the converse must be true also: that Christ must love us as we know we ought to love one another. In other words, the law of love from God to us is exactly the same as the law of love from us to one another. What love demands from me to my brothers and sisters is what love demands from God to me. This is a far more vital point than might appear at first, for wrong views of the love of God lie, I am convinced, at the root of most of our spiritual difficulties. We take the worst elements in our own characters—selfishness, impatience, suspiciousness, and hard thoughts of one another—as the key to interpret God, instead of taking our best elements of love, self-sacrifice, and patience, as the key. And so we subvert every single law of love in our interpretation of God, who is love itself. (*EDR*, 179–80)

JULY 10
YIELDING AND REJOICING

To my mind the greatest cause for rejoicing that our poor world can have is that God has chosen to give us His holy, blessed, and lovely law and has taught us to say, "Thy will be done." Without the will of God, this world would indeed be a place of misery; but the presence and accomplishment of His will transforms it into an outer court of heaven.

If we but knew our God and His love, I am sure we would "make great mirth" as soon as we understood the words that He declared to us (see Neh. 8:12).

I feel more deeply than I can express the grievous wrong that is done to our heavenly Father by the dread His own children have of His blessed will. If those who profess to know and trust Him dread His will, we cannot wonder that the world looks on the will of God as something to be feared and resisted more than anything else, and we need not question why they are driven away from Him. If God's own children regard Him as a tyrant, what can His enemies be expected to think?

It is grievous that Satan has so veiled the goodness of the will of God from the eyes of many Christians; instead of clinging to it as their chiefest good, they often shrink from it in fear and sorrow. This is an obstacle that must be overcome in the lives of believers; for no matter what the circumstances, God's will is always best. (*OTT*, 259–60)

JULY 11
DISCIPLINING FOR HEALING

Some believers can look at the trials that come to sinners around them and perhaps reason why sinners go through what they do, yet when suffering comes their way they are mystified. They are conscious of the integrity of their hearts and cannot see the justice of or the need for their trials. "I was doing what I believed to be right," such a person will say, "why should these things happen to me?"

But the subtle forms of self-life that would ruin us if left undiscovered and unchecked are often most vigorous in those whose outward walk is all that could be desired, and it sometimes takes sharp discipline to uproot them. In this fact lies hidden the secret of much that is mysterious in the dealings of the Lord with the souls of His servants. He loves us too much to permit any evil to linger undiscovered and uncured in our natures, and He will probe us sharply before He will allow our hurt to be healed.

This is not severity but mercy. For the great object of discipline is character building. We are to be the friends of God throughout all eternity. To be His friends means something far grander than merely being saved by Him and requires a far deeper harmony with His will. Therefore it is an unspeakable boon for us that He loves us enough to take the necessary pains to make us fit for companionship with himself. (*OTT*, 280–81)

JULY 12
HELPING, NOT CHIDING

The secret of God's presence is a secret open to all but not opened to everyone. Nature was an open secret before all men in Newton's day, but it was opened to Newton only. The soul that has discovered this secret of God's presence has entered into a place where nothing can ever disturb its rest.

Have you ever thought of what it means to be "closed in" by God? If God "besets" us (cf. Ps. 139:5), it must mean that He is so close to us in love and care that no coldness or rebuffs on our part can drive Him away. God surrounds us; He goes after us to set straight the things we have made crooked and to undo the mistakes and failures that lie behind us. Mothers do this for their children all their lives, beginning with picking up the scattered toys in the nursery and then going "behind" them as they grow older to undo and atone for all their mistakes. When a troubled, frightened child tells his mother of his wrong doings and asks her for sympathy and help, how ready is the mother's ear to listen and her heart to devise ways to help. Suppose the trouble has been all the child's fault; none the less is the mother willing and eager to help him. And none the less is God willing and eager to help us, even though our troubles have come from our own fault.

If we have made any mistake or committed any sin which has caused us anxiety or remorse, let us submit it with confidence to the God who is "behind" us; He will make all things, even these very failures, to "work together for good" (Rom. 8:28) if we will but trust Him. (*VU*, 222–23)

JULY 13
CONSECRATING AND REJOICING

Consecration brings rejoicing. At the first sight of consecration, the soul shrinks and is afraid; but when one has looked more deeply into the beauty and blessedness of the will of God, he learns to rejoice. This was the case of the Israelites in Nehemiah's time.

After a long time of backsliding on the part of the children of Israel, during which the book of God's law had been lost, it was found again, and the people were assembled in the public square of the city to hear it read. At first they wept; but as they understood it better, they saw it was a cause of rejoicing and not of sorrow, and they made "great mirth, because they . . . understood the words that were declared unto them" (Neh. 8:12).

God's will is always our highest joy. He would have us always to rejoice in our feasts (cf. Deut. 16:14). How can we do other than love the will of our God after we become acquainted with Him and learn that His will is the will of infinite love? Not the most loving mother's will for her child was ever half as lovely as this sweet, beloved will of our God for us. It is something to delight in, not to fear; and the words "Thy will be done," when once we understand them, become the dearest words our lips can utter. (*VU*, 58–59)

JULY 14
SELF-EXAMINING, SELF-JUSTIFYING

Self-examination is sometimes extolled among Christians as a most commendable and necessary duty; but in my view it is often a very great evil. It leads either to self-justification and self-commiseration or to discouragement and despair. It fills our lives with chapters full of the personal pronouns "I" and "my," as Job's was. The soul who looks away from self and examines the Lord instead, finds his mouth filled with God's name, His praises, and His glorious power. Compare Job 29 With Psalm 71. One reads, "I," "my," "me." The other reads, "thee," "thy." If you will take a pencil and underline these respective words, you will see how striking the contrast is.

The commands to look to Jesus, to behold His glory, to have our eyes ever toward Him, are literal. When we are looking to Jesus, we cannot see ourselves, for if our faces are to Him, our backs will necessarily be to one another. By "beholding as in a glass the glory of the Lord," we are to be changed into His image (2 Cor. 3:18). By keeping our eyes "ever toward the Lord," our feet are to be plucked out of the net. By looking to Him, all the ends of the earth are to be saved. (*OTT*, 295–96)

JULY 15
DIRECTING IS ASSURING

"Sanctify yourselves therefore, and be ye holy: for I am the LORD your God. And ye shall keep my statutes and do them: I am the LORD which sanctify you" (Lev. 20:7–8).

These promises are precious because they show us that our God loves us enough to care about every little detail of our lives and that to belong to Him means to have each step of our way regulated by His sweet control. To the heathen nations it might have seemed almost intolerable to have God entering so minutely into all their affairs. But to the soul who knew God's love nothing could have been more blessed. The surveillance of true and unselfish love is always most lovely and can bring nothing but blessing and joy.

We do not care for the details of any lives but of those we love. The majority of people around us may live, eat, dress, and act as they please, and so long as they do not interfere with us, we are perfectly indifferent. But the moment we begin to love, all is changed, and the least detail in the life or ways of our loved ones becomes of deepest interest to us. It is because God loves us that He cares what we do, and it is one of our greatest joys to have a command of His for every day and hour of our lives. (*OTT*, 67–68)

DISCOURAGING AND DEFEATING

The soul who has been translated out of the kingdom of darkness into the kingdom of God's dear Son and brought face to face with the wonderful promises and blessings of the gospel longs to go up and possess them. For instance, the glorious liberty and triumphs of the eighth chapter of Romans confront us, and we ask, "Is it not our privilege to enter into these things now?" But we are met on every hand by spies who tell us of the giants in our way and of the difficulties that we will not be able to overcome. Thus our brethren so "discourage our hearts" (cf. Deut. 1:28) that we finally give up in despair, as Israel did, and turn back to wander in the wilderness. We become afraid to take possession of the very land of promise which the Lord our God declares He has given us and into which it was the very purpose of our redemption that we should be brought.

I know what it is to have been discouraged in the early part of my Christian course by the story of these spies bringing up a bad report of the land. When I was first converted, I never dreamed of anything but of taking possession of all the rich and glorious things I saw promised in the Bible to believers in the Lord Jesus Christ. I supposed in my simplicity that to be in the kingdom of heaven meant to be in a kingdom of righteousness, peace, and joy in the Holy Ghost. When the giants began to appear in my land, and I found myself surrounded by a "people greater and taller" (cf. Deut. 1:28) than I was, I concluded this must be because I had not learned the whole gospel and that I needed to be taught something more in order to get the victory. (*OTT*, 84–86)

JULY 17
MEASURING BY BELIEVING

It is nothing to God to work with many or with few, and no giants or walled cities can successfully oppose Him. It was unbelief, therefore, and unbelief alone that prevented the Israelites from going into the Promised Land. It may have sounded like humility to themselves to talk of their own weakness and of the strength of their enemies, but it was really unbelief.

While to us also it may seem humble to dwell on our own weakness and on the strength of sin and to be thereby hindered from realizing the gospel's richest blessings, it is as really unbelief in our case as in theirs. For the Lord our God who goes before us will fight for us and bring us in and plant us in the land of our inheritance just as actually as He was to do it for Israel. Without Him we can do nothing. With Him we can do all things, and depending on Him we are always "more than conquerors" (Rom. 8:37) over every enemy. He has blessed us, "with all spiritual blessings in heavenly places in Christ" (Eph. 1:3), and it only remains for us to go up by faith and possess them.

If we do not, it will not be because of our weakness or the strength of our enemies but because of unbelief. It will be because we measure our enemies with ourselves instead of measuring them with the Lord. We may be "grasshoppers" (cf. Num. 13:33) in their sight, but what are they in the sight of God? By the greatness of His arm they will all be as "still as a stone" (cf. Exod. 15:16), before the soul who dares to step out on His promises and trust all to Him. (*OTT*, 88–89)

JULY 18
FAILING BY DISBELIEVING

The New Testament tells us that the Israelites failed to enter into the riches of the Promised Land because of unbelief. It was not their own weakness or their enemies' strength that hindered their entrance. They were "grasshoppers" and their enemies were "giants" (Num. 13:33), and it was indeed manifest that they were not able to overcome. But the Lord was able, and it was He who was to fight for them and bring them in. They had recognized this when they sang that triumphant song just after they had crossed the Red Sea: "The LORD is a man of war, the LORD is his name" (Exod. 15:3). "Thy right hand, O LORD, is become glorious in power: thy right hand, O LORD, hath dashed in pieces the enemy" (v. 6). "The people shall hear, and be

148

afraid; sorrow shall take hold upon the inhabitants of Palestine"
(v. 14). "Fear and dread shall fall upon them: by the greatness
of thine arm they shall be as still as a stone; till thy people pass
over, O LORD, till the people pass over, which thou hast purchased. Thou shalt bring them in, and plant them in the mountain of thine inheritance, and in the place, O LORD, which thou
hast made for thee to dwell in" (vv. 16–17).

The Israelites' enemies were as great and they themselves
were as weak when this song was sung, as when the borders of
the land were reached. But the people, fresh from the Red Sea
victories, had no fear. The Lord was to do it all; and what
mattered to the Lord—the giants' strength or Israel's weakness?
(*OTT*, 87–88)

JULY 19
CONSECRATING

God's purpose in our redemption is our entire consecration.
Christians too often look on consecration as something extra
added to salvation, not necessarily an essential part. They, therefore, think it is optional to enter into it. But the Bible declares
that salvation is nothing if it does not ultimately lead to holiness,
for salvation in God's thought is holiness.

It is striking to notice that of the many announcements made
concerning the work Christ came to accomplish, nearly every
one declares it to be deliverance from sin rather than escape of
punishment. It is a salvation to holiness rather than a salvation
to heaven. Of course punishment is escaped and heaven is gained
when we are saved from sin, since the greater always involves
the lesser. But the vital thing in the redemption of Christ is the
redemption "from all iniquity" and the "purifying unto himself
a peculiar people, zealous of good works" (Titus 2:14).

The thought of God in the deliverance of Israel was not that
they should wander in the wilderness but that they should be
brought into the Promised Land, which typifies the life of full
consecration.

Entire consecration, therefore, is binding on every Christian,
and sooner or later each one must come to know it, for there is
no entering heaven without it. (*VU*, 54–56)

JULY 20
FEARING IS DOUBTING

The "spirit of fear" (2 Tim. 1:7) does not belong to the Christian religion. It is never enumerated among the "fruit of the Spirit" (see Gal. 5:22–23). It is not given to us from God. On the contrary, it is always condemned as being alien to the whole idea of Christianity and as coming purely and only from unbelief.

All doubts are a "speaking against God." A great many of my readers will start at this and exclaim, "Oh, no, that is a mistake. Doubts often arise from humility. We feel ourselves to be so unworthy of the love and care of God that we cannot believe it is possible for Him to love or care for us. It is not that we doubt Him, but we doubt ourselves." This sounds very plausible; but let us see what it amounts to. Does God's love for us depend on the kind of people we are? Does He love only good people, or does He love sinners? The Bible says, "God commendeth his love toward us, in that, while we were yet sinners, Christ died for us" (Rom. 5:8). And again it says, "But God, who is rich in mercy, for his great love wherewith he loved us, even when we were dead in sins, hath quickened us together with Christ" (Eph. 2:5). Can it be called humility to question this and to doubt whether, after all, He really does love us who are sinners? We would not think it humility on the part of our children if, when they were naughty, they began to doubt our love for them, and because they had been disobedient, became anxious that we would neglect them and fail to protect their interests. True humility, no matter how unworthy it may feel, extinguishes doubts instead of créating them, because it would not presume to doubt God's promises of love and care. (*EDR*, 220–21)

JULY 21
CONSECRATING OR SURRENDERING

However widely Christians may differ on other subjects, there is one point on which every thoughtful soul will agree: We all are called to an entire surrender of ourselves to the will of God. We are made for union with Him, and union must mean oneness of purpose and thought, so the only pathway to this union must be a perfect harmony between our will and His. For "can two walk together, except they be agreed?" (Amos 3:3).

Therefore, God's commands to be holy are all based on the fact that He to whom we belong is holy. In order to be one with God, which is our final destiny, we must be like Him in character; and since He is holy, we cannot be "partakers of the divine nature" (2 Peter 1:4) without ourselves being holy.

It is because we are the Lord's, and not in order that we may become His, that we are called to be holy. "I am the Lord your God" is always the ground of His appeal. He doesn't say, "I will be your God if you will be holy," but He says, "Be ye holy, because I already am the Lord your God." It is because we have been bought with a price, and not in order to induce our Lord to buy us, that we are entreated to be holy.

Having this glorious hope of being one day like Him, we are incited now to purify ourselves even as He is pure. (*VU*, 51–52)

JULY 22
CONSECRATING AND BELONGING

The preliminary step to consecration must be to settle once for all the questions as to whether we belong to the Lord and whether the promises of the gospel are really ours. And then, when this is settled—but not before—we will be able to present ourselves in glad and loving surrender to the divine Master who laid down His life to make us His own.

The children of Israel were not called to consecrate themselves until after they were saved from Egypt. The law could not be given while they were in bondage to the Pharaoh. Therefore, in their history, which is a wonderful type of our spiritual life, they came to consecration only after many other steps had been taken.

We can trace these steps in the books of Exodus, Leviticus, Numbers, and Deuteronomy. In Exodus the Israelites came out of Egypt (a type of our deliverance from the bondage of sin). In Leviticus they received the commands of God as to how they should order their worship and their lives in the Land of Promise into which God was leading them (a type of true worship of Christian hearts). In Numbers they failed through unbelief to enter into the Promised Land and in consequence wandered in the wilderness forty years (a type of the common Christian experience of failure and wandering). In Deuteronomy they came a second time to the borders of the land and were called to an entire consecration before they could enter in. (*VU*, 52–53)

JULY 23
BELONGING AND BECOMING

How few of us know that we are not our own and that we actually do belong to God! We have heard it and read of it often and have perhaps thought we believed it; but really knowing it is a different matter. It is essential to our peace and well-being that we do know that we belong to God. Any doubt about our position in relation to God is a grievous hindrance to our spiritual prosperity and development. To make us in His own image is the object of God's workmanship, and nothing short of this will accomplish His divine purpose in our creation.

We can never understand a complicated machine until we know what purpose its maker had for it. How did he mean it to work? What was it intended to accomplish? How has he arranged for it to run? When we walk through an exhibition of machinery, we ask continually, as we stop to look at one machine after another, "What is this for?" and "What is that for?" We are sure that the maker intended it to accomplish some special end, and we cannot imagine any man being stupid enough to make a machine that is not meant to accomplish anything.

Our divine Maker has made us for something, and it is essen-

tial for us to find out what his purpose is in order that we may
aim after its accomplishment. (*VU*, 172, 201)

JULY 24
CONSECRATING, NOT DOUBTING

Having consecrated ourselves to the Lord, we must from that
moment reckon that we are always the Lord's no matter how
things may seem. We must refuse to admit a question or a doubt
and choose always, with an unfaltering purpose of heart, to have
no will but the will of God. We may not always feel as if we are
consecrated, but we may always choose to be. It is the attitude
of our will not the state of our emotion that is the vital thing in
our soul life. If in my will I choose to be the Lord's, then I am
His no matter how I may feel about it.

Let us from this time onward accept His will as our only
portion. It is safest to come to a definite point in this matter and
to make a definite transaction of it.

A great many Christians acknowledge that they ought to be
consecrated, and they are always meaning to do it, but because
they do not come to the definite point of doing it, it is never
really done. I may want and intend to give a gift to a friend with
all the earnestness possible, but until I come to the point of
actually giving it, it will remain in my own possession.

When could we find a better time than now to consecrate
ourselves? Every hour that we delay, we are holding ourselves
back from blessing and are grieving the heart of our Lord. (*VU*,
61–62)

JULY 25
DELIVERING AND EMPOWERING

I had found in the Lord Jesus a deliverer from the *guilt* of sin,
but I wanted to find in Him a deliverer from the *power* of sin,
and I did not know how to set about it. I went therefore to a
"spy" to find out. He was a beloved Christian teacher who must
know, I supposed, all about it. But I will never forget my disappointment! After I had told my need, saying that I knew it

was because of my ignorance and because I had not taken in the fullness of the gospel that I was in so sad a case, my friend said, "Oh no! You are all right. You cannot expect such a deliverance as you are seeking. All of us are more or less under the power of sin all our lives, and we must not expect the early joy of conversion to last for ever." I thought my friend knew, and I received his report as final and at once settled down to my condition as being inevitable and therefore to be endured with the best grace I could. But my heart sank as I left the house, and, like the children of Israel, I could have lifted up my voice and cried, so great was my disappointment. Many times in the years that followed would I recall with saddest longing the blessedness I had felt when first I knew the Lord.

So ignorant was I of God's ways that I in turn became a spy, bringing a bad report of the land to the Christians who came to me for counsel, telling them it was indeed a good land but adding the fatal "nevertheless" of unbelief, that the people who lived in the land were too strong for them, and the cities were walled and very great. Many a one did I thus turn back, causing them to wander with me in the wilderness for many years. (*OTT*, 86–87)

JULY 26
APPROPRIATING AND RECEIVING

God promised His people that when they entered the Promised Land every place that they would tread had already been granted to them. He didn't say that He *would* give it to them; He said that He *had* given it to them. It was all theirs in the purpose and mind of God, but unless they actually went there and set their feet on it, it did not become theirs practically and experientially.

This is necessarily true of any gift. The giver may give it with all the sincerity and good will possible, but unless the one to whom he gives it actually receives it, appropriates it, and calls it his own, it never really comes into his possession at all. Even though a gift should be laid on the table or put in the pocket of a friend, unless that friend closes the hand of acceptance over it and says mentally, "It is mine," he will not possess it.

154

The children of Israel were going in to take possession of their own land. The Lord had given it to them centuries before, and it was theirs all the while, only waiting for their coming. And so of ourselves we read that God "hath blessed us with all spiritual blessings in heavenly places in Christ" (Eph. 1:3). We very well know that until the hand of faith really closes over and appropriates these blessings and we begin to say "they are mine," we do not actually come into their enjoyment at all. (*OTT*, 118–19)

JULY 27
TRIUMPHING OR LANGUISHING

God's promise to us is that we will be delivered by the power of our Lord from the hands of all our enemies and will be enabled to triumph in every contest with our foe. But if we, as they, refuse to avail ourselves fully of this promised strength, we will suffer the same results.

This accounts for the condition of so many Christians who find themselves continually enslaved and oppressed by their inward enemies, and whose victories are followed by ever-recurring defeats. They groan and cannot understand it. But the secret is this: They have not utterly driven out their enemies. They have thought perhaps that they could not. They have said, "My circumstances are so peculiar" or "My temperament is so sensitive" or "My temptations are so great." They have not expected to be entirely delivered from their irritable tempers or their roots of bitterness or their sharp tongues but have felt very successful if they have been able to keep them under control by constant watchfulness and prayer.

And so they compromise with the Enemy instead of utterly driving him out. In this way many Christians compromise with doubt, with the disobedience of timidity, with a shrinking from saying "Thy will be done," with anxiety, or with a hundred other forms of evil against which God's commands of utter renunciation and death have plainly gone forth. As a consequence, He no longer drives out the enemies we have consented will remain, and they are snares and traps to us. (*OTT*, 138–39)

JULY 28
POSSESSING AND INHERITING

If we as Christians say that deliverance from all our inner enemies is impossible, we in effect declare that what God has promised, He is not able to perform, and thus bring dishonor on His great name.

It is the Lord's command to us that we go in and possess the land of our inheritance. To me God's commands are even more comforting than His promises; for if He commands me to do a thing, I am sure He will give me the power of His Spirit to do it. His commands are not grievous, we are told, but surely they would be grievous if we were unable to obey them. It would have been grievous if God had commanded the children of Israel to go in and possess the land of Canaan, and knowing that they were unable to do it, had not himself intended to supply them with power. But, in fact, His very command was the reason why they should have no fear in undertaking what He had told them to do.

The command of our Lord to us as Christians is that we should drive out every enemy from our hearts and lives. If we refuse to do this and seek merely to make them tribute to us, we will find ourselves continually enslaved and oppressed by those very enemies whom we have allowed to remain. The promise to Israel was that no man would be able to stand before them all the days of their lives, for the Lord would be with them and His strength would always give them the victory. (*OTT*, 138)

JULY 29
CONQUERING THEN RESTING

As the temple could not be built until the land had rest from its enemies and the reign of peace had begun, neither can the heart know the conscious indwelling of Christ, being "filled with the Spirit," until it has "entered into rest" and has been made more than a conqueror through Him. As long as our Christian life is one of conflict, without settled peace of soul, we cannot know the experience of being "filled with all the fullness of God" (Eph. 3:19). The inner life of conscious communion can only exist where peace reigns. The Comforter manifests His abiding presence only to those who have overcome the world by faith and whose hearts are at rest.

The Lord goes with us in all our wanderings and is beside us in every battle to fight and conquer our enemies for us; but He does not take up His abode in our hearts in conscious presence until the kingdom of peace is established there. He cannot. He is the Prince of Peace, and His kingdom is and must always be a peaceable kingdom. If, therefore, we would know that experience, of which the building of the temple and the Lord coming in to fill it with His glory is a type, we must advance beyond the reign of conflict into the reign of peace. We must know what it is to have the peace of God which passes all understanding and keeps our hearts and minds through Christ Jesus continually (Phil. 4:7). (*OTT*, 217)

JULY 30
BAPTIZING AND FILLING

The freeing of the self to love God, I believe, is typical of what took place on the Day of Pentecost when the disciples were "all filled with the Holy Ghost" (Acts 2:4). What takes place in every believing heart now when it is emptied of self and opened for Christ to come in and take up His abode there, filling it with His presence, is a picture, in short, of the baptism of the Holy Ghost. This is, in a sense, true for Christians as a whole, for on the Day of Pentecost the Holy Ghost came to the church, "which is the house of God" (cf. Heb. 10:21), to abide in her midst forever. But in individual experience, the power of the Holy Ghost is not always known, and each soul needs to come to its own Pentecost. The conscious presence of the abiding Comforter is not realized by every Christian. All, of course, must have the Spirit, because the new birth is impossible without His presence and power. But to some souls, there comes at a certain stage in their progress, a wonderful experience, which they seem instinctively to call the baptism of the Holy Spirit. It lifts them up into a region of spiritual life that is as far above their former level as the mountaintop is above the valley, and from which few ever descend.

This baptism does for souls now, just what it did for the disciples on the Day of Pentecost. It purifies, transforms, endues with power from on high, satisfies, comforts, inspires, and controls. It bestows on those who receive it, a "well of water springing up into everlasting life" (John 4:14) for the soul's own comfort and "rivers of living water" (John 7:38) flowing out for the blessing of others. (*OTT*, 215–16)

JULY 31
BELIEVING AND BAPTIZING

The promise of the baptism of Pentecost is "unto you and to your children, and to all that are afar off, even as many as the Lord our God shall call" (Acts 2:39). It is surely needed, for the Christian life without it is but poor and dwarfed. Do not be satisfied without it then for even so much as another day.

The steps to reach baptism in the Holy Ghost are simple. First, convince yourself from the Scriptures that the baptism of the Spirit is a gift intended for you. Next, come to the Lord in simple faith to ask for it. Then, having put your case into His hands, leave it there in childlike trust, knowing that He will attend to your request and that He is more willing to give you the Holy Spirit than parents are to give good gifts to their children. Take 1 John 5:14–15, and act on it: "And this is the confidence that we have in him, that, if we ask any thing according to his will, he heareth us: and if we know that he hear us, whatsoever we ask, we know that we have the petitions that we desired of him." You are asking for that which is according to His will; therefore you know that He hears you. Knowing this, you must know still more and must believe that you have the petitions you desired of Him. Claim it by faith as your present possession.

Begin to praise God for His wondrous gift, and it will come to pass for you as it did to Israel, that when every power of your being is as one—"to make one sound to be heard in praising and thanking the LORD" (2 Chron. 5:13)—"the glory of the

LORD [will fill] the house of God'' (v. 14), and your hungry soul will be filled and satisfied with His presence. (*OTT*, 221–22)

AUGUST 1
TRUSTING AND OBEYING

No position in grace, no height of Christian attainment can keep the soul from failing; that is something that only the indwelling Holy Ghost can do. And nothing but continual faithfulness to the Lord can secure His abiding presence. We never, at any stage of our experience, reach a place where we may relax in our obedience or become indifferent in our trust. Obedience must keep pace with knowledge, and our trust must be daily and hourly fixed on our keeping Savior, or all will go wrong.

Sanctification is not a state so much as a walk, and every moment of that walk we need the Spirit's power and the Spirit's presence as much as we did at first. Not even after living in the land of promise for many years, are we strong enough to do without His indwelling. From the beginning to the end of our Christian life, obedience and trust are the two essential conditions of our triumph. We must make no more compromise with evil at the end than at the beginning. And failure, if it comes, will always arise from one or the other of these two causes: lack of consecration or lack of trust. It is never the strength of our enemies or our own weakness that causes us to fall.

While the Lord continues to be with us, no one can stand before us forever. If we will only steadfastly abide in Him, we need not be in the least discouraged at the thought of the temptations that surround us on every hand. (*OTT*, 152–53)

AUGUST 2
ABIDING AND FLOURISHING

The environment of spiritual life is subject to a definite law. Every plant has its own laws of life and can only flourish in certain localities and under certain soil and climate conditions. On a higher plane this is equally true of the spiritual life. Outward localities and climate make no difference here, although Christians often think they do. We find ourselves in uncongenial surroundings and are tempted to think our spiritual life cannot flourish in such an environment. But no outward circumstances can affect the life of the soul. Its true environment is inward and spiritual; and this environment is none other than God and His love. "For ye are dead, and your life is hid with Christ in God" (Col. 3:3). This may sound mystical, but it is also the profoundest common sense. The sources of one's life, that is, the objects and aims and underlying springs of action, must be either in self or in God. If in self, then our life is hid in self; if in God, then our life is hid in God. To "dwell in God," or, in other words, to "abide in Christ," means simply that we have the underlying spring of all our thoughts, words, and actions in Him.

The reason there are so many "withered" lives is that they do not "abide in Christ." If a branch does not abide in the vine, it must necessarily wither. The only environment in which the spiritual life can flourish is God. To abide in God means to maintain an unfaltering trust in Him and obedience to His will. "If ye keep my commandments, ye shall abide in my love" (John 15:10) is an unalterable law. (*EDR*, 109–10)

AUGUST 3
RESTING AND WORKING

No height of spiritual blessing or power can for a moment absolve us from the need of obedience and watchfulness. The temptation to carelessness has often overwhelmed persons after periods of great blessing.

We can never forsake the written law of the Lord with impunity, let our advancement in spiritual life be what it may. We need to watch, lest, when seated in heavenly places in Christ, we should feel so lifted above the usual temptations of life that we become careless and fail to walk in the law of our God. Some have grievously failed here.

Those who teach a life of perfect rest and peace are sometimes misunderstood to mean that there are no more assaults from our Enemy in such a life. It is difficult to explain just what we do mean, so I do not wonder that we are misunderstood. For it is

one of those marvelous paradoxes in which two apparently ir-
reconcilable things exist at the same moment and perfectly harmonize. Peace and war, rest and labor, are one here. We fight,
but it is the fight of faith not of effort, for our God fights for us,
and therefore we are at perfect peace. We work, but it is not we
who work but God who works in us and through us, and therefore we rest. We work as the instrument works in the hand of
the skillful workman. To understand this, it must be experienced. (*OTT*, 224–26)

AUGUST 4
COMMUNING AND KNOWING

Words cannot describe the blessedness of the inner life of
divine union, and the spirit stands amazed before such glorious
possibilities of experience! With Solomon we exclaim, "But
will God in very deed dwell with men on the earth? behold,
heaven and the heaven of heavens cannot contain thee; how
much less the house which I have built!" (2 Chron. 6:18). And
the Lord answers, as He did to Solomon during the night after
his prayer of dedication had been made: "I have heard thy prayer,
and have chosen this place to myself for a house of sacrifice. . . . Now mine eyes shall be open, and mine ears attent
unto the prayer that is made in this place. For now have I chosen
and sanctified this house, that my name may be there for ever:
and mine eyes and mine heart shall be there perpetually" (7:12–
16).

"If ye abide in me, and my words abide in you, ye shall ask
what ye will, and it shall be done unto you" (John 15:7). "By
this know we that we dwell in him and he in us, because he hath
given us of his Spirit" (1 John 4:13). "God is love; and he that
dwelleth in love dwelleth in God and God in him" (v. 16). "At
that day ye shall know that I am in my Father, and ye in me,
and I in you" (v. 20). These are a few of the New Testament
expressions of this glorious hidden life of conscious union and
communion with God. (*OTT*, 221)

AUGUST 5
RESTING, NOT WORRYING

Among the peaks of the Sierra Nevada mountains, not far from the busy whirl of San Francisco, lies Lake Tahoe. It is twenty-three miles long, ten miles wide, and so deep that a line dropped nineteen hundred feet does not touch bottom; and it lies five thousand feet above the neighboring ocean. Storms come and go in waters that are lower down the mountains, but this lake is so still and clear that the eye can penetrate, it is said, a hundred feet into its depths. Around its mild verdant sides are the mountains, ever crowned with snow. The sky above is as calm as the motionless water. Nature loses scarcely anything of its clear outline as it is reflected there. Here the soul may learn something of what rest is, as day after day one opens one's heart to let the sweet influence of nature's sabbath enter and reign. This is but a faint type of what we may find in Christ.

In the pressure of the greatest responsibilities, in the worry of the smallest cares, in the perplexities of life's moments of crisis, we may have the Lake Tahoe rest in the security of God's will. Learn to live in this rest. In the calmness of spirit it will give, your soul will reflect, as in a mirror, the beauty of the Lord; and the tumult of men's lives will be calmed in your presence, as your tumults have been calmed in His presence. (*VU*, 81)

AUGUST 6
DWELLING AND CLEANSING

Peace and holiness will be the result of God's recognized presence. His presence will drive out sin just as sunshine drives out darkness, if the heart will but open itself to its shining.

Having learned the transforming fact of God's continual presence and unceasing care, the soul is brought into so profound a union with Him that we love what He loves and hate what He hates. We eagerly appeal to Him to search us and try us, so that there may be no area of our being that is out of harmony with Him.

162

To be the temple of God means to be His dwelling place, the habitation of God. It is almost impossible for the heart of man to conceive of anything so amazing, but if we believe the Bible at all, we must believe that our hearts are the home of our God and that He does continually seek to find a dwelling place there.

As the sunlight fills the air all around us and enters wherever there is an opening, the presence of God fills the whole universe and enters every heart that opens to receive Him. George Macdonald says concerning this, "The spirit of God lies all about the spirit of man like a mighty sea ready to rush in at the smallest chink in the walls that shut Him out from His own." (*VU*, 223–24)

AUGUST 7
RELATING AND SHARING

Christians are continually trying to feed their spiritual lives with all sorts of things other than Christ. They feed on the dry husks of dogmas and doctrines, on forms and ceremonies, on religious duties well performed, on Christian work, on good resolutions, or on fervent emotions; and then they wonder at their starved condition. Nothing can really satisfy the hunger of the soul but Christ. He can be to the soul all that the soul needs. To draw our life from Christ means to be so united to Him in oneness of nature that the same spiritual life flows through our spiritual veins as flowed through His.

This is a subject often regarded as mystical and difficult to understand. I have no intention of dealing with any mystical meanings, but there is a practical way of looking at the matter that seems to me simple and easy to understand. We feed ourselves on the writings of a great author by becoming familiar with them and by adopting their teachings as our own; in the same way we must feed on Christ. We know what it is to become one in thought and feeling with a beloved friend and to share that friend's inmost life; similarly we must become one with Christ. We can understand how an artist can feed his mind on the life and work and teaching of some great master in art and so become like him and able, after his measure, to follow in that master's footsteps; and we must do just that with Christ. (*EDR*, 164)

AUGUST 8
BEING, THEN DOING

God's purpose in our salvation is that we should bring forth fruit. A husbandman plants the vine for the sake of the grapes it will bear; the farmer plants his apple orchard in order to gather fruit; Christ has chosen us that we should bring forth fruit. A fruitless Christian life is an impossibility. Many are apt to think far more of being saved than of being fruitful, but God does not separate these things; to be saved is to be fruitful, and to be fruitful is to be saved.

No matter how good our outward appearance, how clear our doctrines, or how great our activities, unless we bear fruit we cannot be acceptable to God. But the question arises here as to what this fruit is, and on this point many mistakes are made. The fruit God desires is character. It is being right even more than it is doing right; the doing will follow the being. Most people have too much reversed this order and have made the doing the vital thing, limiting the meaning of fruit-bearing to service or quantity of work done. But God's primary idea of fruit is a Christlike character.

We need to understand that no amount of preaching, praying, or singing will do instead of being gentle, meek, long-suffering, and good. A great many people want to work for the Lord but do not want to be good for Him; but He cares far more for goodness than for work. If you cannot do both, choose being good, for it is infinitely more important. (*VU*, 145–46)

AUGUST 9
BEARING AND ABIDING

What is the secret of true fruit-bearing?

Here again we have the inexorable nature of things: "The branch cannot bear fruit of itself" (John 15:4). Try as hard as we may, no fruit is possible except we "abide in Christ." Other things are possible—wonderful works, eminent service, great benevolences—but not the fruit of the Spirit. This fruit cannot come from any other source than from the indwelling Spirit alone.

It is the husbandman's business to prune and purge the vine in order to make it fruitful. We must accept all the storms and sorrows of life as the purgings necessary to make us bring forth more fruit (cf. John 15:2). To an inexperienced eye, the trimming and cutting of the gardener often seem ruthless, and we cry out to him to spare the vine. But in the autumn, when the rich clusters of fruit are hanging from the same vine, we acknowledge his wisdom and applaud his will. In our soul life we may similarly be tempted to question the wisdom or the goodness of the divine Husbandman when He sees it necessary to cut off our most flourishing branches or to trim our life of its dearest joys. But the Husbandman knows what is best for His vine, and we must leave it all to Him. (*VU*, 152–53)

AUGUST 10
LIVING IS FRUIT-BEARING

A living plant always bears fruit. It is the law of its life that it should do so; and it is equally a law that this fruit should come not by effort but by spontaneous growth.

"Ye have not chosen me but I have chosen you, and ordained you, that ye should go and bring forth fruit, and that your fruit should remain: that whatsoever ye shall ask of the Father in my name, he may give it you" (John 15:16).

We need not trouble ourselves about our fruit-bearing. It is "ordained" that we will bring forth fruit just as it is ordained that a fig tree will bear figs. It is the law of our spiritual life. We can no more have real spiritual life within us without bearing fruit than the oak tree can have life without bearing acorns. Very few seem to understand this; and as a consequence there is a vast amount of effort among Christians to hang fruit on their branches by some outside performances of one sort or another. It is as if a man should buy apples and hang them on his apple trees and think thus to secure to himself a good crop of fruit!

Fruit must be "brought forth," not fastened on. This is the law of fruit-bearing, and to try to violate this law can only bring confusion and death.

The law of fruit-bearing is clearly this, that our fruit can only be the outcome of what we are. Therefore, the thing for me to be concerned about is not so much whether my fruit is good or evil but whether I am good or evil. (*EDR*, 165–66)

AUGUST 11
FRUIT-BEARING, NOT COMPLAINING

One of the laws of life is that all plants must yield fruit after their own kind. I must be content, therefore, to be the type of plant and bear the type of fruit the divine Husbandman pleases. We do not always like to be what God has made us to be. Perhaps I would like to be a rosebush and blossom out in roses, but He has made me a potato plant and wants me to yield potatoes. I might be tempted, in such a case, to get paper roses and sew them on. But what folly! A million paper roses could not turn my potato plant into a rosebush, and the first person who tried to pick one would find me out! All I have to do is to see to it that, whatever kind of plant I may be, whether a homely potato plant or a gorgeous rosebush, I become a healthy vigorous plant and fulfill without grumbling the law of my being. Be content to be what God has made you, but do not be content until you are the best of its kind.

The law of the spiritual life is that divine strength will be made perfect in human weakness. Our part is to supply the weakness; God's part is to supply the strength. We are, however, continually trying to usurp God's part and to supply the strength ourselves. Because we cannot do this, we are plunged into depths of discouragement. We think that in order to work effectively for the Lord, we ought to feel strong in ourselves, and when instead we find ourselves feeling weak we are in despair. But the Bible teaches us that, if we only knew it, our weakness is in reality our greatest strength. (*EDR*, 166–67)

AUGUST 12
FORCING OR FULFILLING

What are we made to be, and what are we made to do?

A machine that fails to fulfill the purposes of its maker does not bring honor but dishonor on him. And we who fail in fulfilling the purpose of our Creator are bringing dishonor on Him. What then is His purpose?

He has made us to have dominion. We are to be "kings" (Rev. 1:6). We are to sit on the throne with Christ and reign with Him over the things of time and sense. We are to conquer the world instead of being conquered by it. We are to know what it is to be made "always to triumph" (cf. 2 Cor. 2:14) through Christ. If we fail in this victory; if, instead of our having dominion over sin, sin has dominion over us; if the world and the things of it master us and bring us into bondage instead of being mastered by us, then we are not fulfilling the purposes of our Creator but are bringing disgrace on His name.

We ask of a complicated machine, "How does it go?" We want to know how its different parts move in reference to one another. If a machine "goes" the way its maker meant it to go, it will move easily and without friction. My hand was made to shut inward on my palm, and if I try to shut it outward over its back, I cannot do it without breaking my bones. My heart was made to love and serve its Creator, and when I do this, all my inward machinery moves without friction. But if I love and serve the creature more than the Creator, all goes wrong, and something is sure to break. A great deal of the friction and failure in our spiritual lives arises from the fact that we do not "go" as God meant us to. (*VU*, 201–3)

AUGUST 13
BEARING, NOT ATTACHING

Christ said, "A good tree cannot bring forth evil fruit, neither can a corrupt tree bring forth good fruit" (Matt. 7:18). Notice the word "cannot"; it expresses an impossibility in the very nature of things. No outward putting on, therefore, will avail anything in the matter of fruit-bearing. The tree itself must be good or the fruit it bears cannot be good.

Some people walk on spiritual stilts when before others. If they are in a public place, they take out their Bibles in order to look pious; when they write a letter, they try to put in some expressions that will show their religion; they interlace their conversation with religious words. They can never afford to be natural in the presence of others for fear they might not be considered as religious as they really are. They do their works to be seen of others, and they do indeed have their reward. People see and praise; but God sees and condemns.

Persons can never be more than their character makes them. They can never do more nor better than deliver or embody that which is their character. Character must stand behind and back up everything—the sermon, the poem, the picture, the book. None of them is worth a straw without it.

Character, then, is the essential thing. What is in the heart and what comes "out of the abundance of the heart" (Matt. 12:34) are the only realities in life. If we fail to see this, we are yet, as our Lord said, "without understanding" (see Matt. 15:16). (*VU*, 150–52)

AUGUST 14
STRENGTHENING BY QUICKENING

It is of vital importance to the children of God that they understand that God's strength can be made perfect only in human weakness. For in the spiritual life the natural man never can feel strong in himself, and if we think we ought to, we will be continually troubled. Understanding the law, however, we will learn, like Paul, to "take pleasure" in our infirmities and our weaknesses (2 Cor. 12:10), because we will see that only when we are weak are we really spiritually strong.

The choice lies between the strength of our own human nature and the strength of the divine nature within us; and we may well be glad to lose the one in order to gain the other. It is like the difference between the power of a lifeless seed to push away the clods above it and the power of the life in that seed when it is quickened. To the tiny unquickened mustard seed the weight of earth above it would seem like an immovable mountain; but when quickened the life within the same tiny seed pushes aside those mountains of earth without any apparent effort. Life carries all before it, and no obstacles can withstand its progress. It is life, more life that we want, not more effort. (*EDR*, 168–69)

AUGUST 15
COMMUNING, NOT COMMANDING

When communion fails, teaching comes in to take its place. Doctrines are looked to as the remedy for spiritual coldness and wandering. The effect at first seems blessed, but truth alone, without the Spirit, cannot reach the central home of the soul; and sooner or later, therefore, teaching also fails.

I remember a time when just this thing happened to me. It was before I knew the secret of the life hid with Christ in God. I found in my experience that the learning of new truth helped me for a time into greater warmth and earnestness of Christian life, and I sought eagerly for every opportunity of being taught. But continually I was disappointed by finding that, in a little while, the freshness of the new discovery in truth would wear off; and with its freshness, its power would seem to go, and my soul would be left drier than ever. The only remedy of which I then knew, was to go on hoping that at last I would discover something that would have permanent effects and from which I would have no adverse reaction.

But this can never be. It takes an experience far deeper than the learning of new truth alone to keep the soul alive. The result of repeated disappointments unless a more vital experience is known, is to drive the soul into seeking by some outward rule to supply the empty place from which the Lord is lost. The commandments and traditions of men take the place of the commandment of God; and the soul endeavors by the "law of a carnal commandment" (Heb. 7:16) to remedy the state into which it has been brought by the loss of inward communion. (*OTT*, 175–76)

AUGUST 16
SELF-EXAMINING, SELF-DENYING

Nothing hinders us more in our Christian lives than to keep our eyes fixed on ourselves, trying to search out evidences of our own goodness and fitness for the mercy of the Lord or tokens of our growth in grace. If we think we find any, at once we are frightened at the danger of pride; and if we do not find any, we are plunged into the depths of discouragement. We must give up self at first, as Job did at last, as hopelessly bad, and have no eyes or thoughts for anything but the Lord and His salvation. This, I think, is what the Scriptures mean by self-denial and self-crucifixion. It is to say to this "I," "I am a stranger to you," and refuse to listen for a moment to his pretensions or claims.

Few will understand this, and fewer still will act on it. Self is so enticing to us, and self-examination is such an interesting and absorbing occupation that it is very difficult for us to give it up. But from experience I can say that I never have any peace or victory, except when I utterly ignore even the existence of self and turn my eyes and thoughts only on the Lord.

Most Christians commit things to the Lord when on their knees, and then the moment they rise from their knees they take the burden all back on their own shoulders. Of course no proceedings as this can bring peace. We must not only commit our cares to the Lord, but we must also leave them with Him, and it is in the leaving that most people fail. (*OTT*, 295; *VU*, 67)

AUGUST 17
MISUNDERSTANDING TEMPTATION

If there is one thing more than another that we need to have common sense about, it is the subject of temptation, for nothing is more misunderstood. Moreover, temptation is an everyday occurrence, and in a book of lessons for everyday life it is a subject of vital importance.

The first common-sense thing that I would say concerning

temptation is that temptation is not sin. The second thing I would say is the same, and the third thing is the same also. It may seem to some that this hardly needs to be said so emphatically since everyone must already know it; but I believe, on the contrary, that very few really know it. People often assent to a thing as a theory, which practically they do not in the least believe; and this is just one of these things. Do we not feel that we must be dreadful sinners just because we are tempted? A flood of evil thoughts is poured into our souls—proud thoughts, unkind thoughts, malicious thoughts. They are thoughts we loathe and yet which we seem to originate.

It is as if a burglar, breaking into a man's house to steal, would, when the head of the house tries to resist him, turn around and accuse the owner himself of being the thief! It is the Enemy's grand ruse for entrapping us. He says, "It is very plain you cannot be a child of God; for if you were, it would have been impossible for such dreadful thoughts to have entered your heart." This reasoning sounds so very plausible that the Christian feels as if it must be true, but the divine teaching about temptation is very different. (*EDR*, 228–29)

AUGUST 18
LOVING AND SUFFERING

The apostle Paul did not think of his trials as heavy crosses to be borne, but he "took pleasure" (2 Cor. 12:10) in them. The true lover takes pleasure in suffering, if need be, for the one he loves; and if we love our Lord, it is not anything very mystical for us to "take pleasure" in suffering endured for His sake.

Although we may not all have attained this attitude of taking pleasure in our trials, it is of the utmost importance that we should not hinder our advance toward it by cherishing false notions of what we are called to as children of God. Neither must we degrade the grand Scripture idea of denying ourselves and taking up our cross, to the poor paltry fact of being compelled to give up things we love and to do things we dislike. If things are wrong we ought to hate them and want to give them up; and if duties are right, we ought to love them and delight to do them.

We will do this if we have truly "taken up our cross" (Matt. 16:24) and are indeed "crucified with Christ" (Gal. 2:20).

The expressions "crucified with Christ" and "dead to sin" (Rom. 6:2) are looked on as being very mysterious and occult; and simpleminded Christians think they describe experiences that few can comprehend or attain to. But whatever mystical meaning they may have, there is a practical common-sense meaning as well that the most simpleminded can understand: They mean just what is meant by the ordinary expression of being "dead" to anything.

Just as we have "taken up the cross" (Matt. 16:24) to some of the things that are contrary to the will of God and are now "dead" to them, so must we "take up the cross" and be "dead" to all that is opposed to His will. (*EDR*, 144–45)

AUGUST 19
BELIEVING, NOT EXPERIMENTING

"According to your faith" (Matt. 9:29) it shall be unto you. We are familiar with these declarations of our Lord and have repeated them many times to ourselves and to others. But have we not looked on them too much as magical words involving a sort of continuous miracle, for which there is no law, and about which there can be no certainty? Has not the feeling concerning faith been more or less that it is a capricious, uncertain factor which may work or may not and on which no real dependence can ever be placed? Has not the exercise of it been somewhat of an experiment, even with the most devout souls? Is not the wonder and admiration with which we regard a successful result to faith's ventures an indication that the truth has hardly yet dawned on us of a law of faith about whose working there can be no experiment and no doubt?

Jesus told His disciples that faith could move mountains and that whatever they asked in His name in faith would be done. These astounding assertions from the lips of our Lord himself contain a deeper truth than the church has yet comprehended. If we had, our achievements in the region of faith could not possibly be so meager. I believe that Christ was here telling us of a mighty, irresistible spiritual law that is inherent in the nature

172

of God and is shared, according to our measure, by everyone who is begotten of God and is a partaker of His divine nature. (*EDR*, 147–49)

AUGUST 20
BELIEVING AND CONFESSING

"Then said they unto him, What shall we do, that we might work the works of God? Jesus answered and said unto them, This is the work of God, that ye believe on him whom he hath sent" (John 6:28–29).

We must believe two things: first, what God says concerning Christ; and second, what He says concerning us.

We aren't really believing a person if we only believe half he says; yet many who would consider it the worst of sins to disbelieve God's testimony concerning Christ consider it no sin at all, but rather virtuous humility, to doubt His testimony concerning themselves. They dare not doubt that Jesus is the Christ but find no difficulty doubting whether they are themselves born of God. Yet God joins the two inseparably together.

But you may say, how can I know that I believe? Could you write a paper saying, "I do not believe that Jesus is the Christ?" and sign it with your name? Would it not be a lie if you should do so? If the alternative were presented to you of denying Christ or going to prison, would you not choose the prison? I'm sure you would.

You do believe, therefore, that Jesus is the Christ; and God says that whosoever does believe is born of Him. Does not this settle the question?

Could language be plainer than this? If you confess that Jesus is the Son of God, God lives in you now. (*VU*, 48–49)

AUGUST 21
EXERCISING BELIEVING

Faith is not a thing to be seen or touched or handled. It is not a grace or a gracious disposition. It is nothing mysterious or perplexing. It is simply and only believing God. To exercise faith one has only to exercise toward God the same believing faculty one exercises toward man.

Neither are there different kinds of faith. Men talk about a feeling faith, a living faith, a saving faith, an intellectual faith, a historical faith, and a dead faith. But it is all a waste of words; for either we trust or we do not trust. If we trust, we have faith; and if we do not trust, we do not have faith; and that is all there is to it.

The difficulty is that we neither "say" the word of faith or "pray" the prayer of faith. We generally say the word of doubt and pray the prayer of experiment, and then we wonder why our faith and our prayers are so ineffectual.

It is of no use to fight against inevitable law. As well might the architect try to work in opposition to the law of gravitation and undertake to build his house from the top downwards, as for the Christian to try to accomplish anything in the spiritual realm by means of doubt. It simply cannot be done; and the sooner Christians know this, the better for them. How much can be done by faith may perhaps remain an open question, but it is a settled matter forever that nothing can be done by doubt. (*EDR*, 151, 154)

AUGUST 22
DENYING DOUBTING

You must hand your doubting over to God just as you do your temper or your pride; and you must trust Him to deliver you from doubting just as you trust Him to deliver you from getting angry. The great point is that you must give up the liberty to doubt. The trouble is that most people reserve to themselves a little liberty because they feel it is impossible always to trust and never to doubt. We say, "I do not want to doubt any more" or "I hope I will not doubt any more"; but it is hard to come to the point of saying, "I will not doubt. I give up all liberty to doubt forever." But no surrender is really effectual until it reaches the point of saying "I will not." Therefore, our only hope for victory lies in an utter surrender of all liberty to doubt forever.

I do not mean that doubts will not come. As long as we are

in this body of flesh we will be subject to the temptation to doubt, but while we cannot stop the temptation from coming, we can help entertaining it and giving it an abiding place in our hearts. We must treat every temptation to doubt as a temptation to sin and must refuse to entertain it for a single moment. We will be helped in this if we begin to assert by faith the exact opposite of our doubt. Doubts always fly when faith appears on the scene. If the doubt, for instance, says, "God does not love you," faith must declare more emphatically than ever, "God does love me. He says He does, and I know it is true." Kill your doubts by refusing to listen to them for a moment. Doubts cannot live where they find no nourishment. (*EDR*, 224–25)

AUGUST 23
TREMBLING OR TRIUMPHING

When Rahab helped the spies who had been sent by Joshua escape from the king of Jericho, she made this confession: "I know that the LORD hath given you the land, and that your terror is fallen upon us, and that all the inhabitants of the land faint because of you" (Josh. 2:9). If we were gifted with eyes that could see the unseen kingdom of evil, I believe we would find that a terror and faintness has fallen on all the forces of evil and that they see in every man and woman of faith, a sure and triumphant conqueror.

It is because we do not know this secret that we meet our spiritual enemies with such fear and trembling and suffer such disastrous defeats.

We are told that "for this purpose the Son of God was manifested, that he might destroy the works of the devil" (1 John 3:8); and "Ye know that he was manifested to take away our sins; and in him is no sin" (1 John 3:5); and again "Now once in the end of the world hath he appeared to put away sin by the sacrifice of himself" (Heb. 9:26). We must accept it as a fact, therefore, that sin is for us a conquered foe. If our faith will only lay hold of this fact and reckon sin to be dead to us and ourselves to be dead to sin, and will dare to raise the shout of victory when we face temptation, we will surely find, as the

Israelites did, that every wall will fall down flat and a pathway will be opened up for us to take the city! (*GAC*, 197–98)

AUGUST 24
TRUSTING, NOT THWARTING

God is love, and His will can be nothing but love. He is full of wisdom, and His will must always be wise. He is omnipotent, and His will is baffled by nothing that can oppose. He is just, and His will must be truly and perfectly just. When I think of who and what our God is, I am amazed that it ever entered into the head of any of us to fear or combat His will. We do not know what we are doing when we indulge in such feelings. The idea that our Father who loves us can want anything but our truest happiness is inconceivable. His will for us must be all that is best and most satisfying. Surely we can trust ourselves to it without a single shrinking or fearing thought.

When once we have opened our ears to listen to God's will, we will find as the children of Israel did that "his commandments are not grievous" (1 John 5:3) as we may have feared, but that peace, rest, and even "very great gladness" (Neh. 8:17) follow quickly in the keeping of His law.

Thy wonderful grand will, my God,
With triumph now I make it mine!
And faith shall cry a joyful, Yes!
To every dear command of Thine. (*OTT*, 260, 105)

AUGUST 25
HELPING OR HINDERING

Many Christians love God's will in the abstract but carry great burdens in connection with it. From this there is deliverance in the wonderful life of faith, for in this life no burdens are carried, no anxieties felt. The Lord is our Burden-bearer, and on Him we must lay every care.

God says, in effect, "Be careful for nothing, but make your requests known to me, and I will attend to them all" (Phil. 4:6, para.). Don't worry about anything, He says, not even your service. Above all, we are tempted to worry about our service, because we know we are so helpless in regard to it. But why should we worry whether we are fit for service? The Master Workman surely has a right to use any tool He pleases for His own work, and it is plainly not the business of the tool to decide whether it is the right one to be used or not. He knows; and if He chooses to use us, of course we must be fit. If we only knew it, our chief fitness is in our utter helplessness. His strength is made perfect not in our strength but in our weakness. Our strength is only a hindrance. (*SEC*, 191–92)

AUGUST 26
REJECTING THE OLD, CONFESSING THE NEW

"If any man be in Christ, he is a new creature: old things are passed away; behold, all things are become new. And all things are of God, who hath reconciled us to himself by Jesus Christ, and hath given to us the ministry of reconciliation" (2 Cor. 5:17–18).

The "old things" spoken of as "passing away" are everything that belong to the "old man," or carnal life—the old activities of the flesh; the old efforts to generate something in a religious way to recommend us to God; the old way of relying on exercises, ordinances, and duties of various kinds to beget and feed the life of God in the soul. Those who have been born into the resurrection life must learn that none of these things are of any avail in the new sphere they have entered.

Our "things," for example, our feelings, our experiences, and our exercises of various sorts, seem often to have a "show of wisdom," and it is hard for us to count them as really nothing and to say truly, when we seem to have so many things, that we have nothing. But anything that is what the apostle calls "rudiments of the world" (Col. 2:8, 20), that is, anything that is wrought out by "flesh," must always be "nothing" in the sight of God. As soon as we have learned to see things with His eyes, they will be nothing in our own sight. The simple fact is that our possessions of any kind are literally and truly "nothing."

So we must say with the apostle that we serve Christ ''as having nothing'' (2 Cor. 6:10). (*EDR*, 130–31)

AUGUST 27
CHASTENING BUT LOVING

Our sinfulness brings out a fresh expression of God's love in the form of chastening. Only those we love do we care to make perfect. Who of us would take the pains with the training and disciplining of the children of strangers whom we do not love that we do with our own children? Christ rebuked the scribes and Pharisees because they attributed less loving care to the heavenly Father than they did to the human fathers He had made.

God's love, therefore, seeks to make us good and cannot be satisfied until we are good. His reason for loving us is in himself and not in us. We all know how much we delight in anything we create, how we like to look at it and show it to our friends, how tender we are of its safety, and how jealous we are of any criticism of it. This joy of ours in creation and ownership will help us to understand and believe in the love of our Creator for us who are ''the work of his hands'' (Job 34:19 et al.).

God's love was not *caused* by the work of Christ, it was simply ''manifested'' (cf. 1 John 4:9), and all we can do is ''perceive'' it (cf. 1 John 3:16). In spiritual things we perceive by believing. Our friends may love us and tell us so and give us continual proof, but unless we believe in their love we shall never really perceive it or possess it. Faith is necessary to the possession of human love, and faith is equally necessary for the possession of divine love. God gives us His love always, but we cannot perceive and possess it unless we believe it. (*VU*, 22–27)

AUGUST 28
WINNING BY LOVING

The first way we can return love is by believing it and accepting its goodness. Nothing grieves love so much as a want of trust on the part of its beloved one. You wound the Lord more by your doubts of His love than by all your other sins together.

If a naughty child should let in doubts of his mother's love, this would be the hardest of all to bear. Let our uttermost confidence, then, be the first return we make to the wondrous love of God. God's love thus known and believed in will draw out ours in return.

God *wins* our love. Just as a bridegroom wins the love of his bride by assurances and proofs of his love for her, so does our God win our love. We love God because He first loved us (1 John 4:19).

If we love we will obey. Obedience is always the test of love. It is easy to talk about our love to God and even to work ourselves up into an emotion of love, but unless it stands the test of "walking in all the commandments" (cf. Luke 1:6), it is nothing but an unreal sentimentality.

We have seen children sometimes who would make great professions of loving their parents who yet, when asked to perform some little act of service, would say complainingly, "Oh, can't somebody else do it?" Real love delights to serve.

Let us ask ourselves the searching question as to whether all fear that "hath torment" (1 John 4:18) has been cast out of our hearts. Do we trust God's love for us to deliver us from fear, care, and anxiety and to keep our hearts in perfect peace? (*VU*, 28–29)

AUGUST 29
TOTALLY CONSECRATING

Lord, I am Yours, Yours wholly and Yours forever! I am Yours by the purchase of Your blood, and I give myself to You now as a living sacrifice—body, soul, and spirit—to be as clay in Your hands.

I give You my *heart*, Lord, to love only what You love, to hate what You hate, to endure all things, to suffer long and be kind, to be not easily provoked. To think no evil, not to seek my own, help me, oh my God!

I give You my *mind* to be wholly devoted to Your service and perfectly under Your control, to think only those thoughts that will please You, to devise only such plans as You suggest, to

179

yield the management of all its affairs to You. To bring every thought to the obedience of Christ, help me, oh my God!

I give You my *body* to be used by You—my eyes to see only what You would have them see, my ears to hear only what You would have them hear, my feet to go only where You lead, my hands to do such work only as can be done in fellowship with You, my tongue to speak only words that please You. I give my time to You, Lord, to be all Yours. Help me, oh my God!

I give You my children, my husband, and all whom I love, to be disposed of according to Your will. I leave to You the ordering of my whole life, and with Your help will follow You *wherever* You lead. I will give You the control of my feelings and of my prejudices. I submit in short my whole being and life—all that I am, and have, and will be, to Your control; and ask only that Your will may be perfectly done in me, through me, and by me! Take me and keep me, oh my God! (*Diaries*, 1859)

AUGUST 30
THANKING AND ACCEPTING

If brought face to face with the fact that they are to be thankful in everything, most Christians will say, "Oh, but that is an impossible command. If everything came directly from God, one might do it, but most things come through human sources and often are the result of sin. It would be impossible to give thanks for these." It is true we cannot always give thanks for the things themselves, but we can always give thanks for God's love and care in them. He may not have ordered what seem to us like adverse situations, but He is in them to compel even the most grievous matters to work together for our good.

The "second causes" of the wrong may be full of malice and wickedness, but faith never sees second causes; it sees only the hand of God behind the second causes. They are all under His control, and not one of them can touch us without His knowledge and permission. The thing itself that happens cannot perhaps be said to be the will of God, but by the time its effects reach us, they have become God's will for us and must be accepted as from His hands.

The story of Joseph is an illustration of this. Nothing could have seemed more entirely an act of sin or more utterly contrary to the will of God than Joseph's being sold to the Ishmaelites by his wicked brothers; and it would not have seemed possible for Joseph, when he was being carried off into slavery in Egypt, to give thanks. Yet if he had known the end from the beginning, he would have been filled with thanksgiving. (*GAC*, 204)

AUGUST 31
THANKING, NOT COMPLAINING

The greatest heights to which most Christians, in their shortsightedness, seem able to rise, is to strive for resignation to things they cannot alter and to seek for patience to endure them. As a result, thanksgiving is almost an unknown exercise among the children of God; and instead of giving thanks in everything, many of them hardly give thanks in anything. Christians as a body are a thankless set. It is considered in the world a very discourteous thing for us to receive benefits from others and fail to thank them; and I cannot see why it is not just as discourteous a thing not to thank God.

Yet we find people who would not for the world omit an immediate note of thanks on the reception of any gift, however trifling, from a human friend, but who have never given God real thanks for any one of the innumerable benefits He has been showering on them all their lives.

Moreover, I am afraid a great many not only fail to give thanks, but they do exactly the opposite and allow themselves instead to complain about God's dealings with them. Instead of looking for His goodness, they seem to delight in picking out His alleged shortcomings and think they show a spirit of discernment in criticizing His laws and His ways. We are told that "when the people complained, it displeased the LORD" (Num. 11:1); but we are tempted to think that our complaining is special because it is spiritual complaining and is a sign of our great zeal and deep spiritual insight. (*GAC*, 205–6)

SEPTEMBER 1
PRAISING OR BLAMING

Complaining is always the same whether it is on the temporal or the spiritual plane. It always has in it the element of fault-finding. Webster says to complain means to make a charge or accusation. It is not merely disliking the thing we have to bear; it contains the element of finding fault with the agency that lies behind it. If we will carefully examine our complainings, I think we will generally find that they are founded on a subtle fault-finding with God. We secretly feel as if He were to blame; and almost unconsciously we make mental charges against Him.

Have you ever noticed how much we are urged in the Bible to praise the Lord? It seemed to be almost the principal part of the worship of the Israelites: "Praise the LORD, for the LORD is good: sing praises to his name; for it is pleasant" (Ps. 135:3). This is the continual refrain all through the Bible. I believe that if we counted we would find there are more commands given and more examples set for the giving of thanks than for the doing or the leaving undone of anything else.

From the teaching of Scripture it is evident that the Lord loves to be thanked and praised just as much as we like it. I am sure that it gives Him real pleasure just as it does us and that our failure to thank Him for His "good and perfect gifts" (James 1:17) wounds His loving heart just as our hearts are wounded when our loved ones fail to appreciate the benefits we have so enjoyed bestowing on them. What a joy it is to us to receive from our friends an acknowledgment of their thanksgiving for our gifts, and it is a joy to the Lord to receive thanks and praise from us. (*GAC*, 206–7)

SEPTEMBER 2
TRUSTING, NOT COMPLAINING

Instead of thanking God, we complain against Him, though we generally direct our complaints not against the Physician himself who has ordered our medicine but against the "bottle"

182

in which He has sent it. This "bottle" is usually some human being whose unkindness, carelessness, neglect, or cruelty, has caused our suffering, but who has been after all only the instrumentality or "second cause" that God has used for our healing.

Good common sense tells us that it would be folly to rail against the bottles in which the medicines prescribed by our earthly physicians come to us; and it is equal folly to rail against the "second causes" that are meant to teach us the lessons our souls need to learn.

God is the great Cause behind all second causes. The second causes are only the instrumentalities that He uses; and when we murmur against these, we are really murmuring not against the instrumentalities but against God himself. Second causes are powerless to act except by God's permission; and what He permits becomes His arranging. The psalmist tells us that when the Lord heard the complainings of His people "he was wroth" (Ps. 78:21), and His anger came up against them "because they believed not in God, and trusted not in his salvation" (v. 22). All complainings mean just this: that we do not believe in God and we do not trust in His salvation. (*GAC*, 208–10)

SEPTEMBER 3
RESTING, NOT WRESTLING

I cannot but feel that we need more sitting still in Christian experience. There is too much restless anxiety about our prayers, too much of a feeling that unless we help in some way or at least unless we wrestle and agonize over it, the matter cannot be finished satisfactorily at all.

I was visiting a mother in her nursery where her little boy was playing. We were talking about prayer and asking each other what sort of praying was right—the trusting kind or the agonizing kind—when we were interrupted by the child's asking for a cookie. His mother said yes at once and went to the closet for them but found the cookie jar empty. She said she would send for some, and the child saw the nurse take the money and start out to make the purchase. A good child would have gone back to playing again and would have waited trustingly until the cookie came. But this child stood at his mother's elbow, saying over and over, first in a plaintive tone, which rapidly rose to an agony of entreaty, "Mother, give me a cookie. I want a cookie. Please let me have a cookie. I must have a cookie." Finally our conversation was drowned in the noise of his wailing. My question about prayer was answered; and never from that time have I dared to agonize over any request I have made of the Lord.

I do not mean, however, that we are to forget our prayers or be indifferent to their results, but simply that, having made our request known, we must then wait in a quiet and patient faith, sure that the Lord will not rest until He has finished the matter we have put into His hands. (*OTT,* 164–65)

SEPTEMBER 4
WOOING, NOT COMPELLING

Christ prayed for His followers that they might be one even as He and the Father are one (John 17:21). The promise is ours. Let us boldly make our claim, for we may rest assured our Lord will not rest until He has perfected that which concerns us. He has made our souls capable of a marvelous oneness with himself, but He will not force it on us. A compelled marriage can never be other than a wretched one, and the glory of our destiny is that, on our part, it is to be a voluntary and glad surrender to a love that woos and wins our hearts by its compelling constraint. We love Him because He first loved us (1 John 4:19), and we can come to Him with unshrinking faith to claim that which He himself has already told us is His own purpose and prayer.

"That they all may be one" (John 17:21)—it is all shut up in this. Imagine such similarity of thought, feeling, desire, loves, and hates! We may have it all, dear Christian, if we are but willing. We may walk through this world so united to Christ that our cares and interests, sorrows and joys, purposes and wishes will be the same—one will to govern us, one mind to control us. He will be in us and we in Him until our lives are so intermingled and conjoined that we can say at last, "Not I, but Christ." For self will vanish in such a union as this, and this great "I" of ours, which so fills up the present horizon, will wilt down into nothing before the glory of His overcoming presence. (*OTT*, 169–70)

SEPTEMBER 5
CHEERING, NOT DISCOURAGING

An old Quaker has said, "All discouragement is from the devil"; and I believe he has stated a far deeper and more universal truth than we have yet fully understood. Discouragement cannot have its source in God. The religion of the Lord Jesus Christ is a religion of faith, good cheer, courage, and hope that maketh not ashamed. "Be discouraged," says our lower nature, "for the world is a place of temptation and sin." "Be of good cheer," says Christ, "I have overcome the world" (John 16:33). There cannot possibly be any room for discouragement in a world which Christ has overcome.

We must settle it then, once for all, that discouragement always comes from an evil source. This is not the idea held by all Christians, at least in spiritual things. In temporal things, perhaps, we have more or less learned that discouragement is foolish and even wrong; but when it comes to spiritual things, we are apt to reverse the order and make what is commendable in one case, reprehensible in the other; and we even succeed in persuading ourselves that to be discouraged is a very pious state of mind and an evidence of true humility. (*GAC*, 174)

SEPTEMBER 6
CLAIMING AND CONQUERING

Christ's word gives us the ground for our triumphant shout of faith. "Be of good cheer," He says, "I have overcome the world" (John 16:33)—not "I will overcome" but "I have overcome." It is already done; and nothing remains but for us to enter into the power of it. Joshua did not say to the people, "Shout, for the Lord will give you the city," but "Shout, for the LORD hath given you the city" (Josh. 6:16). It must have drained all Joshua's will power to his lips for him to make such a statement in view of the fact that the walls of the city were at

185

that very minute standing up as massive and as impregnable as ever. But God was a reality to Joshua, and he was not afraid to proclaim the victory that had been promised, even before it was accomplished.

There is a great difference between saying, "The Lord will give," and "The Lord hath given." A victory, promised in the future, may be hindered or prevented by a thousand contingencies, but a victory already accomplished cannot be gainsaid. When our Lord assures us, not that He will overcome the world but that He has already done so, He gives an assured foundation for a shout of the most triumphant victory. Henceforward the forces of sin are a defeated and demoralized foe; and, if we believe the words of Christ, we can meet them without fear, since we have been made more than conquerors through Him who loves us.

The secret then lies in this, that we must meet sin not as a foe that has yet to be conquered but as one that has already been conquered. (*GAC*, 173–74)

SEPTEMBER 7
CONSECRATING AND ABANDONING

The Lord is leading me on, step by step. He has created in me a willingness and ability to consecrate myself to Him, to be His wholly and forever—to be His, not only in *some* of the special circumstances of my life or in *some* of the activities of my soul, but to be His *myself*—to abandon my whole self to Him, with all my powers and all my circumstances, to resign my whole will to Him without any possible reservation.

He has now taught me that He himself has taken possession of me, and that He is having His own way in me, to make me just what He pleases. "This is His will, even my sanctification" (cf. 1 Thess. 4:3); therefore, if He has possession of me, it is impossible that He should leave me unsanctified for a single moment. It was only myself who hindered the work; and if I give myself up to Him, the work must be accomplished. I cannot but believe it. An actual transaction has taken place between God and my soul. I have abandoned myself to Him; so He has taken possession of me and—I *must* believe it—has sanctified me.

A *real* work has taken place: on my part, consecration; on the Lord's part, sanctification. For it is all His work from beginning to end! I say *my* part because the conscious asking of my soul was to give itself up; but it was God who did it in me. It is not a *belief*, but a *reality* in which I am rejoicing. I have abandoned myself to God, and He has taken possession of me. All the rest must follow. He cannot but do His will in me, which is my *sanctification*.

Blessed Lord Jesus, what a perfect works was Yours! Oh, show me more and more of its completeness! (Diary, 1868)

SEPTEMBER 8
DESPAIRING AND DAUNTING

Our enemies are "giants" now just as truly as they were in Israel's day, and cities as great as Jericho, with walls as high, confront us in our spiritual pathway. Like the Israelites of old, we have no human weapons with which to conquer them. Our armor, like theirs, must be the "armour of God" (Eph. 6:11). Our shield is the same invisible shield of faith that protected them, and our sword must be as theirs was, the "sword of the Spirit" (v. 17) which is the Word, that is, the promises and declarations of God. When our faith puts on the armor of God and lays hold of the "sword of the Spirit," and we confront our enemy with a shout of undaunted faith, we cannot fail to conquer the mightiest giant or take the strongest city.

How different is the usual method of our Christian warfare. Instead of a triumphant shout of victory, we meet our temptations with feeble resolutions, futile arguments, or half-hearted self-upbraiding; or we cry, "O Lord, deliver me!" When no deliverance comes and the temptation has swept aside all our arguments and resolutions and we have been grievously defeated, we cry out in despair that God has failed us. This is the usual and the unsuccessful way of meeting temptation, as many of us know to our cost.

But what we ought to do is very different. Where we prayed before that the Lord would save us, we must make now the

187

assertion that He does save us and that He saves us now. We must add the letter "s" to the word save and make it the present instead of the future tense. (*GAC*, 198–99)

SEPTEMBER 9
THANKSGIVING OR COMPLAINING

Thanksgiving or complaining—these words express two contrasting attitudes of God's children in regard to His dealings with us; and they are more powerful than we realize in furthering or frustrating His purposes of comfort and peace toward us. The soul who gives thanks can find comfort in everything; the soul who complains can find comfort in nothing.

God's command is, "In every thing give thanks"; and the command is emphasized by the declaration, "For this is the will of God in Christ Jesus concerning you" (1 Thess. 5:18). It is a command; if we want to obey God, we have to give thanks in everything.

But a great many Christians have never realized this. Although they may be familiar with the command, they have always looked on it as a sort of counsel of perfection to which mere flesh and blood could never be expected to attain. They unconsciously change the wording of the passage and make it say "be resigned" instead of "give thanks," and "in a few things" instead of "in everything." They leave out altogether the words, "for this is the will of God in Christ Jesus concerning you." (*GAC*, 203–4)

SEPTEMBER 10
THANKSGIVING FOR TESTING

When the apostle Paul is exhorting the Ephesian Christians to be "followers of God, as dear children" (Eph. 5:1), one of the exhortations he gives in connection with being filled with the Spirit is this: "[Give] thanks always for all things unto God and the Father in the name of our Lord Jesus Christ" (v. 20). "Always for all things" is a sweeping expression, and it is impossible to suppose it can be whittled down to mean only the scanty thanks which seem to be all that many Christians manage to give. It must mean that there can be nothing in our lives that lacks in it somewhere a cause for thanksgiving, and no matter who or what may be the channel to convey it, everything contains for us a hidden blessing from God.

But even when we realize that things come directly from God, we find it very hard to give thanks for what hurts us. Do we not, however, know what it is to thank a skillful physician for his treatment of our diseases, even though that treatment may have been very severe? Surely we should no less give thanks to our divine Physician when He is obliged to give us bitter medicine to cure our spiritual diseases or to perform a painful operation to rid us of something that harms. (*GAC*, 207)

SEPTEMBER 11
PURGING YET LOVING

How well we know the strength of love it requires for us to discipline our children in order to make them what they ought to be, and how often we fail through a selfish weakness. Let us be thankful, then, that we have a holy God who will not tolerate inequity and whose love is so strong that He will not withhold the hand of His discipline until He has purely purged away all our dross, taken away all our sin, and presented us to himself, a "glorious church, not having spot, or wrinkle, or any such thing" (Eph. 5:27).

Job shows us the divine method by which God does this purifying process. By all that happened to Job, he was brought to a knowledge of his own heart and was made to abhor himself in dust and ashes. The instrument used was Satan, but the hand that used this instrument was the Lord's. When Job's possessions were taken and when his own body was smitten with sores, Satan's power extended only as far as the Lord permitted.

At first the Lord said, "Behold, all that he hath is in thy power; only upon himself put not forth thy hand" (Job 1:12). Then He said, "Behold he is in thine hand; but save his life" (Job 2:6). Therefore, while Satan seemed to do it all, there was One behind Satan who overruled everything and made it all work together to accomplish His purposes of grace toward Job. (*OTT*, 281–82)

SEPTEMBER 12
HURTING BUT HEALING

The story of Job is enacted over and over. The righteous suffer, and we do not know why. Mysterious providences darken and attempt to ruin the lives of those who have seemed too good to need such discipline. Even to ourselves come afflictions that we cannot understand, and Satan seems so busy in the matter that it is hard to trace the hand of the Lord in it at all. But His hand is in it nevertheless, and He overrules everything. No trial comes except by His permission and for some wise and loving purpose which perhaps only eternity will disclose.

Earthly parents deal this way continually with their children. Their watchful eyes discover incipient diseases long before their children feel any uncomfortable symptoms themselves, and they administer the needed medicines, often when it seems very mysterious and unreasonable to their children. Yet a parent's closet may be full of medicines that remain untouched for months if no need is discovered. A parent's love is too tender to inflict unnecessary doses and too strong to spare the dose that is needed.

Here lies the secret of all that seems so mysterious in the discipline of our lives. Our loving and wise Physician has discovered in us some incipient disease that He knows will ruin us if it remains unchecked, and He is applying the remedy. Would we stay His hand even if we could? Surely not. For more than anything else, we want soul health; and any remedy that will bring it to us is more than welcome. (*OTT*, 283–84)

SEPTEMBER 13
CONSECRATING DEFINITELY

I thank the Lord that He has made my consecration to Him a reality thus far, and that He has given me more and more light upon the subject, both as respects its importance and its effects.

I see now plainly that although I fully desired and intended, before this act of consecration, to be wholly given up to the Lord and to lose my will in His, yet from the fact of not having actually and definitely yielded myself up to Him, I left a loophole for the flesh. Whenever temptation overcame me, it did not seem so very dreadful a thing.

But now, although I can make no more *promises* for the future than I did before, yet I find a great difference in my way of looking at it. I feel that the future belongs to God as really as my present; and to contemplate the taking back of any moment of it into my own hands, fills me with horror of soul. Before, I might be able to say at any given moment, "I am the Lord's now, altogether and unreservedly." But my will always took comfort in the thought of a future, when perhaps I would not be entirely His; secretly and almost unconsciously, I made a future provision for the flesh, to fulfill the desires thereof. But now!

Oh, my Lord and Maker, teach me the depth and reality of this giving up of my whole self to You! Dimly I begin to see it, and I find that my will is slain in a manner I never before experienced. It can rest nowhere but in You. For all my future, I contemplate no moment when I will not be given up to You, as in the present. (Diary, 1868)

SEPTEMBER 14
ACCEPTING WITHOUT MURMURING

Nothing but seeing God in everything will make us loving and patient with those who annoy and trouble us. They will be to us then only the instruments for accomplishing His tender and wise purposes toward us, and we will even find ourselves inwardly thanking them for the blessings they bring.

Nothing else will put an end to our rebellious thoughts and complaining. Christians often feel at liberty to murmur against other people when they would not dare to murmur against God. Seeing God in all things, therefore, will make it impossible even to murmur. If our Father permits a trial to come, it must be because the trial is the sweetest and best thing that could happen to us, and we must accept it with thanks from His dear hand. This does not mean, however, that we must enjoy the trial itself, but that we must be thankful for God's will in the trial. It is not hard to do this when we have learned that His will is the will of love and is therefore always lovely.

Believe God is faithful not because you feel it or see it but because He says He is. Believe it even when it seems to you that you are believing something that is absolutely untrue. Believe it actively and persistently.

It is an inexorable rule in the spiritual life that according to our faith so is it unto us. Of course, this rule must work both ways; therefore we may fairly expect that it will be to us according to our doubts. Doubts and discouragements are inlets by which evil enters, while faith is an impregnable wall against all evil. (*SEC*, 151–52)

SEPTEMBER 15
TRUSTING AND ACCEPTING

I thank the Lord that He enables me still to keep the consecration of myself and all my powers on the altar. And I thank Him that He has allowed me to meet with so many things that confirm me in the belief.

It seems indeed that when I look at myself I find that I am too weak, too full of imperfection and sin, to dare to make such a dedication of myself to the Lord. But when I look at Christ, every thought vanishes but the one longing desire to live and walk so as to please Him and to bring glory to His name. I know it is His will that I should live like that, and that He is able to keep me from falling. And so all I can do is trust Him.

Satan constantly suggests to my mind that I have not made this consecration in the best way; but the Lord knows that I try to do it in the best way I am able. And besides, it is not my *way* of making the sacrifice that makes it acceptable, but the fact that it is in Christ. Christ knows; I trust Him; and He *will not let me be confounded.*

"But," says Satan, "you would *feel* differently if your sacrifice were accepted." The Lord never promised that I should *feel* He accepted the sacrifice; He only told me to make it. So I know He will receive it, and *has* received it. Even if He leaves me without any evidence of acceptance for years or always, I will

not withdraw my sacrifice from the altar; nor will I doubt that
He accepts it. If it be more for His glory that I should always
live a life of simple faith, He will give me strength to do it, and
I will trust Him. (*Diaries*, 1859)

SEPTEMBER 16
LISTENING AND OBEYING

Subjection to a voice is one of the surest ways of learning to
know it. Each time we obey the voice of our Shepherd it will
become easier for us to distinguish it the next time.

We must bow our necks to the yoke of divine guidance if we
want to learn to walk in the true "way of life." No one can do
this fully who has not learned that self must be dead and Christ
all in all. Our own wisdom must fail utterly before we can submit in all things to divine wisdom; therefore few reach this stage.

Believers cry out everywhere, "Oh, that I might know the
Shepherd's voice!" But they shrink from the steps that must be
taken in order to learn it. There is no other way. If we want to
walk where Christ walks, we must have on His yoke, and if we
will not take it on lovingly and gladly, He will be compelled to
put it on us with chastisements and severity. To take the yoke of
Christ on us means that we give our freedom of will to Him and
consent to be guided by His voice in all things. This voice will
be made known to us, in three ways: through Scripture, through
providential circumstances, and through a divine conviction
produced in the soul by the Holy Spirit. We have a right to ask
that we may clearly distinguish it before being required to act.
When once we know it, nothing but obedience will do, and to
the truly obedient soul the yoke proves to be indeed an easy one
and the burden light (Matt. 11:30). (*OTT*, 327–29)

SEPTEMBER 17
YIELDING, NOT WORKING

God does not tell us that we are workmen who are to use and
manage instruments. Instead we are the instruments to be used
and managed by the divine Master Workman who made us, and

who alone, therefore, understands for what work we are best fitted and how we are best used. The only thing the instrument can do is yield itself perfectly to the will of the Master Workman. The Master surely knows how best to use His instruments, and it is plainly not the business of the tool to decide these questions for itself. Neither must it try to help by its own efforts to do the work.

One absolutely necessary characteristic of a tool is its pliableness. The moment resistance is felt in any tool, the moment it refuses to move just as the master wants, that moment it becomes unfit for use. If I am writing with a fine gold pen and it begins to catch and sputter and move with difficulty, I will soon lay it aside and use gladly in its place even a stub end of a lead pencil if only it will move easily in obedience to my will. The strength of an instrument lies in its helplessness. Because it is helpless to do anything of itself, the master can use it as he pleases. (*VU*, 141)

SEPTEMBER 18
PRAYING WITH SIMPLICITY

When we love an earthly friend, we are not satisfied with only a few minutes' conversation at a time; nor can we come to know that person's true character or appreciate the deeper parts of one's nature, even if those passing words should occur every few minutes. Neither can we know *God* in this way. How often we say of our earthly friends, "How I long to have a good, long, quiet talk with you!" And shall we not have the same with our heavenly Friend, so that we may really get to know Him?

I desire to realize the *simplicity* of prayer. I must not look at it as a religious exercise, but as a child's going to its father to get what it needs in answer to prayer. Especially, I must remember that my having access to God depends not upon *my* feelings but upon *His*—He welcomes my approaches because of the ground upon which I draw near to Him, not because of the mere flow of emotion in my heart.

If my prayers should be without one wandering thought, with most heavenly feelings I would probably be tempted to congratulate myself, saying, "What a grand prayer!" But if, on the other hand, I am plagued with many wandering thoughts and much coldness, then I shall *know* that God can hear me only for Jesus' sake. And I shall say, "What a grand plea the name of Jesus is! It makes my otherwise worthless prayer to be acceptable!"

Oh, Lord, when I pray, let me feel it to be a *privilege*, not an exercise or duty. (*Diaries*, 1859)

SEPTEMBER 19
CONSECRATING BRINGS REJOICING

"Thy will be done in earth, as it is in heaven" (Matt. 6:10)—to me these words are among the most beautiful ever put into mortal lips. The perfect doing of God's will is what makes heaven what it is, and to have His will done perfectly here would turn this earth into a heaven also. In so far as God's will is done in any individual life, it does bring heaven down into that life and makes that person live in a perpetual kingdom. For he does indeed "always reign who sides with God," since God's way is his way.

How sad it is that anyone should ever have a different thought from this. Yet we all know how common it is even for Christians to look at consecration as a stern demand and to shrink from the will of God as from the worst evil that could befall them. I knew of a Christian teacher once who was asked by one of his friends to speak on the subject of consecration. "Oh, do not ask me to do that!" was his shuddering reply. "Do you know what consecration means?" he continued. "It means that all that is bright and pleasant in your life will be taken out of it and that every hard and sad thing you can conceive of will come into it. It means that you will have to do impossible things and that your ease and comfort will be gone forever."

How little could such a soul have known about the Lord. How is it that we can so misunderstand and misjudge our Lord, whose will can be nothing but goodness and love, since He himself is these and these only? (*OTT*, 103–4)

SEPTEMBER 20
DELIGHTING, NOT GRUDGING

Do we "delight" to do God's will (cf. Ps. 40:8)? Is it our "meat" to do it (cf. John 4:34)?

We need to watch against a grudging service. The Enemy is always trying to get us to think "duty" instead of "delight." He says a stern "you must" instead of the loving "you may." When a mother cares for her child from duty only, the tender sweetness of mother love has gone. When a husband or wife begins to say "I ought" instead of "I delight to" in their relations toward one another, the home becomes a prison.

There is no slavery like the slavery of love, but its chains are sweet. It knows nothing of "sacrifice" no matter what may be given up. It delights to do the will of the beloved one. Our Lord can never be satisfied until this is the attitude of our souls toward Him. His purpose of grace for us is harmony between our will and His—not two wills crossing one another but two wills made one. Has it become so with us as yet? Can we say that it is our "meat" to do His will? If not, the choice is before us now, and we must decide it.

May the Lord enable us to settle the question at once and forever on the side of His will and not our own. (*VU*, 59–60)

SEPTEMBER 21
WILLING OUR BLESSING

Faber says, "God's will on earth is always joy, always tranquility." The soul that has learned to know God can say amen to this with eager gladness. For the will of God is the will of love, and the will of love can never be anything but richest blessing to the loved one.

We all know this truth, even in our meager human experience of love. We know that where we love, our will toward the object of our affections embraces and demands only his blessing and happiness. Our own happiness is as nothing in comparison, and our only trouble is that we cannot find ways enough in which to express our love. We know that the one question of our hearts is not, "What can he do for me?" but, "What can I do for him?" His good is our good, his suffering is ours, and every joy that lights up his face lights ours as well. If he would let us have our way, how happy we would make him, along what smooth pathways we would lead him, and how tenderly we would guard him from danger or pain.

If this is true of our paltry human love, what must it be with the infinite, unspeakable, and unknowable love of God? If therefore, we have ever been able to trust ourselves gladly to an earthly lover or to surrender our wills to the call of human affection, surely we might with a fearless devotion abandon ourselves to the disposal of our Lord and Savior and say to Him with the gladdest joy, "Thy will be done in earth, as it is in heaven" (Matt. 6:10). (*OTT*, 102–3)

SEPTEMBER 22
SURRENDERING AND RESTING

Surrender, faith, and obedience are necessary at every step of divine progress. Without them rest is impossible. A young child rests in its mother only when it yields unquestioning submission to her control and trusts implicitly in her love. The ox that yields to the yoke without chafing, rests under it, while the young bullock, "unaccustomed to the yoke" (Jer. 31:18), finds it a galling burden. Truly many Christians have less sense than dumb animals; for the animals, when they find the yoke inevitable, yield to it, and thus it becomes easy. But we who ought to have more sense are tempted to chafe and worry under it as long as life lasts.

Learn to "take" the yoke on you. Do not wait for it to be forced on you. Say, "Yes, Lord," to each expression of His will in all the circumstances of your lives. Say it with full consent to everything: to the loss of your health, to the malice of enemies, or to the cruelty of friends. Take each yoke as it comes, and in the taking you will find rest.

Notice the expressions "I will give you rest" and "ye shall find rest" in Matthew 11:28–29. This rest cannot be earned, bought, or attained. It is simply given by God and found by us.

All who come to Christ in the way of surrender and trust "find" it without any effort. They "enter into rest" (cf. Heb. 4:3), for in His presence there is never any unrest. (*VU*, 80)

SEPTEMBER 23
HAVING BUT LOSING

Sooner or later the child of God who knows the embrace of the Father's love comes to the place of insight where thoughts of self vanish in the wondrous revelation of the heart of God.

But the "I" religion is not lost all at once, nor is it confined only to the unenlightened sinner. In the parable of the Prodigal Son, the "elder brother" who lived at home with his father and shared all his possessions thought only of himself at the supreme moment of his father's joy. He felt himself to be badly used and declared that his rights had not been recognized or his merits appreciated. "Lo, these many years did I serve thee, . . . and yet thou never didst such things for me" (Luke 15:29, para.). Self was uppermost in the heart of this son. He had been in one sense a good son, faithful in his father's service, but he had kept his "I" religion. He could not forget himself.

There are some of God's children even now who, like this "elder brother," think of themselves first in every emergency and feel that their own rights and deserts ought always to have the first claim, both inwardly and outwardly. (*VU*, 228–29)

SEPTEMBER 24
LOSING AND FINDING

The "not I" religion forgets self in its absorption in God. It expects nothing from self but everything from God; it demands nothing for self but seeks to lavish all on the Lord; it learns to recognize in God the same blessed attributes and begins to have an insight into His heart of self-forgetting love and tenderness. It pours out its most precious gifts as a love offering to its Lord and asks for no return, but it receives most abundant and un-expected measure.

Some of the most religious people of the day have the "I" religion. "I am altogether right," they say, "and you, if you differ from me, are altogether wrong. I ought to be put foremost, for I know the best. I am the one to have place and authority, for I am the best fitted to assume it. My rights must be considered, for they are the most important." The "I" religion compels everything to come up to its own standard. The "not I" religion covers all things with a mantle of Christlike love; it "suffereth long, and is kind"; it "envieth not"; it "vaunteth not itself, is not puffed up"; it "seeketh not [its] own, is not easily provoked, thinketh no evil"; it "beareth all things, believeth all things, hopeth all things, endureth all things" (1 Cor. 13:4–7).

In each event that meets us, self clamors for recognition, and at each clamor it may be crucified and its claims ignored. Always and everywhere we may put off the old man of the "I" religion and put on the new man of the "not I" religion. (*VU*, 236–39)

SEPTEMBER 25
DYING AND LIVING

There is one principal center around which life revolves and for the sake of which it acts. Generally this center is the "I," or self. Everything is calculated with reference to its influence on self. What gain or what improvement to my personal standing or prospects will come from certain courses of action? How will it affect me? These are the continual underlying questions.

The Prodigal Son is an illustration of this. The returning son had no thought of his father's love or sorrow or longing; his only care was to get comfort and food for himself. His expectations could rise no higher than to be a servant in his father's household where he would find "bread enough and to spare" (Luke 15:17).

This is always the first selfish way of the human heart. We do not consider how our heavenly Father loves us, longs for us, and grieves over our wandering, or how He will rejoice at our return; instead we ask what we will get by returning, what personal gain will accrue to us, how much better off we will be for giving our allegiance to Christ. It is the "I" religion only that we can comprehend at first.

In the father's embrace the "I" religion was swept away, and all the son's previous thoughts of being a hired servant vanished before the "best robe" (Luke 15:22), the "fatted calf" (v. 23), and the merry feast of welcome over himself, the son who "was lost, and is found" (v. 24). (*VU*, 227–28)

SEPTEMBER 26
GAINING BY GIVING

In order to enter into the kingdom of heaven, all dependence on earthly riches, whether money, reputation, or good deeds, must be given up. The "poor in spirit" (Matt. 5:3) alone can find the kingdom. "To gain the whole world," in any sense, however subtle, is to lose one's soul in the same subtle sense (Matt. 16:26).

Some of God's own children make great outward gains in things that minister to self even in their religious lives. They have wonderful religious experiences, do great religious works, and receive honor from men, yet in this gaining they have so degraded their finest impulses and deadened their spiritual life that they have buried their souls under a mountain of selfhood until they have to all intents and purposes lost their own lives.

A "not I" religion is the religion that denies self, that says to this "I," "I am a stranger to you and do not wish to have anything to do with you." It denies self not in the sense of making self miserable but in the sense of utterly refusing to recognize its claims, enthroning the Christ-life in its stead always and everywhere. (*VU*, 233–34)

SEPTEMBER 27
LIVING IN DYING

The only way out of an "I" religion into a "not I" religion, is by a death to self. We must die that we may live. Practically, this means that we are not to care what self gains or what becomes of self but only how God is treated and what brings gain and joy to Him.

The trouble with our religion is its tendency to selfishness. Its first and foremost thought is always for self; and this cannot but taint the whole character. If it is right to think of self first in the most sacred of all things, we naturally feel that it cannot be wrong to think of self first in all minor things. We continually seek to please ourselves and to save ourselves.

Christ saved others, but He couldn't save himself. Christ didn't please himself. If we are living the Christ-life, we will know that we also are not to please ourselves or save ourselves but to save and please others. How far we are from this Christlike burden bearing. Our own burdens fill the whole horizon for us, and we can scarcely see, much less carry, the burdens of others.

This selfishness of our "I" religion taints our views of God. We are so selfish that we are unable to give one single generous or unselfish attribute to Him. We think He must be all the time looking out for His rights and His glory just as we are for ours. We are afraid to trust Him to save us, because we know our own selfish unwillingness to save others. We think He is like us. This is the "I" religion. (*VU*, 234–35)

SEPTEMBER 28
SURRENDERING AND SANCTIFYING

When we have heard the call to surrender and have confessed that the Lord is our God and that we will walk in His ways and keep His commandments, He declares us to be His peculiar people and promises to make us holy. From that moment He takes full possession of us. What can He do but take possession of the soul that surrenders itself to Him? And of course He sanctifies that which is His own. Everything given to God becomes, by that very act, holy and set apart for His use alone.

Having once given it to the Lord, a devoted thing was reckoned by all Israel as being His, and no one dared stretch forth a hand to retake it. The giver might have felt his offering to be a very poor one or to have been very poorly made, but having made it, the matter was taken out of his hands, and the devoted thing, by God's own law, became "most holy unto the LORD"

(Lev. 27:28). It was not the intention of the giver nor the quality of the gift that made it holy but the holiness of the receiver. God's possession of anything sanctifies it. "The altar sanctifieth the gift" (Matt. 23:19). Just as we used to read in our fairy tales of a certain kind of water that turned all things that it touched into gold, so God makes everything that is given to Him holy no matter what its former condition may have been. "Whatsoever toucheth the altar shall be holy" (Exod. 29:37). (*VU*, 60–61)

SEPTEMBER 29
ABIDING AND ASSURING

Often in our childhood, when we were afraid to go somewhere or do something, our mothers comforted us by saying, "I will be with you." God stills all the fears of His people by the same simple announcement: "Lo, I am with you alway, even unto the end of the world" (Matt. 28:20).

Repeated assurances of God's presence with His people under all their varying circumstances must be meant to assure us that because He is thus with us, we may be also sure that all His wisdom and power are at our disposal and engaged on our behalf. No good mother could be present with her child and fail to use all her resources in that child's behalf; her mother heart would make it impossible. The heart of God toward us makes it far more impossible for Him to be present with us and fail to help us in every need.

God promised Israel that He was as steadfast as the mountains that surrounded Jerusalem. What are the mountains around Jerusalem like? Are they there one day and gone the next? Are they there in sunshine but forsake Jerusalem when it storms? Are they there when all eyes see them but gone when night makes them invisible? What foolish questions! But the things many Christians think and say are far more foolish.

The mountains are around Jerusalem whether anyone sees them or not; and it is equally true that God is now and always will be around us whether we see and feel Him or not. (*VU*, 216–17)

SEPTEMBER 30
BELIEVING AND SEEING

The king of Syria came up against the man of God with horses and chariots that were visible to everyone, but God had chariots that could be seen by none but the eye of faith. The servant of the prophet could see only the outward and visible, and he cried, as so many under similar circumstances have done since, "Alas, my master! how shall we do?" (2 Kings 6:15). But the prophet himself sat calmly within his house without fear, because his eyes had been opened to see the invisible. He asked for his servant, "LORD, I pray thee, open his eyes, that he may see" (v. 17).

This is the prayer we need to pray for ourselves and for one another—"Lord, open our eyes that we may see" —for the world around us is full of God's horses and chariots, waiting to carry us to places of glorious victory.

But they do not look like chariots. They look instead like enemies, sufferings, trials, defects, misunderstandings, disappointments, and unkindnesses. They look like Juggernauts of misery and wretchedness waiting to roll over us and crush us into the earth. But they really are chariots of triumph in which we may rise to those very heights of victory for which our souls have been longing and praying.

Only the chariots of God are equal to such lofty riding as this. Earthly chariots are subject to the laws of matter and may be hindered or overturned; God's chariots are controlled by spiritual forces and triumph over all would-be hindrances. No words can express the glorious places to which that soul will arrive who travels in the chariots of God. (*VU*, 241–42)

OCTOBER 1
HOLDING AND UPHOLDING

The Lord's relationship to us is like that of a mother holding the hand of her little child as they walk together. She holds his hand so that he won't trip and fall. It is the mother holding the child that makes him safe not vice versa. An infant in a mother's arms is safe because of her upholding. His tight clinging when danger is near does not make him any safer, for his safety consists in that his mother holds him; everything depends on whether she is able to keep him safe.

Mothers are not always able to keep their children from falling, but God is always able to keep His children from falling. People in their ignorance sometimes say, "If I get religion, I am afraid I cannot keep it." This is true, but if you get the right kind of religion, God will keep you.

Often we are tempted to think that God's keeping is not true keeping unless it is in our own way and according to our own ideas, but our Lord himself has taught us that it must be in God's way and not ours, or it would be no keeping at all.

We must give up all care of our own by an absolute surrender to His keeping and by an implicit trust of our needs day by day. If this is done and steadfastly persisted in, the peace of God will keep as in a garrison our hearts and minds. (*VU*, 63–70)

OCTOBER 2
CRUSHING OR UPLIFTING

We may make out of each event in our lives either a Juggernaut to crush us or a chariot of God in which to ride to heights of victory. It all depends on how we take things—whether we lie down under our trials and let them roll over and crush us or whether we climb up into them as into a chariot and make them carry us triumphantly onward and upward.

Whenever we climb into God's chariots, the same thing happens to us spiritually that happened to Elisha: we are translated—not into the heavens above us as Elisha was but into the heaven within us, which after all is almost a grander translation than his. We will be carried up and away from the earthly plane of life where there is hurt and sadness into the "heavenly places in Christ" (Eph. 1:3), where we will ride in triumph over all below.

These "heavenly places" are interior not exterior; and the road that leads to them is interior also. But the chariot that carries the soul over this road is generally some outward loss, trial, or disappointment—some chastening that is not joyous, but that nevertheless afterwards yields the peaceable fruits of righteousness.

Look on these chastenings then, no matter how grievous they may be for the present, as God's chariots sent to carry your soul into the "high places" of spiritual achievement and uplifting. (*VU*, 242–43)

OCTOBER 3
SEEING AND TRIUMPHING

You can take each thing that is wrong in your life as a chariot of God for you. No matter who the originator of the wrong may be, whether men or devils, by the time it reaches your side it is a chariot of God for you and is meant to carry you to "heavenly places" (Eph. 1:3) of triumph in the Lord. Shut out all the second causes and find the Lord in it. Somewhere in the trial His will must be hidden, and you must accept His will whether known or unknown and so hide yourself in His invisible arms of love. Say, "Thy will be done! Thy will be done!" over and over. Shut out every other thought except submission to His will and trust in His love. Then your trials will become your chariots, and you will find your soul riding on the heavens with God in a way you never dreamed could be.

If our eyes were opened today we would see our homes, our places of business, and the streets we walk, filled with the "chariots of God." That cross person in your household who has made life a burden for you and has been the Juggernaut to crush your soul into the dust, may henceforth be a glorious chariot to carry you to the heights of patience and long-suffering. Misunderstanding, unkindness, disappointment, loss, defeat—all these are chariots waiting to carry you to places of victory you have so longed to reach.

Get into these chariots, then, with thankful hearts, and lose sight of all second causes in the shining of His love. He will carry you in His arms safely and triumphantly over it all. (*VU*, 250–51)

OCTOBER 4
KNOWING BEFORE FEELING

Many people believe that we must have the witness and then we can believe. They put the witness before believing. But God's order is to believe and then have the witness. We can never reverse this order, for it is in the very nature of things and in the Book.

In earthly things we require the fact before the feeling. We do not start on a journey haphazardly and then shut our eyes to feel whether or not we are going the right way. We do not sit down to feel whether we have money in the bank with which to pay our debts. "Give us the facts" is always our cry in earthly things. But when it comes to spiritual things we are tempted to reverse this order. Instead of asking, "What is the fact?" we say plaintively, "How do I feel?"

No one can sing a song of rejoicing unless the cause for rejoicing has first been ascertained to be a fact. The Israelites did not say, "We will feel happy and sing songs, and then we shall be in our own land." We cannot conceive of any one in his senses doing such a silly thing, yet many children of God say something very nearly akin to this: "If I could only feel happy, then I could believe that God is my Father and that He loves me." A moment's thought will show us the folly of this; for we can only know that God loves us by His saying so, not by our feeling so. We can only know that our earthly friends love us from their own words. We believe them when they tell us that they love us, and then we feel happy because we believe it. (*VU*, 122–23)

OCTOBER 5
BELIEVING, NOT FEELING

The foundation for the assurance of faith is not what we feel but what the record is, not what our experiences are but what has been "written."

We all know the curious experience of being "turned round"

when walking in the streets of a city or traveling in a car. We feel as if we are going in one direction when we are actually going in exactly the opposite. Our feelings in this case contradict the facts, and we may even know this; yet it is almost impossible not to yield to these feelings and take the wrong direction. I have discovered that I can conquer these feelings and turn myself in the right direction by just repeating the facts over to myself in a very emphatic way. When I feel as though I am going north but am actually going south, I repeat over and over, "I am, I am, I know I am going south." In a minute or two my feelings come under the control of the fact, and I begin to feel as well as know that I really am going south.

In the same way, when we have convinced ourselves from God's Word that our sins are forgiven and that we are reconciled to Him, we can then, by a similar process, control our deceptive feelings. We can assert on the authority of God's Word, "My sins are forgiven; I am God's child; I am reconciled to Him; I am a Christian."

Such a course, persevered in regardless of feeling, will always bring peace and deliverance to every soul who is willing to take God at His Word and risk all on His trustworthiness. (*VU*, 49–50)

OCTOBER 6
KEEPING, NEVER NEGLECTING

Our divine Keeper never slumbers nor sleeps (cf. Ps. 121:3-4) and, therefore, never neglects those for whom He cares. Think of the fatal consequences of neglect on the part of keepers of a prison, keepers of a flock of sheep, keepers of a vineyard on a frosty night, or sentinels keeping a dangerous outpost, and then see by contrast what sort of keeper our Lord must be.

We can all realize the responsibilities of the human keeper to whose care anything has been committed. When something is given to us to keep, we feel that we must care for that thing in preference to our own. From these high ideals of responsibility in our own case we may learn what our divine Keeper must necessarily do.

If we know Him, we cannot fail to trust Him. Knowledge of

the trustworthiness of the one to be trusted is, after all, the true secret of confidence. We act on this in our earthly affairs and are never so silly as to look inside ourselves to see whether we can or ought to trust another. Instead we look at others and try to find out their character and ways. But in our relationship with the Lord we are tempted to act on an entirely different principle. We look at ourselves for a warrant and ground of trust instead of at Him. When we behold self and its untrustworthiness, we are filled with doubts and despair. But a single look at God in His utter trustworthiness would fill us with perfect peace. (*VU*, 66–67)

OCTOBER 7
BEING NAMED HIS

What are some of the names by which God calls us? To ponder them and accept them is to know what we really are in His sight.

He calls us His children.
He calls us His heirs.
He calls us His friends.
He calls us His brethren.
He calls us His sheep.
He likens us to birds.
He calls us branches of the vine.
He likens us to trees.
He likens us to flowers.
He calls us clay.
He calls us vessels.
He calls us instruments.
He calls us His treasure.
He calls us His bride.
Finally, He declares that we are *one* with himself.

In every one of these names there is included a whole world of comfort to those who consent to *be* what they are thus *called*. (*VU*, 134–35)

OCTOBER 8
KNOWING AND BEING

It is of vital importance that we find out what we really are in order that we may know what we ought to be. This we can do by considering the names by which God calls us.

God calls us His children. Let us be children, then, in the blessed ease, security, and childlikeness of childhood. Let us take the children's happy place of freedom from care and anxiety, and let us live as the children do, in the present moment, without taking thought for tomorrow.

God calls us His heirs. Let us be heirs, then, in the sense of entering into possession of our inheritance. No earthly heir fails or delays to take possession of that which he inherits. He may be amazed at the good fortune that has befallen him or may feel unworthy of it; but nevertheless, if he is the heir, he takes possession of his inheritance and rejoices in it. We who are declared to be the heirs of God must do the same.

God calls us His friends. Let us be God's friends, then, in the best way we know how. Let us trust Him as we like our friends to trust us. Let us lean on Him as we urge our friends to lean on us. Let us try to please Him for love's sake as love leads us to try to please our earthly friends. Moreover, let us recognize that if we are His friends, He is necessarily our Friend also, and the duties and responsibilities of friendship are on His shoulders as well as on ours. (*VU*, 133–36)

OCTOBER 9
RELATING AND BECOMING

God calls us His brethren. Let us be His brethren, then, and take to our hearts the wonderful comfort and joy of having such an elder Brother to bear our burdens and share our sorrows. Some of us know the comfort of earthly brothers and are not afraid to roll our cares off on them. Let us take to ourselves the comfort of the heavenly Brother as well and roll every care off on Him.

209

God calls us His sheep. Let us be sheep, then, and abandon ourselves to the care of the Shepherd to whom we belong. The sheep cannot care for themselves, protect themselves, nor provide food for themselves; the shepherd must do it all. The responsibility of their well-being is all on his shoulders not on theirs. They have nothing to do but to trust him and follow him. The Lord is our shepherd.

God calls us branches of the vine. Be branches, then, and realize that you have no life apart from the Vine. Realize also that you have nothing to do in order to "bring forth much fruit" (cf. John 15:5) but to abide in the Vine. The branch cannot bear fruit of itself. Do not try, then, to do it, but abide steadfastly in the Vine and let the life-giving sap flow through you without effort or anxiety on your part. Only see to it that you do not hinder its flow by doubt or rebellion. Do not try to make the fruit but consent to bear it. Let it grow. (*VU*, 136–39)

OCTOBER 10
BELIEVING AND HAVING

All exhortations to holiness and service are based on the assured knowledge of our reconciliation with God. God wants from us the service of heirs, not of servants. A servant works for wages, an heir from love. A servant works to gain something; an heir works because all has been given to him. How can we render an heir's service unless we know we are heirs?

The assurance of faith is the only normal condition of a child of God. It comes simply by believing God. He says certain things about himself and about us; faith believes these things, and assurance follows on faith. Notice that in the Scriptures "believing" and "having" are always joined together. "He that believeth hath" (cf. John 3:36 et al.) is the continual declaration!

Notice that Scripture never says, "He who feels has. . . ." Our feelings are no guide whatever in our assurance of faith. In all matters of fact it is folly to depend on feelings; we never do so in our earthly affairs. We never say over a piece of good or bad news, "Do I feel it is true?" Rather we confine ourselves to simply, "Is it true?"

The state of our feelings cannot alter the facts, and our sole aim is always to find out the facts. In order for the assurance of faith, then, as to our relations with the Lord, we must not depend on our feelings but must find out the facts. (*VU*, 45–47)

OCTOBER 11
BELIEVING AND INHERITING

We must reject the clamorings of our feelings that declare that God's facts are but dreams of the imagination. And we must take our stand without wavering on the unalterable truths of God's record, receiving His witness with at least as much confidence as we accord to the witness of men, and resting our souls absolutely on His testimony.

> *In hope, against all human hope,*
> *Self desperate, I believe;*
> *Thy quickening word shall raise me up.*
>
> *The thing surpasses all my thought,*
> *But faithful is my Lord;*
> *Through unbelief I stagger not.*
>
> *Faith, mighty faith, the promise sees,*
> *And looks at that alone;*
> *Laughs at impossibilities,*
> *And cries—"It shall be done!"*

Someone has said that the only thing necessary for the children of God to do in order to enter into full possession of their inheritance in Christ is simply to be what they are, in other words, to "apprehend that for which they are apprehended" of Christ Jesus (cf. Phil. 3:12). In all human relations this principle holds good. If a man is a king in fact, he must be one in outward recognition, or his kingship avails him nothing. In all conditions of life our success depends on our being who we really are. In our relationship to the Lord we must be just who we declare we are. (*VU*, 132–33)

OCTOBER 12
BELIEVING IS LIVING

Faith is the vital principle of the spiritual life just as truly as breathing is the vital principle of the bodily life. We can no more live spiritually without faith than we can live our bodily life without breathing.

Is it not reasonable to suppose that there must be laws of the spiritual life just as there are laws of the natural life, and that the laws of one must be as sure and dependable in their working as the others? Too often the Christian life is only a series of rather doubtful experiments whose results are hoped for but can never be depended on with any sort of certainty. There seems to be but little conception in most minds that there is an ascertainable and dependable law of life, which, if discovered and understood, will remove our experience out of the region of doubtful chances into the region of assured certainties.

Nothing could be plainer. Our spiritual life is begotten of God. Therefore it has its source in Him and derives its nature from Him. Few of us realize this as a fact. If we do, why is it that we struggle so hard to beget a spiritual life in ourselves by our own efforts? We often act as if we were to be born "of the will of man," and try by wrestlings, agonizings, resolutions, prayers, and religious exercises of all sorts, to bring about the new birth. No wonder religion has become such a hard and apparently hopeless task to so many. The soul, therefore, who tries by his own efforts to create spiritual life in himself is attempting an impossible task and can land himself nowhere but in despair. (*EDR*, 155–59)

OCTOBER 13
KNOWING, BELIEVING, FEELING

God's order and the order of good common sense as well is always: (1) fact, (2) faith, (3) feeling. But in matters of religion, man reverses this order and says: (1) feeling, (2) faith, (3) fact.

There is in all spiritual things a divine order and a human order, and very frequently these two are in exact contrast to one another.

In the three F's we are considering, this is strikingly the case. God's order reads: (1) fact, (2) faith, (3) feeling. In man's order this is reversed: (1) feeling, (2) faith, (3) fact.

In the divine order God gives us first the fact of His salvation; then we believe these facts; and as a consequence, we have the feelings suitable to the facts believed.

But we reverse this order and say, "I must have the feeling first and then I can believe in that feeling, and thus I will get hold of the facts."

Of course this is absurd; but it is a very common temptation and is the cause of most of the pitiful uncertainty and doubt that characterizes so much of Christian experience. (*VU*, 122)

OCTOBER 14
BELIEVING IS TRUSTING

Just as gravitation is a law of matter, inherent in matter and absolutely unerring and unremitting in its working, so is faith a law of spirit, inherent in spirit and equally unerring and unremitting in its working. When Christ says, therefore, that "nothing shall be impossible" (Matt. 17:20) to faith, He is not only stating a marvelous fact, He is revealing a tremendous law.

We know that all things are possible to God, and here our Lord tells us that all things are possible to us also if we only believe. No assertion could be more distinct or unmistakable. The great thing for us, therefore, is to discover the law by which faith works, in order that we may know how to exercise this tremendous spiritual force that is declared by our Lord to be our birthright as children of God and partakers of His nature.

In all sorts of ways, the subject of faith is often so mixed up with mystery that a plain, common-sense wayfaring man can make neither head nor tail of the matter in his everyday life. But in truth, faith is neither more nor less than trust or confidence. We have faith in ourselves when we trust ourselves; we have faith in a friend when we trust that friend; we have faith in a bank when we trust that bank. Faith in the Bible sense, therefore, is simply trust or confidence in God. Faith in man and faith in God are precisely the same thing in their nature; the difference consists only in the different persons believed in. Faith in man links us to and makes us one with mere humanity; faith in God links us to and makes us one with divinity. (*EDR*, 149–50)

OCTOBER 15
SERVING, NOT TALKING

The work to which we are called is the Christlike work of helping and saving, and the talents given us to be used are those common to humanity—the power of ministering to the sick, helpless, needy, and sinful. In Christ's description of God's principles of judgment, the difference between the sheep and the goats was that the sheep utilized their humble talents and did Christlike work, but the goats did not.

It is easy to talk about doing things, but the doing is the vital point. It is possible to be very pious in all religious performances and yet to have very little "pure religion . . . before God" (James 1:27).

All the talking, fasting, weeping, or wearing of sackcloth in the world will not do as a substitute for the Christlike life of love and kindness toward our fellow men. The "fast [God] has chosen" (cf. Isa. 58:5-6) is to help the needy and raise the fallen; and no amount of religious emotion, be it ever so fervent, will take the place of this.

A great many Christians never do anything for anyone but themselves. Whether they fast or whether they eat and drink, it is all for themselves; they never lift a hand to help anyone else. Their religion is all for self-exaltation in one way or another, either now or hereafter, and not truly for the glory of God at all. They are so absorbed in self, that they do not even know that they are condemned. "When saw we" (cf. Matt. 25:38), they ask; never dreaming that because they have not served their fellow men, they have therefore failed to serve their Master. (*VU*, 165–68)

OCTOBER 16
KNOWING HIM, NOT OURSELVES

What matters most is not knowing what we are, what we do, or what we feel; it is becoming acquainted with God, getting to know what He is and what He feels. Comfort and peace can never come from anything we know about ourselves but only and always from what we know about God.

We may spend our days in what we call our religious duties, and we may fill our devotions with fervor, yet still be miserable. Nothing can set our hearts at rest but a real acquaintance with God, for everything in our salvation must ultimately depend on Him. According to His worthiness of our confidence, so must our comfort be.

If we were planning to take a dangerous voyage, our first question would be what kind of captain we were to have. Our common sense would tell us that if the captain were untrustworthy, no amount of trustworthiness on our part would make our voyage safe. It would be his character and not our own that would be the thing of paramount importance to us.

The vital question of all ages is "What is His name?" The fate of humanity hangs on the answer to this question. Everything in a universe will depend on the sort of creator and ruler who has brought that universe into existence. If the God who created us is a good God, then everything must of necessity be all right for us. But if He is a bad God, a careless God, or an unkind God, then we cannot be sure that anything is right and cannot have peace or comfort anywhere. (*GAC*, 9–11)

OCTOBER 17
ADDING AND ENJOYING

In the Gospel of John, Christ takes the name "I Am" as His very own. This unfinished name of God seems to me like a blank check signed by a rich friend, given to us to be filled in with whatever amount we may desire. Every attribute of God, every revelation of His character, every proof of His undying love, every declaration of His watchful care, every assertion of His purposes of tender mercy, every manifestation of His loving kindness—all are the filling in of this unfinished "I Am."

God tells us through all the pages of the Bible what He is. He says, "I am all that my people need: I am their strength, wisdom, righteousness, peace, salvation, and life. I am their all in all." This unfinished name allows us to add to it without any limitation whatever we feel the need of.

But if our hearts are full of our own wretched "I ams," we will have no ears to hear His glorious, soul-satisfying "I Am." We say, "I am so weak," "I am so foolish," "I am so good for nothing," or "I am so helpless"; and we give these pitiful "I ams" as the reason for the wretchedness and discomfort of our religious lives. And all the while we ignore the blank check of God's magnificent "I Am," which authorizes us to draw on Him for an abundant supply for every need. (*GAC*, 14–15)

OCTOBER 18
KNOWING BRINGS COMFORTING

If you are an uncomfortable Christian, the only thing to give you a thoroughly comfortable religious life is to know God. The psalmist says that they who know God's name will put their trust in Him, and it is impossible for anyone to really know Him and not trust Him. A trustworthy person commands trust not in the sense of ordering people to trust him but by irresistibly winning their trust by his trustworthiness.

What our Lord declares is eternally true, "I, if I be lifted up from the earth, will draw all men unto me" (John 12:32). When once you know Him, Christ is absolutely irresistible. You can no more help trusting Him than you can help breathing. Could the world but know Him as He is, the whole world, sinners and all, would fall at His feet in adoring worship.

How then can we become acquainted with God? There are two things necessary: first, God must reveal himself; and second, we must accept His revelation.

Christ is the revelation of God. None of us has ever seen God, and we never can see Him in this present stage of our existence, for we do not have the faculties that would make it possible. But He has incarnated himself in Christ, and we can see Christ, since He was human like us. (*GAC*, 15–16)

OCTOBER 19
KNOWING IS ADORING

A man wanting to talk with ants might stand over an ant hill and harangue for a whole day, yet not one word would reach the ears of the ants. They would run back and forth utterly unconscious of his presence. As far as we know, ants have no faculties by which they can receive human communications. But if a man could incarnate himself in the body of an ant and could go about among them, living an ant's life and speaking the ants' language, he would make himself intelligible to them at once. Incarnation is always necessary for a higher form of life to communicate with a lower.

Christ revealed God by what He was, what He did, and what He said. From the cradle to the grave, every moment of His life was a revelation of God. We must go to Him then for our knowledge of God, and we must refuse to believe anything concerning God that is not revealed to us in Christ. All other revelations are partial and therefore not wholly true. Only in Christ do we see God as He is; for Christ is declared to be the "express image" of God (Heb. 1:3).

Just what God would have said and done under the circumstances is what Christ said and did. "I do nothing of myself" was His continual assertion. "I speak not of myself: but the Father that dwelleth in me, he doeth the works" (John 14:10); "I and my Father are one" (John 10:30); "He that seeth me seeth him that sent me" (John 12:45).

Other words could not tell us more plainly than the Bible that in order to know God we have only to look at Christ and receive His testimony. (*GAC*, 16–17)

OCTOBER 20
SEEING IS KNOWING

Over and over we are assured that God and Christ are one. When the Jews came to Christ as He was walking in the porch of Solomon's temple and asked Him to tell them plainly who He was, He answered, "I and my Father are one" (John 10:30). And in answer to His disciples' questions at His last supper with them, He said, "If ye had known me, ye should have known my Father also: and from henceforth ye know him, and have seen him" (14:7). But Philip could not understand this, and said, "Lord, shew us the Father, and it sufficeth us" (v. 8). And then Jesus repeated His former statement even more strongly, "Have I been so long time with you, and yet hast thou not known me, Philip? he that hath seen me hath seen the Father; and how sayest thou then, Shew us the Father?" (v. 9).

Nothing is more emphatically stated in the New Testament than that we are to behold the "light of the knowledge of the glory of God in the face of Jesus Christ" (2 Cor. 4:6) and that we can behold it fully nowhere else. He alone is the earthly translation of God. He alone is the image of the invisible God.

It is evident, therefore, that we must never accept any conception of God that is contrary to what we see in Christ. We must utterly reject any view of God's character or acts or any statement of His relationships with us, no matter how strongly upheld, that is at variance with what Christ has revealed. (*GAC*, 17–18)

OCTOBER 21
REVEALING BY EMBODYING

Christ alone tells us the true name of God. In His last wonderful prayer He said: "I have manifested thy name unto the men which thou gavest me out of the world: . . . Now they have known that all things whatsoever thou hast given me are of thee. For I have given unto them the words which thou gavest me" (John 17:6-8). Could we ask for greater authority than this?

218

In the whole life of Christ, nothing is plainer or more emphatic than that He claimed continually to be a complete manifestation of God. "The words that I speak unto you," He said, "I speak not of myself: but the Father that dwelleth in me, he doeth the works" (John 14:10). Over and over Jesus asserted that He said only what the Father told Him to say. The apostle Paul declared most emphatically that it "pleased the Father" (Col. 1:19) that in Christ should "dwell all the fullness of the Godhead bodily" (2:9). Although we may not understand all that this means theologically, we cannot fail to see that we need only to become acquainted with Christ's ways and Christ's character in order to become acquainted with God's ways and God's character.

"He that hath seen me," Christ said, "hath seen the Father" (John 14:9). This settles beyond doubt that Jesus is God incarnate. We may have all sorts of imaginings about God, but we are wasting our energy, for we cannot know Him except through the revelation of Christ. We may know a good many things about God, but that is very different from knowing God himself as He really is in nature and character. (*GAC*, 18–19)

OCTOBER 22
MANIFESTING BY LIVING

Witnesses have told us of God's visible acts, but from these we often get wrong impressions of His true character. No other witness but Christ can tell us of the real secrets of God's bosom, for of none other can it be said, as it is of Him, that "the only begotten Son, which is in the bosom of the Father, he hath declared him" (John 1:18). It will make all the difference between comfort and discomfort in our Christian lives whether we believe this to be true. If we do believe it, then the stern Judge and hard Taskmaster whom we have feared, even while we tried to follow Him, and whose service we have found so irksome and so full of discomfort, will disappear; and His place will be taken by the God of love who is revealed to us in "the face of Jesus Christ" (2 Cor. 4:6). He is the God who cares for us as He cares for the sparrows and for the flowers of the field and who tells us that He even numbers the hairs of our heads. No human being could be afraid of a God like this.

If we have been accustomed to approaching God with mistrust of His feelings toward us; if our religion has been poisoned by fear; if unworthy thoughts of His character and will have filled our hearts with suspicions of His goodness; if we have pictured Him as an unjust despot or a self-seeking tyrant; if, in short, we have imagined Him in any way other than that which has been revealed to us in "the face of Jesus Christ," we must go back to the records of that lovely life and bring our conceptions of God into perfect accord with the character and ways of Him who came to manifest the name of God to men. (*GAC*, 20–21)

OCTOBER 23
SEEING IS RECEIVING

No one who believes in Christ can doubt that Christ knew God, and no one can question whether or not we ought to receive His testimony. He has assured us over and over again that what He said is to be received as the absolute truth, because He came down from heaven and therefore knew about heavenly things.

None of us would dare to openly question the truth of Christ's testimony; yet a great many of God's children ignore it and choose instead to listen to the testimony of their own doubting hearts, which tells them that God could not be as loving in His care for us or as ready to forgive our sins as Christ revealed Him to be. But since Christ declared that He was a living manifestation of the Father, all He said and did assures us that He was simply saying and doing that which the Father would have said and done had He acted directly from His heavenly throne.

In the face of such an assertion as this out of the lips of our Lord himself, it becomes not only our privilege but our duty to cast out of our conception of God every element that could in any way conflict with the blessed life and character and teaching of Christ. (*GAC*, 21–22)

OCTOBER 24
BELIEVING THEN ACTING

As we look at the life of Christ and listen to His words, we can hear God saying, "I am rest for the weary; I am peace for the storm-tossed; I am strength for the powerless; I am wisdom for the foolish; I am righteousness for the sinful; I am all that the neediest soul on earth can want; I am exceeding abundantly beyond all you can ask or think, of blessing and help and care."

Here the doubter may say, "Ah, yes, this is no doubt all true; but how can I get hold of it?" You cannot get hold of it at all, but you can let it get hold of you. It is a piece of magnificent good news declared to you in the Bible; and you only need do with it exactly what you do when any earthly good news is told you by a reliable earthly source. If the speaker is trustworthy, you believe what he says and act in accordance. You must do the same here. If Christ is trustworthy when He tells you that He is the manifestation of God, you must believe what He says and act accordingly.

You must take your stand on Christ's trustworthiness. You must say to yourself and to your friends if necessary, "I am going to believe what Christ says about God. No matter what the seemings may be, what my own thoughts and feelings are, nor what anybody else may say, I know that what Christ says about God must be true, for He knew, and nobody else does. I am going to believe Him come what may. He said that He was one with God [cf. John 10:30], so all that He was God is, and I will never be frightened of God any more." (*GAC*, 22–23)

OCTOBER 25
RECEIVING HIS IMAGING

If we will take our stand on the fact that Christ and God are one, intelligently comprehend what it involves, and refuse unwaveringly to cherish any thought of God that is at variance with what Christ has revealed, life will be transformed for us.

We may often have to set our faces like a flint to hold stead-

221

fastly here, for our old doubts and fears will be sure to come back and demand admittance. We must turn our backs on them and declare that now we know the name, or character, of our God, and that such things would be impossible to Him. We must refuse to listen for a moment to any libels on His character or His ways.

It is unthinkable to suppose that when God told Moses His name was "I Am," He could have meant to say, "I am a stern Lawgiver and am indifferent to the sorrows and fears of my people." But don't the doubts and fears of some Christians say exactly these things in secret every day of their lives?

> *Jesus is God! Oh could I now*
> *But compass land and sea,*
> *To teach and tell this single truth,*
> *How happy should I be!*
> *Oh, had I but an angel's voice,*
> *I would proclaim so loud,—*
> *Jesus, the good, the beautiful,*
> *Is the image of our God! (GAC, 24-25)*

OCTOBER 26
COMFORTING, NOT DISCOMFORTING

Among all the names that reveal God, the "God of all comfort" (2 Cor. 1:3) seems to me one of the loveliest and the most absolutely comforting. The words "all comfort" admit of no limitations and no deductions. One would suppose that however full of discomforts the outward lives of the followers of such a God might be, their inward religious lives must be comfortable under all circumstances.

But, in fact, the opposite is often the case; religious lives of large numbers of God's children are full not of comfort but of the utmost discomfort. This discomfort arises from anxiety about their relations to God and doubts about His love. They torment themselves with the thought that they are too good for nothing to be worthy of His care. They suspect Him of being indifferent to their trials and of forsaking them in times of need. They are anxious and troubled about everything in their religious

222

lives. Although God declares himself to be the God of all comfort, they continually complain that they cannot find comfort anywhere, and their sorrowful looks and doleful tones of voice show that they are speaking the truth.

Such Christians spread gloom and discomfort around them wherever they go. It is out of the question for them to hope that they can induce anyone else to believe that this beautiful name by which He has announced himself is anything more than a pious phrase that means nothing at all. The uncomfortable religious lives of so many Christians are, I am afraid, responsible for a large part of the unbelief of the world. (*GAC*, 26)

OCTOBER 27
THE MEANING OF COMFORTING

What do we mean by the comfort God gives? Is it a sort of pious grace that may perhaps fit us for heaven but is somehow unfit to bear the brunt of our everyday life with its trials and pains? Or is it an honest and genuine comfort that enfolds life's trials and pains in an all-embracing peace? With all my heart I believe it is the latter.

Comfort, whether human or divine, is pure and simple comfort and nothing else. None of us care for pious phrases; we want realities; and the reality of being comforted and comfortable seems to me more delightful than almost any other thing in life. We all know what it is. When we were little children we cuddled up into our mother's lap after a fall or a misfortune and felt her soft kisses in our hair. That was comfort. When, as grown-up people, after a hard day's work, we have put on our slippers and seated ourselves with a book in an easy chair by the fire, we have had comfort. When, after a painful illness, we have begun to recover and have been able to stretch our limbs and open our eyes without pain, we have had comfort. When someone we dearly love has been ill almost to death and has been restored to us in health again, we have had comfort. Probably a thousand times in our lives, we have said with a sigh of relief, "Well, this is comfortable," and in that word "comfortable" there has been comprised more rest, relief, satisfaction, and pleasure, than any other word in the English language could possibly be made to express. (*GAC*, 28–29)

OCTOBER 28
ACCEPTING COMFORTING

We have failed to believe that God is the "God of all comfort" (2 Cor. 1:3). It has seemed too good to be true. The joy and delight of it has been more than our poor suspicious natures could take in. We may venture to hope sometimes that little scraps of comfort may be vouchsafed to us; but we have run away frightened at the thought of the "all comfort" that is ours in the salvation of the Lord Jesus Christ.

Yet what more could God have said about it than He has said: "As one whom his mother comforteth, so will I comfort you; and ye shall be comforted" (Isa. 66:13). Notice the "as" and "so" in this passage: "As one whom his mother comforteth, so will I comfort you." It is real comforting that is meant here— the sort of comforting that a child feels when he is "dandled on his mother's knees and borne upon her sides" (v. 12, para.); yet how many of us have really believed that God's comforting is actually as tender and true as a mother's comforting, or even a half or a quarter as real?

Instead of thinking of ourselves as being "dandled" on God's knees and hugged to His heart, have we not rather been inclined to look at Him as a stern, unbending judge, holding us at a distance and demanding our respectful homage as He criticizes our slightest faults? Is it any wonder that our religion, instead of making us comfortable, has made us thoroughly uncomfortable? Who could help being uncomfortable in the presence of such a judge? But I rejoice to say that that stern judge does not exist. (*GAC*, 29)

OCTOBER 29
ABIDING AND COMFORTING

Our Comforter is not far off in heaven where we cannot find Him. He is close at hand. He abides with us. When Christ was going away from this earth, He told His disciples that God would not leave them comfortless but would send "another Comforter" who would abide with them forever (John 14:16). This Comforter, He said, would teach them all things and would bring all things to their remembrance (v. 26). And then He declared, as though it were the necessary result of the coming of this divine Comforter: "Peace I leave with you, my peace I give unto you; not as the world giveth, give I unto you. Let not your heart be troubled, neither let it be afraid" (v. 27). Oh, how can we, in the face of these tender and loving words, go about with troubled and frightened hearts?

A "Comforter"—what a word of assurance, if we only could realize it. Let us repeat it over and over to ourselves until its meaning sinks into the very depths of our being. And He is an abiding Comforter, not one who comes and goes and is never on hand when most needed. He is always present and always ready to give us "joy for mourning, [and] the garment of praise for the spirit of heaviness" (Isa. 61:3).

The very words "abiding Comforter" are an amazing revelation. Try to comprehend them. We think ourselves happy when we are in trouble if we can have a human comforter to stay with us for only a few days; but here is a divine Comforter who is always staying with us and whose power to comfort is infinite. Never, for a single minute, should we be uncomfortable. (*GAC*, 32–33)

OCTOBER 30
REPROVING BUT COMFORTING

You may ask whether our divine Comforter sometimes reproves us for our sins and whether we could get any comfort out of that. In my opinion this is exactly one of the places where the comfort comes in, for what sort of creatures would we be if we had no divine Teacher always at hand to show us our faults and awaken in us a desire to get rid of them? It is a comfort to know that there is always abiding with me a divine, all-seeing Comforter who will reprove me for all my faults and will not let me go on in a fatal unconsciousness of them. Ralph Waldo Emerson says it is far more in persons' interests that they should see their own faults than that anyone else should see them. A moment's thought will convince us that this is true and will make us thankful for the Comforter who reveals them to us.

We need the Holy Spirit's comforting all the more because we are not worthy. Christ came into the world to save sinners not good people, and our unworthiness is our greatest claim for His salvation. In the same passage in Isaiah in which He tells us that He has seen our ways and was "wroth" with us, He assures us that He will heal us and restore comfort to us (Isa. 57:16-18). It is just because He is wroth with us (wroth in the sense in which love is always wroth with any fault in those it loves) that He therefore restores comfort to us. He does it by revealing our sin and healing it. This explains to me better than anything else the reason why the very God who loves us allows sorrow and trial to come to us. The consolations of God mean the substituting of a far higher and better thing than the things we lose to get them. (*GAC*, 33-35)

OCTOBER 31
DISBELIEVING IS DISCOMFORTING

Strangely enough, while it is easy for us when we are happy and do not need comforting to believe that our God is the "God of all comfort" (2 Cor. 1:3), as soon as we are in trouble and need it, it seems impossible to believe that there can be any comfort for us anywhere. It would almost seem as if in our reading of the Bible we have reversed its meaning and made it say not "Blessed are they that mourn: for they shall be comforted" (Matt. 5:4) but "Blessed are they that rejoice, for they, and they only, shall be comforted." It is strange how often in our secret hearts we almost unconsciously alter the Bible words a little and make the meaning exactly opposite to what it actually

226

is; or else we put in so many "ifs" and "buts" that we take the whole point out of what is said. Take, for instance, the beautiful words, "God, that comforteth those that are cast down" (2 Cor. 7:6), and ask whether we have never been tempted to make it read in our secret hearts, "God who forsaketh those who are cast down," or, "God who will comfort those who are cast down"; or, "God who will comfort those who are cast down if they show themselves worthy of comfort"; and whether, consequently, instead of being comforted we have not been plunged into misery and despair.

The psalmist tells us that God will "comfort [us] on every side" (Ps. 71:21); yet in times of special trial, how many Christians secretly read this as though it says, "God will comfort us on every side except just the side where our trials lie"? But God says *every* side, and it is only unbelief on our part that leads us to make an exception. (*GAC*, 35–36)

NOVEMBER 1
ACCEPTING COMFORTING

You may ask how you are to get hold of divine comfort. My answer is that you must take it. God's comfort is being continually and abundantly given, but unless you accept it, you cannot have it. Divine comfort does not come to us in any mysterious or arbitrary way; it comes as the result of a divine method. The indwelling Comforter brings to our remembrance comforting things concerning our Lord, and if we believe them we are comforted by them. A text is brought to our remembrance, perhaps, or the verse of a hymn or some thought concerning the love of Christ and His tender care for us. If we receive the suggestion in simple faith we cannot help being comforted. But if we refuse to listen to the voice of our Comforter and insist instead on listening to the voice of discouragement or despair no comfort can reach us.

It is very possible for even a mother to lavish all her stores of motherly comfort on a weeping child in vain. The child sits up stiff and sullen and refuses to be comforted. All her comforting words fall on unbelieving ears. To be comforted by comforting words it is necessary for us to believe these words. God has spoken comforting words enough, one would think, to comfort a whole universe, and yet we see all around unhappy Christians, worried Christians, and gloomy Christians, into whose comfortless hearts not one of these comforting words seems to be allowed to enter. In fact, a great many Christians actually think it is wrong to be comforted; they feel too unworthy. If any rays of comfort steal into their hearts, they sternly shut them out and refuse to be comforted. (*GAC*, 37–38)

NOVEMBER 2
BELIEVING BRINGS COMFORTING

In the matter of comfort it is exactly as it is in every other experience in the religious life: God says, "Believe, and then you can feel." We say, "Feel, and then we can believe." God's order is not arbitrary; it exists in the very nature of things. In all earthly matters we recognize this and are never so foolish as to expect to feel we have anything, until we first believe that it is in our possession.

Let me illustrate. Let us suppose we are overwhelmed with cares and anxieties. To comfort us in these circumstances the Lord assures us that we need not be anxious about anything but may commit all our cares to Him, for He cares for us (1 Peter 5:7). One would think there was comfort enough here for every care or sorrow all the wide world over. What could possibly be a greater comfort than to have the almighty God, the Creator of heaven and earth, who can control everything and foresee everything and consequently manage everything in the very best possible way, declare that He will undertake for us?

Yet few people are really comforted by God's promises of care because they do not believe them. They are waiting to have an inward feeling that His words are true before they will believe them. They look on them as beautiful things for Him to say; but if they should speak out honestly, they would confess that since they have no such inward feeling, they do not believe His words apply to them. "Oh, if I could only feel it is all true," they say; and God says, "Oh, if you would only believe it is all true!" (*GAC*, 39–40)

NOVEMBER 3
PERSEVERING BRINGS COMFORTING

God comforts us on every side (cf. Ps. 71:21), but we do not believe His words of comfort. The remedy for this is plain. If we want to be comforted, we must believe every word of comfort God has ever spoken and refuse to listen to any words of discomfort spoken by our own hearts or by our circumstances. We must set our faces like a flint to believe under each and every sorrow and trial is the divine Comforter and to accept and rejoice in His all-embracing comfort. I say, "set our faces like a flint," because when everything around us seems out of sorts it is not always easy to believe God's words of comfort. We must put our wills into this matter of being comforted just as we put our wills into all other matters in our spiritual lives. We must choose to be comforted.

It may seem impossible when things look all wrong to believe that God really can be caring for us as a mother cares for her children. Although we know perfectly well that He says He does care for us in just this tender and loving way, we say, "Oh, if I could only believe that, of course I would be comforted." This is where our wills must come in. We must believe it. We must say to ourselves, "God says it, and it is true, and I am going to believe it no matter how it looks." Then we must never allow ourselves to doubt or question it again.

Whoever will adopt this plan will come, sooner or later, into a state of abounding comfort. (*GAC*, 40–41)

NOVEMBER 4
REMEMBERING SHEPHERDING

"The LORD is my shepherd; I shall not want" (Ps. 23:1). Perhaps no aspect in which the Lord reveals himself to us is more full of comfort than the aspect set forth in the Twenty-third Psalm. Amazingly, the highest and grandest truths of the religion of the Lord Jesus Christ are often shut up in the simplest and most common texts in the Bible, those texts with which we have been familiar from our childhood. What we all need, there-fore, is to take up our childhood verses once more and while reading them with the intelligence of our adult years believe them with childlike faith.

Can we not recall even now something of the joy and pride of our childish hearts when we were first able to repeat the Twenty-third Psalm without mistake? Since then we have always known it, and at this moment its words may sound so familiar to you that you cannot see what meaning they convey. But, in fact, they tell us the whole story of our religion in words of such wondrous depth of meaning that I doubt whether any mortal has yet conceived of all they reveal.

Repeat these familiar words over to yourselves afresh: "The LORD is my shepherd; I shall not want." (*GAC*, 43–44)

NOVEMBER 5
NAMING MEANS FULFILLING

There came a critical moment in my life when I was sadly in need of comfort but could see none anywhere. I could not at the moment lay my hands on my Bible, and I cast about in my mind for some passage of Scripture that would help me. Immediately there flashed into my mind the words, "The LORD is my shep-herd; I shall not want" (Ps. 23:1). At first I turned from it almost with scorn. "Such a common text as that," I said to myself, "is not likely to do me any good." I tried hard to think of a more appropriate text, but none would come, and at last it almost seemed as if there was no other text in the whole Bible. I began to repeat to myself over and over, "The LORD is my shepherd; I shall not want." Suddenly, as I did so, the words were divinely illuminated, and there poured out on me such floods of comfort that I felt as if I could never have a trouble again.

The moment I could get hold of a Bible I turned over its leaves with eagerness to see whether it could possibly be true that such untold treasures of comfort were really mine. Then I did some-thing I have often found great profit in doing: I built up a pyra-mid of declarations and promises concerning the Lord being our Shepherd that, once built, presented an immovable and indestructible front to all the winds and storms of doubt or trial that could assail it. I became convinced beyond a shadow of doubt that the Lord really was my Shepherd and that in giving himself this name, He assumed the duties belonging to the name. I knew that He really would be what He declared himself to be: a "good shepherd [who] giveth his life for the sheep" (John 10:11). (*GAC*, 45–46)

NOVEMBER 6
DISCOVERING HIS SHEPHERDING

Surely one would think that no Christian could ever accuse our divine Shepherd of being as faithless and unkind as their remarks sometimes imply. Although they do not put it into words and perhaps hardly know themselves their feelings about Him, at the bottom they really do look on Him as a faithless Shepherd.

What else can it mean when Christians complain that the Lord has forsaken them; that when they cry to Him for spiritual food, He does not hear; that when they are beset by enemies on every side, He does not deliver them; that when their souls find themselves in dark places, He does not come to their rescue; that when they are weak, He does not strengthen them; and that when they are spiritually sick, He does not heal them? Are not all these doubts and discouragements secret accusations against our Good Shepherd of the very things which He himself so scathingly condemns?

A Christian who had just discovered what it meant to have the Lord as his Shepherd said to me once, "I read the Twenty-third Psalm as though it was written, 'The Lord is the sheep, and I am the shepherd, and if I do not keep a tight hold on Him, He will run away.' When dark days came, I never for a moment thought that He would stick by me, and when my soul was starving and cried out for food, I never dreamed He would feed me. I see now that I never looked on Him as a faithful Shepherd at all. But now all is different. I myself am not one bit better or stronger, but I have discovered that I have a good Shepherd, and that is all I need." (*GAC*, 47–48)

NOVEMBER 7
TRUSTING AND TAKING

Hundreds of times you have said, "The LORD is my shepherd" (Ps. 23:1), but have you ever really believed it to be an actual fact? Have you felt safe and happy and free from care, as a sheep must feel when under the care of a good shepherd? Or have you felt like a forlorn sheep without a shepherd or with an unfaithful, inefficient shepherd, who does not supply your needs and leaves you in times of danger and darkness?

Answer these questions honestly in your own soul. Have you had a comfortable religious life or an uncomfortable one? If the latter has been your condition, how can you reconcile it with the statement that the Lord is your Shepherd and therefore you shall not want? You say He is your Shepherd, yet you complain that you do want. Who has made the mistake—you or the Lord?

But here, perhaps, you will meet me with the words, "Oh, no, I do not blame the Lord, but I am so weak and foolish and ignorant that I am not worthy of His care." Don't you know that sheep are always weak, helpless, and silly, and that the very reason they must have a shepherd is because they are so unable to take care of themselves? Their welfare and their safety do not in the least depend on their own strength or wisdom but wholly and entirely on the care of their shepherd. If you are a sheep, your welfare also must depend altogether on your Shepherd and not at all on yourself. (*GAC*, 48–49)

NOVEMBER 8
SHEPHERDING IS CARING

Let us imagine two flocks of sheep meeting at the end of the winter and comparing their experiences. One flock is fat and strong and in good condition, and the other flock is poor and lean and diseased. Will the healthy flock boast of themselves, saying, "See what splendid care we have taken of ourselves, what good, strong, wise sheep we must be"? Surely not. Their boasting would all be about their shepherd. "See what a good shepherd we have had," they would say, "and see how he has cared for us. Through all the storms of the winter he has protected us. He has defended us from every wild beast and has always provided us with the best of food."

On the other hand, would the poor, wretched, diseased sheep blame themselves and say, "Alas! what wicked sheep we must be, to be in such a poor condition"? No, they too would speak only of their shepherd. "Our shepherd was very different from yours. He fed himself, but he did not feed us. He did not strengthen us when we were weak, heal us when we were sick, bind us up when we were broken, or look for us when we were lost. In times of danger or of storm, he forsook us and fled."

We all understand the responsibility of a shepherd toward his sheep, but the moment we transfer the figure to our religion, we shift all the responsibility from the Shepherd and lay it on the sheep. We demand of the poor human sheep the care and power to provide what can only be provided by the divine Shepherd. Of course, the poor sheep fail, and their religious lives become miserable. (*GAC*, 49–50)

NOVEMBER 9
REFUSING SHEPHERDING

I freely confess that there is a difference between sheep and ourselves when it comes to shepherding. Sheep have neither the intelligence or the power to withdraw themselves from the care of their shepherd.

We cannot imagine one of them saying, "Oh, yes, we have a good shepherd who says he will take care of us; but then we do not feel worthy of his care, and therefore we are afraid to trust him. He says he has provided for us green pastures and a safe and comfortable fold; but we are such poor, good-for-nothing creatures that we have not dared to enter his fold or feed in his pastures. We have felt it would be presumption; and in our humility we have been trying to do the best we could for ourselves.

"The strong, healthy sheep may trust themselves to the shepherd's care; but that is something such miserable, half-starved sheep as we are dare not do. We have had a very hard time and are in a sad and forlorn condition; but then we are such unworthy

233

creatures that we must expect this and must try to be resigned to it."

Silly though sheep are, we well know that no sheep would talk this way. Herein comes the difference between the sheep and us: We are so much wiser than sheep, in our own estimation, that we think the sort of trust sheep exercise will not do for us. In our superior intelligence, we presume to take matters into our own hands and so shut ourselves out from the Shepherd's care. (*GAC*, 50–51)

NOVEMBER 10
AMAZING SHEPHERDING

When Paul wrote to the Ephesians that he had been called to preach to the Gentiles the unsearchable riches of Christ and to "make all men see what is the fellowship of the mystery, which from the beginning of the world hath been hid in God" (Eph. 3:9), he added that the object of it all was "to the intent that now unto the principalities and powers in heavenly places might be known by the church the manifold wisdom of God, according to the eternal purpose which he purposed in Christ Jesus our Lord" (vv. 10-11). Well may we be lost in amazement at the thought that God has purposed such a glorious destiny for His sheep as to make known to the universe His "manifold wisdom" by means of what He has done for us!

We should be eager to trust God for salvation so that He may receive great glory and the whole world may be won to trust Him. If we will not let Him save us, if we reject His care and refuse to feed in His pastures or lie down in His fold, then we will be a starved and shivering flock, sick, wretched, and full of complaints. We will bring dishonor on Him and, by our forlorn condition, hinder the world from coming to Him.

Realize to yourself what your ideal Shepherd would be—all that you would require from anyone filling such a position of trust and responsibility—and then know that an ideal far beyond yours was in the mind of our Lord when He said, "I am the good shepherd" (John 10:14). (*GAC*, 52–54)

NOVEMBER 11
SHEPHERDING AND ASSURING

Christ, better than any other, knew the Shepherd's duties. He knew that the Shepherd is responsible for His flock and that He is bound, at any loss of comfort, of health, or even of life itself, to care for them and bring them all safely home to the Master's fold. Therefore He said, "The good shepherd giveth his life for the sheep" (John 10:11). And again, "My sheep hear my voice, and I know them, and they follow me: and I give unto them eternal life; and they shall never perish, neither shall any man pluck them out of my hand" (vv. 27-28).

Christ has undertaken His duties, knowing perfectly well what the responsibilities are. He knows that He is dealing with very silly sheep who have no strength to protect themselves, no wisdom to guide themselves, and nothing to recommend them but their utter helplessness and weakness. But none of these things baffle Him. His strength and His skill are sufficient to meet every emergency that can possibly arise.

There is only one thing that can hinder the Good Shepherd: refusal of the sheep to trust Him and let Him care for them. If they stand off at a distance and look at the food He has provided and long for it and cry for it but refuse to eat it, He cannot satisfy their hunger. If they linger outside the shelter He has made and are afraid to go in and enjoy it because they feel too distrustful or too unworthy, He cannot protect them. No sheep is so silly as to act in this way, but we human beings, who are so much wiser than sheep, do it continually. (*GAC*, 55–56)

NOVEMBER 12
SHEPHERDING IS CARING

No sheep, could it talk, would say to the shepherd: "I long for the food you have provided and for the shelter and peace of your fold. I wish I might dare to enjoy them; but, alas! I feel too unworthy. I am too weak and foolish. I do not feel grateful enough. I am afraid I do not feel quite hungry enough. I dare not presume to think you mean all these good things for me.''

One can imagine how grieved a good shepherd would be at such talk as that. Surely our Lord gave us a glimpse into His sorrow over those who would not trust Him when He beheld Jerusalem and wept over it, saying: ''If thou hadst known, even thou, at least in this thy day, the things which belong unto thy peace! but now they are hid from thine eyes'' (Luke 19:42).

If Christ is your Shepherd, then He wants to care for you in the very best possible way. What you think or feel does not matter; you are not the Shepherd. The important point is what He thinks and feels. Lose sight of yourself for a moment, and try to put yourself in the Shepherd's place. Consider your condition as He considers it. See Him coming out to seek you in your far-off wandering. See His tender yearning love, His unutterable longing to save you. Believe His own description of himself, and take Him at His own sure word.

> *If our faith were but more simple,*
> *We would take Him at His word;*
> *And our lives would be all gladness*
> *In the sunshine of our Lord.* (GAC, 56–57)

NOVEMBER 13
TRUSTING AND FOLLOWING

The sheep's part is simple; all they have to do is trust and follow. The Shepherd does all the rest. He chooses their paths for them and sees that those paths are paths where they can walk in safety. Then He goes before them. The sheep have none of the planning to do, none of the decisions to make, none of the forethought or wisdom to exercise. They have absolutely nothing to do but to trust themselves entirely to the care of the Good Shepherd and to follow Him wherever He leads. It is very simple. There is nothing complicated in trusting when the One we are called on to trust is absolutely trustworthy. And there is nothing complicated in obedience when we have perfect confidence in the Power we are obeying. Abandon yourself to Christ's care and guidance as a sheep in the care of a shepherd, and trust Him utterly.

You need not be afraid to follow Christ wherever He leads, for He always leads His sheep into green pastures and beside still waters. Do not worry if you seem to be in the midst of a desert, with nothing green about you inwardly or outwardly. You will not have to make a long journey to get to green pastures, for the Good Shepherd will turn the very place where you are into green pastures. He has power to make the desert rejoice and blossom as the rose. He has promised that "instead of the thorn shall come up the fir tree, and instead of the briar shall come up the myrtle tree" (Isa. 55:13), and "in the wilderness shall waters break out, and streams in the desert" (35:6). (*GAC*, 57–58)

NOVEMBER 14
SHEPHERDING IS BLESSING

Thousands of the flock of Christ can testify that when they have put themselves absolutely into His hands, He has quieted the raging tempest and has turned their deserts into blossoming gardens. I do not mean that there will be no more outward trouble or care or suffering; but these very places will become green pastures and still waters to the soul. The Shepherd knows what pastures are best for His sheep, and they must not question or doubt but must trustingly follow Him. Perhaps He sees that the best pastures for some of us are to be found in the midst of opposition or earthly trials. If He leads you there, you may be sure they are green pastures for you and that you will grow and be made strong by feeding in them.

Words fail to tell even half of what the good Shepherd does for the flock that trusts Him. According to His promise, He makes a covenant of peace with them and causes the evil beasts to leave the land. His flock will live safely in the wilderness and sleep in the woods. He makes them and the places around them a blessing. He causes the shower to come down in His season; and there are showers of blessing. The tree of the field yields her fruit, and the earth yields her increase. His flock is safe in their land and is no longer prey for the heathen. None can make them afraid. (*GAC*, 58–59)

NOVEMBER 15
WILLING, NOT UNDERSTANDING

If you were to ask me how to get the Lord to be your Shepherd, I would answer that you do not need to get Him to be your Shepherd at all, for He already is your Shepherd. You only need to recognize that He is, and yield yourself to His control. Every soul who will begin from today believing in the Good Shepherd and trusting himself to His care, will sooner or later find himself feeding in the Shepherd's green pastures and walking beside His still waters.

If you have difficulty understanding all this, and if the life of full trust looks complicated and mysterious, I would advise you not to try to understand it but simply to begin to live it. Just take your childhood Psalm and say, "This is my Psalm, and I am going to believe it. I have always known it by heart, but it has never meant much to me. But now I have made up my mind to believe that the Lord really is my Shepherd and that He will care for me as a shepherd cares for his sheep. I will not question it again."

We must not forget that while sheep trust unconsciously and by instinct, we will need to trust intelligently and with purpose; for our instincts are all against trusting. We will have to make an effort to trust, and we can do it, no matter how weak and ignorant we may be. We may not understand all it means to be a sheep of such a Shepherd, but He knows. If our faith will but claim Him in this blessed wondrous relationship, He will care for us according to His love, His wisdom, and His power, and not according to our poor understanding of it. (*GAC*, 60–61)

NOVEMBER 16
REVEALING BY NAMING

Among all the names of God, perhaps the most comprehensive is the name Jehovah. The word *Jehovah* means "the self-existing One," the "I Am." In several places an explanatory word is added, revealing one of His special characteristics. For example: *Jehovah-jireh*, "the Lord will see" or "the Lord will provide" (Gen. 22:14); *Jehovah-nissi*, "the Lord my banner" (Exod. 17:15); *Jehovah-shalom*, "the Lord our peace" (Judg. 6:24); *Jehovah-tsidkenu*, "the Lord our righteousness" (Jer. 23:6; 33:16); and *Jehovah-shammah*, "the Lord is there" (Ezek. 48:35).

These names were discovered by God's people in times of great need. The characteristics they describe were discovered, and the names were the natural expression of these characteristics. When Abraham was about to sacrifice his son, the Lord provided a lamb for the sacrifice and delivered Isaac. Abraham made the grand discovery that it was one of the characteristics of Jehovah to see and provide for the needs of His people. Therefore he called Him Jehovah-jireh, "the Lord will see" or "the Lord will provide."

The counterparts to this name in the New Testament are numerous. Over and over our Lord urges us to take no care, because God cares for us. "Your heavenly Father knoweth," He says, "that ye have need of all these things" (Matt. 6:32). If the Lord sees and knows our need, it will be a matter of course with Him to provide for it. As soon as a good mother sees that her child needs anything, she at once sets about supplying that need. She does not even wait for the child to ask; the sight of the need is asking enough. Being a good mother, she could not do otherwise. Being our Father, God could not do otherwise for us. (*GAC*, 75–76)

239

NOVEMBER 17
RELYING, NOT STRUGGLING

God's name Jehovah-nissi ("the Lord my banner"; Exod. 17:15) was a discovery made by Moses when Amalek came to fight with Israel in Rephidim. The Lord gave the Israelites a glorious victory there. Moses realized that the Lord was fighting for them, and he built an altar to Jehovah-nissi, "the Lord my banner." The Bible is full of developments of this name, such as "The LORD shall fight for you, and ye shall hold your peace" (Exod. 14:14), and "God himself is with us for our captain" (2 Chron. 13:12).

Nothing is more abundantly proved in the Bible than that the Lord will fight for us if we will let Him. All He asks of us is to be still and let Him fight for us. This is the only sort of spiritual conflict that is ever successful. But we are very slow to learn this. When temptations come, instead of handing the battle over to the Lord we summon all our forces to fight them ourselves. We believe, perhaps, that the Lord is somewhere near, and if the worst comes to worst, He will step in to help us. But for the most part we feel that we ourselves and we only must do all the fighting. Our method of fighting consists generally in a series of repentings, resolutions and promises, weary struggles for victory, and then failing again—over and over and over. Each time we tell ourselves that now at last we will have the victory, and each time we fail even worse than before. This may go on for weeks, months, or even years, and no real or permanent deliverance ever comes.

God has told us to cease from our own efforts and hand our battles over to Him. (*GAC*, 77–78)

NOVEMBER 18
RESTING, NOT WRESTLING

Our spiritual "wrestling," of which we are often so proud, is really a wrestling not for God against His enemies but against Him on the side of His enemies. We allow ourselves to indulge in doubts and fears, and as a consequence, we are plunged into darkness, turmoil, and wrestling of spirit. Then we call this "spiritual conflict" and look on ourselves as an interesting and peculiar case. The single word that explains our peculiar case is "unbelief," and the simple remedy is found in the word "faith."

But you may ask, what about wrestling Jacob? Did he not gain his victory by wrestling? To this I reply that, on the contrary, he gained his victory by being made so weak that he could not wrestle any longer. It was not Jacob who wrestled with the angel but the angel who wrestled with Jacob. Jacob was the one to be overcome. When the angel found that Jacob's resistance was so great that he could not prevail against him, he was obliged to make him lame by putting his hip out of joint. Then the victory was won. Jacob gained power when he lost it; he conquered when he could no longer fight (see Gen. 32:24-32).

Jacob's experience is ours. The Lord wrestles with us in order to bring us to a place of entire dependence on himself. We resist as long as we have any strength, until at last He is forced to bring us to a place of helplessness where we are obliged to yield. Then we conquer by this very yielding. Paul knew this victory when he said, "And the Lord said unto me, My grace is sufficient for thee: for my strength is made perfect in weakness" (2 Cor. 12:9). (*GAC*, 80–81)

NOVEMBER 19
CHOOSING AND RESTING

Our idea of peace is that it must be outward before it can be inward, that all enemies must be driven away before troubles cease. But the Lord's idea is an inner peace that can exist in the midst of turmoil and can be triumphant over it. The ground of this sort of peace is found in not in that we have overcome the world but that Christ has overcome it. Only the conqueror can proclaim peace, and the people whose battles He has fought can do nothing but enter into it. But, if they choose, they can refuse to believe in it and so fail to let it reign in their hearts.

The Bible tells us that Christ is our peace, and consequently, whether I feel as if I have peace or not, peace is really mine in Christ, and I must take possession of it by faith. "The kingdom of God is . . . righteousness, and peace, and joy in the Holy Ghost'' (Rom. 14:17). The soul who has not taken possession of peace has not yet fully entered into this kingdom.

Practically, we can always enter into peace by a simple obedience to Philippians 4:6-7: "Be careful for nothing; but in every thing by prayer and supplication with thanksgiving let your requests be made known unto God. And the peace of God, which passeth all understanding, shall keep your hearts and minds through Christ Jesus.'' The steps here are plain: First, give up all anxiety; and second, hand over your cares to God. Then stand steadfastly, and peace will come. (*GAC*, 83)

NOVEMBER 20
UNDERSTANDING OUR JUSTIFICATION

If we discover that the Lord is our righteousness, we will have a hold on the secret of victory. In the Lord Jesus Christ we have a full revelation of this wonderful name of God. The apostle Paul declares that God "hath made [Christ] to be sin for us; . . . that we might be made the righteousness of God in him" (2 Cor. 5:21). He says that Christ "is made unto us wisdom, and righteousness, and sanctification, and redemption" (1 Cor. 1:30). Few Christians really understand what this means. We repeat the words as part of our religious vocabulary, and in a vague sort of way think of them as being somehow a part of the salvation of Christ; but of what practical use they are we have no idea.

To me this name of God, the Lord our righteousness, is of such tremendously practical use that I want to make it plain to others. I cannot explain it theologically, but experientially it seems to be like this: We are not to try to have a stock of righteousness laid up in ourselves from which to draw a supply when needed; instead we are to draw continual fresh supplies as we need them from the righteousness that is laid up for us in Christ. The results are triumphant. I have seen sweetness and gentleness poured like a flood of sunshine into dark and bitter spirits; I have seen sharp tongues made tender, anxious hearts made calm, and fretful spirits made quiet by taking by faith the righteousness that is ours in Christ. (*GAC*, 84–85)

NOVEMBER 21
APPROPRIATING BY BELIEVING

The apostle Paul, after proving to us in the third chapter of Romans the absolute impossibility of any satisfying righteousness coming to us by the law (that is, by our own efforts), goes on to say, "But now the righteousness of God without the law is manifested, being witnessed by the law and the prophets; even the righteousness of God which is by faith of Jesus Christ unto all and on all them that believe: for there is no difference" (Rom. 3:21–22).

Faith and faith only can appropriate the righteousness that is ours in Christ. Just as we appropriate by faith the forgiveness that is ours in Christ, so must we appropriate by faith the patience that is ours in Him, the gentleness, the meekness, the long-suffering, or any other virtue we may need. Our own efforts will not procure righteousness for us any more than they will procure forgiveness. Yet how many Christians try! Paul describes them when he says, "For I bear them record that they have a zeal of God, but not according to knowledge. For they being ignorant of God's righteousness, . . . have not submitted themselves unto the righteousness of God. For Christ is the end of the law for righteousness to every one that believeth" (Rom. 10:2–4).

How wonderful it would be if all such zealous souls would discover this wonderful name of God, the Lord our righteousness, and give up at once and forever seeking to establish their own righteousness, and would submit themselves to the righteousness of God. The prophet Isaiah tells us that our own righteousness, even if we could attain to any, is nothing but filthy rags (Isa. 64:6). (*GAC*, 85–86)

NOVEMBER 22
SEEING IS ASSURING

The name Jehovah-shammah, "the LORD is there" (Ezek. 48:35), was revealed by a vision to the prophet Ezekiel in the twenty-fifth year of the Captivity. In it he was shown what was to be the future home of the children of Israel. He described the land and the city of Jerusalem and ended his description by saying, "And the name of the city . . . shall be, The LORD is there."

To me this name includes all God's other names. Wherever the Lord is, all must go right for His children; His presence is enough. We can all remember how the presence of our mother was enough for us when we were children. All the comfort, rest, and deliverance we needed was insured to us by our mother's presence. As she sat in her usual chair with her work, her book, or her writing, we would burst in on her with our doleful list of childish woes. If we could see that the presence of God is the same assurance of comfort, rest, and deliverance, only infinitely more so, a wellspring of joy would be opened up in our religious lives that would drive out every vestige of discomfort and distress.

All through the Old Testament the Lord's one universal answer to the fears and anxieties of the children of Israel was, "I will be with thee." He did not need to say anything more. His presence was a guarantee that all their needs would be supplied; and the moment they were assured of it, they were no longer afraid to face the fiercest foe. (*GAC*, 87)

NOVEMBER 23
TRUSTING AND UNMOVING

The names Jehovah-shammah and Emmanuel mean the same thing. They mean that God is everywhere present in His universe, surrounding everything, sustaining everything, and holding all of us in His safe and blessed keeping.

It will help you if you will put your trust into words. Say,

244

"God is my dwelling place, and I am going to abide in Him forever. It is all settled; I am in this divine habitation and I am safe here and I am not going to move again." You must meet all assaults of doubt and discouragement with the assertion that you know you will not be confounded; and you must declare that, let other people do as they may, you are going to abide in your divine dwelling place forever. Then, having taken this stand, you must refuse to reconsider the matter.

In all this I do not, of course, mean that we are to lie in bed and let things go. I am talking about the inner aspect of our affairs not the outer. Outwardly we may have to be full of active carefulness, but it must all be from the inner basis of a soul that has hidden itself and all its interests in the dwelling place of God and is therefore "careful for nothing" (Phil. 4:6) in the Bible sense of having no anxious thoughts. To be without inner care is the surest foundation for successful outer care. The soul that is hidden in the dwelling place of God, is the soul that will be able to bear triumphantly earth's greatest trials and conquer its strongest foes. (*GAC*, 87–88, 114–15)

NOVEMBER 24
TRUSTING HIS KEEPING

If we trust for ourselves, we must trust for our loved ones also, especially for our children. God is more their Father than their earthly fathers are, and if they are dear to us they are far dearer to Him. We cannot, therefore, do anything better for them than to trust them in God's care, or do hardly anything worse for them than to try to keep them in our own care.

I knew a Christian mother who trusted peacefully for her own salvation but was racked with anxiety about her sons, who seemed entirely indifferent to all religious subjects. One evening she heard about putting those we love into the fortress of God by faith and leaving them there. Like a flash of heavenly light, she saw the inconsistency of hiding herself in God's fortress and leaving her beloved sons outside. At once her faith took them into the fortress with her, and she abandoned them to the care of God.

She did this so fully that all her anxiety vanished and perfect

245

peace dawned on her soul. She told me she felt somehow that her sons were God's sons now and no longer hers. He loved them far better than she could and would care for them far more wisely and effectually. She held herself in readiness to do for them whatever the Lord might suggest, but she felt that He was the One who would know what was best, and she was content to leave the matter in His hands. (*GAC*, 116–17)

NOVEMBER 25
LONGING AND FULFILLING

We are told that "Eye hath not seen, nor ear heard, neither have entered into the heart of man, the things which God hath prepared for them that love him" (1 Cor. 2:9). If God has prepared more for us than it has ever entered into our hearts to conceive, surely we can have no question about obtaining that which has entered into our hearts and "much more" beside. But unbelief leads us to think that God's salvation is "much less' than the things that have entered into our hearts to long for.

Let us settle it then that the language of our souls must henceforth be not the "much less" of unbelief but the "much more" of faith. We will find that God's "much mores" will be enough to cover the whole range of our needs, both temporal and spiritual.

"For if through the offence of one many be dead, much more the grace of God, and the gift by grace, which is by one man, Jesus Christ, hath abounded unto many" (Rom. 5:15). This is a "much more," that reaches, if only we could understand it, into the depth of human need. There is no question in our minds as to the fact that "many be dead," but how is it with the "much more" of grace that is to abound unto many? Are we as sure of the grace as we are of the death? Do we really believe that the remedy is "much more" than the disease? Does the salvation seem to us "much more" than the need? Or do we believe in our hearts that it is "much less"? Which does God declare? (*GAC*, 123–24)

NOVEMBER 26
CONFESSING, NOT DOUBTING

One of the deepest needs of our souls is the need to be saved. Is there a "much more" to meet this need? The apostle Paul says, "But God commendeth his love toward us, in that, while we were yet sinners, Christ died for us. Much more then, being now justified by his blood, we shall be saved from wrath through him. For if, when we were enemies, we were reconciled to God by the death of his Son, much more, being reconciled, we shall be saved by his life" (Rom. 5:8). The question of salvation seems to me to be absolutely settled by these "much mores." Since Christ has died for us and has thereby reconciled us to God (not God to us; He did not need reconciling), He will now save us if we will only let Him. There can be no question as to whether He will or will not, for the greater must necessarily include the lesser.

The practical point here is: Do we really believe it? Have we rid ourselves of all doubts about our salvation? Can we speak with assurance of forgiveness and of eternal life? Do we say with the timidity of unbelief, "I hope I am a child of God"? Or do we lift up our heads with joyous confidence in God as our Father and say with John, "Now are we the sons of God"? (1 John 3:2). (*GAC*, 123–24)

NOVEMBER 27
WILLING OUR FILLING

We long and pray for the gift of the Holy Spirit, but our prayers are not answered. Our Lord gives faith a wonderful "much more" to lay hold of for this. "If ye then, being evil, know how to give good gifts unto your children: how much more shall your heavenly Father give the Holy Spirit to them that ask him?" (Luke 11:13). All of us know how thankful and eager good parents are to give gifts to their children, how they thrust them on their children, often before the child is ready to receive or even knows that he has a need. Yet who of us believes that

God is actually "much more" eager to give the Holy Spirit to those who ask Him? Do we not feel secretly that He is "much less" willing and that we will have to entreat, wrestle, and wait for this sorely needed gift?

If we could only believe this "much more," how full of faith our asking would be in regard to it. We would then truly be able to believe that we actually did receive that for which we had asked. We would find that we were in actual possession of the Holy Spirit as our personal Comforter and Guide, and all our weary struggles and agonizing prayers for this promised gift would be over. (*GAC*, 125)

NOVEMBER 28
BELIEVING AND REIGNING

More critical, perhaps, than any other need is our need of victory over sin and over circumstances. Like Juggernauts they roll over us with irresistible power and crush us into the dust. The language of "much less" seems the only language that our souls dare utter. But God has given us for this a most triumphant "much more": "For if by one man's offence death reigned by one; much more they which receive abundance of grace and of the gift of righteousness shall reign in life by one, Jesus Christ" (Rom. 5:17).

We have known the reigning of spiritual death that comes by sin, but how much do we know of that "much more" reigning in life by Jesus Christ of which the apostle Paul speaks? We have been reigned over by thousands of things—by the fear of man, by our peculiar temperaments, by our irritable tempers, by bad weather, by outward circumstances of every kind. We have been slaves when we ought to have been kings. We have found our reigning to be "much less" rather than "much more."

The lack cannot possibly be on God's side. He has not failed to provide the "much more" of victory. It must be that we have in some way failed to avail ourselves of it. Our failure arises from not believing there really is a sufficiency in the gift of righteousness in Christ to enable us to reign.

What then is our remedy? Only this: to abandon forever our "much less" of unbelief, to accept as true God's declaration of "much more," and to claim at once the promised victory. According to our faith it must and will be to us. (*GAC*, 125–26)

NOVEMBER 29
TRUSTING, NOT FRETTING

The assurances of the "much mores" of God's salvation are not for our spiritual needs only but for our temporal needs as well. Do not be anxious, He says, about earthly things, for "if God so clothe the grass of the field, which to day is, and to morrow is cast into the oven, shall he not much more clothe you, O ye of little faith?" (Matt. 6:30).

God cares for us human beings "much more" than He cares for the universe, and He will watch over and provide for us much more. Incredible yet true! How often we have marveled at the orderly working of the universe and admired the great creative Power that made it and now controls it. But none of us, I suppose, have ever felt it necessary to take the burden of the universe on our own shoulders.

Even where we have fully recognized that the universe is in God's care, we have failed to see that we also are. We have looked at our circumstances, at the greatness of our need, and at our own helplessness, and have been anxious and afraid. We have burdened ourselves with the care of ourselves, feeling in our unbelief that instead of being of "much more" value than the fowls of the air or the lilies of the field, we are infinitely "much less." It seems to us that the God who cares for them is not at all likely to care for us. But God declares that He does care for us and that He even cares for us much more than He cares for the universe. Since we are not so foolish as to be anxious about the universe, we must not be so much more foolish as to be anxious about ourselves. (*GAC*, 127–28)

NOVEMBER 30
CARING IS GIVING

In the Sermon on the Mount, our Lord gives us the crowning "much more" of all. "Or what man is there of you, whom if his son ask bread, will he give him a stone? Or if he ask a fish, will he give him a serpent? If ye then, being evil, know how to give good gifts unto your children, how much more shall your Father which is in heaven give good things to them that ask him?" (Matt. 7:9–11).

In this "much more" we have a guarantee for the supply of whatever our Father sees to be good for us. The illustration used to convince us is one of universal application. In all nations, under all conditions of life, and even in the hearts of birds and beasts, the mother instinct never fails to provide for its offspring the best it can obtain. Under no conditions will a mother, unless she is wicked beyond compare, give a stone when asked for bread or a serpent when asked for fish. Could our God who created the mother heart be worse than a mother? No, no, a thousand times no. What He will do is "much more" than any mother, even the tenderest, could do.

Which of us has fathomed the meaning of this "how much more"? At least, it means this: All human readiness to hear and answer the cry of need can only be a faint picture of God's readiness; therefore, we can never dare to doubt it again. If parents would not give a stone for bread neither would He, so when we ask we must be absolutely sure that we do receive the "good thing" for which we asked, whether what we receive looks like it or not. (*GAC*, 129–30)

DECEMBER 1
GIVING AND GIVING

The mother of Augustine, in her longing for the conversion of her son, prayed that he might not go to Rome, as she feared its dissipations. God answered her by sending him to Rome to be converted there. Things we call good are often God's evil things, and our evil is His good. However things may look, we always know that God must give the best because He is God and can do no other.

"He that spared not his own Son but delivered him up for us all, how shall he not with him also freely give us all things?" (Rom. 8:32). Since God has done the supreme thing of having given us Christ, how much more will He do the lesser thing of giving us all things with Him. Yet we continually hear God's children lamenting their spiritual poverty and even sometimes thinking it to be a mark of true humility. But what is this but glorying in the "much less" of their unbelief instead of in the "much more" of God?

I heard a child of God, when urged to some victory of faith, say, "I am such a poor creature that I cannot expect to attain to the heights you grand Christians reach." "Poor creature," indeed; of course you are, and so are we all. But God is not poor, and it is His responsibility to supply your needs not yours to supply His. He is able, no matter what unbelief may say, to "make all grace abound toward you, that ye, always having all sufficiency in all things, may abound to every good work" (2 Cor. 9:8). "All," "always," "every"—what all-embracing words these are! They include our needs to their utmost limit. How can we, how dare we, in the face of such declarations, ever doubt or question again? (*GAC*, 130–31)

DECEMBER 2
SENSING HIS KEEPING

The psalmist seemed to delight in repeating over and over again, "for the LORD is good." We must join our voices to his: "The Lord is good." But we must not say it with our lips only and then by our actions lie. We must "say" it with our whole being—with thought, word, and action—so that people will see we really mean it and will be convinced that it is a tremendous fact.

A great many things in God's divine providences do not look to the eye like goodness. But faith sits down before mysteries such as these, and says, "The Lord is good, therefore all that

He does must be good no matter how it looks. I can wait for His explanations."

A housekeeping illustration has often helped me here. If I have a friend whom I know to be a good housekeeper, I do not trouble over the fact that at housekeeping time things in her house may seem to be upset—carpets up, furniture shrouded in coverings, and even, perhaps, painting and decorating making some rooms uninhabitable. I say to myself, "My friend is a good housekeeper, and although things look so uncomfortable now, all this upset is only because she means in the end to make it far more comfortable than ever."

This world is God's housekeeping; and although things at present look grievously upset, we know He is good and therefore a good Housekeeper. We may be sure that this present upset is only to bring about in the end a far better state of things than could have been without it. (*GAC*, 99–100)

DECEMBER 3
WRECKING BUT LOVING

A seasoned saint was asked by a despairing Christian, "Doesn't the world look to you like a wreck?" "Yes," was the cheerful and confident reply, "like the wreck of a bursting seed." Any of us who have watched the first sproutings of an oak tree from the heart of a decaying acorn will understand what this means. Before the acorn can bring forth the oak it must become a wreck. No plant ever came from any but a wrecked seed.

Our Lord uses this fact to teach us the meaning of His processes with us, "Verily, verily, I say unto you, Except a corn of wheat fall into the ground and die, it abideth alone; but if it die, it bringeth forth much fruit" (John 12:24).

The explanation of the apparent wreckage of the world at large or of our own personal lives in particular is here set forth. Looked at in this light, we can understand how it is that the Lord can be good yet permit the existence of sorrow and wrong in the world He has created and in the lives of the human beings He loves.

It is God's very goodness that compels Him to permit sorrow and wrong. He knows that only through such apparent wreckage can His glorious purposes for us be brought to pass. And we whose hearts also long for that fruition, will, if we understand His ways, be able to praise Him for all His goodness even when things seem hardest and most mysterious. (*GAC*, 100–101)

DECEMBER 4
RESTING OR WORRYING

Our souls are made for God. He is our natural home, and we can never be at rest anywhere else. We talk about obeying the commands of the Lord and make a great point of outward observances and duties, all the while ignoring or neglecting the commands as to the inner life, which are a thousandfold more important. "Let not your heart be troubled, neither let it be afraid" (John 14:27), is one of our Lord's commands that is almost universally disobeyed; yet I question whether our disobedience of any other command is so grievous to His heart.

I would be far more grieved if my child mistrusted me and felt her interests were unsafe in my care than if in a moment of temptation she disobeyed me. None of us have appreciated how deeply it wounds the loving heart of our Lord to find that His people do not feel safe in His care.

Suppose a friend should commit something to our keeping, receiving from us every assurance that we would keep it safe, and then go away and worry over it as we worry over the things we commit to God. And suppose he then went to others and expressed anxieties about it the way we allow ourselves to express anxiety about the things we put into God's care. How would we feel about it? Would we not be deeply hurt and wounded? Would we not finally be inclined to hand the thing back to our friend and say, "Since it is very plain that you do not trust me, had you not better take care of your things yourself?" (*GAC*, 104, 110–11)

DECEMBER 5
EXPANDING, NOT LIMITING

There is an expression used over and over again in the Bible to describe the salvation of the Lord Jesus Christ, which gives such an amazing view of salvation that I cannot help wondering whether any of us have ever yet grasped its full meaning. It is the expression "much more," and it is used to tell us that there is no need any human being can ever know that cannot be "much more" than met by God's glorious salvation. Anyone who grasps this truth can never be uncomfortable or miserable again.

But we are continually tempted to think that so far from this salvation being "much more" than our needs, it turns out in actual experience to be much less. This "much less" view can endanger our spiritual lives, making them miserable.

Whether this is a biblical view is, I believe, a far more vital question for each one of us than may appear at first sight. For if God declares that the salvation He has provided is "much more" than enough to meet our needs, and if we insist on declaring that it is "much less," we are storing up for ourselves untold discomfort and misery.

"Much less" is the language of the visible; "much more" is the language of the invisible. "Much less" seems on the surface to be far more reasonable than "much more," because every visible thing confirms it. Our weakness and foolishness are visible; God's supply is hidden in the secret of His presence and can only be realized by faith. (*GAC*, 118–19)

DECEMBER 6
SERVING, NOT STRIVING

God declares emphatically that He wants us to keep the sort of "fast" He approves of, by giving up the afflicting of our souls. He says, "If thou draw out thy soul to the hungry, and satisfy the afflicted soul; then shall thy light rise in obscurity, and thy darkness be as the noon day: and the LORD shall guide thee continually, and satisfy thy soul in drought, and make fat thy bones: and thou shalt be like a watered garden, and like a spring of water, whose waters fail not" (Isa. 58:10-11).

All this is exactly what we have been striving after, but our strivings have been in our own way not in God's. The "fast" we have chosen has been to afflict our souls, bow down our heads as bulrushes, and sit in sackcloth and ashes. Consequently, instead of our bones being made fat and our souls refreshed like a watered garden, we have found only leanness and thirst and misery. Our own "fasts," no matter how fervently they may be carried out or how many groans and tears may accompany them, can never bring us anything else.

Now let us try God's "fast." Let us lay aside all care for ourselves and care instead for our needy brothers and sisters. Let us stop trying to do something for our miserable self lives and begin to do something to help the spiritual lives of others. Let us give up our hopeless efforts to find something in ourselves to delight in, and delight ourselves only in the Lord and in His service. If we will but do this, all the days of our misery will be ended. (*GAC*, 142-43)

DECEMBER 7
BELIEVING, NOT WAVERING

Many of God's children are hungering and thirsting for the peace and rest Christ has promised them, but they seem unable to attain to it for more than a few moments at a time. They may now and then get a faint glimmer of faith, and peace seems to be on the way, but then all the old doubts spring up again with tenfold power. "Look at your heart," they say; "see how cold and indifferent it is. How can you for a moment believe that God can love such a poor, unworthy person as you are?" It all sounds so reasonable that they are plunged into darkness again.

A lack of faith is the cause of their trouble. It seems so commonplace to say it, but in the spiritual life we receive always, always, ALWAYS, according to our faith. This is a spiritual law that can neither be evaded nor neglected. It is not an arbitrary law that we hope can be repealed in our own special case, but it is inherent in the very nature of things and is therefore unalterable. Equally inherent in the nature of things is its converse:

if it is to be to us according to our faith, so will it also be to us according to our doubts.

The root and cause then of our wavering experience is not, as we may have thought, our sins, but is simply and only our doubts. Doubts create an impassable gulf between our souls and the Lord just as inevitably as they do between us and our earthly friends. No amount of fervor or earnestness can bridge this gulf in one case any more than in the other. There exists that inherent nature of things that makes it impossible for doubt and confidence to exist together, whether in earthly relations or heavenly, and which neither God nor man can alter. (*GAC*, 163–64)

DECEMBER 8
FLYING ISN'T FEELING

Paul knew what it was to use his wings. Though he was "sorrowful" as to the earthly plane of life, he was "always rejoicing" as to the spiritual plane (2 Cor. 6:10). Do we know anything of the same experience? Do we "mount up with wings" (cf. Isa. 40:31) above all life's trials, or do we plod wearily along on foot through the midst of them, where they overwhelm us at every turn?

We must guard against a mistake here. Do not think that by flying I necessarily mean joyous emotions or feelings of exhilaration. A great deal of emotional flying is not real flying at all; rather it is like a feather which is driven upward by a strong puff of wind but flutters down again as soon as the wind ceases to blow. The flying I mean is a matter of *principle*, not a matter of *emotion*. It may be accompanied by joyous emotions but it does not depend on them. It depends only on an entire surrender to and an absolute trust in the Lord. Everyone who will honestly do these two things and will faithfully persist in them, will find that they *have* mounted up with wings as an eagle, no matter how empty of all emotion they may have felt themselves to be before.

The promise is sure: "They that wait upon the Lord shall . . . mount up with wings as eagles" (Isa. 40:31)—not "may perhaps mount up," but "shall." It is the inevitable result. May all of us prove it for ourselves!

The only creature that sings is the creature that flies. And only the soul on wings can sing the song of the Lord. (*WS*, 5)

DECEMBER 9
SURRENDERING PLUS TRUSTING

Two wings are needed to lift a bird in the air, and two wings are needed to lift the soul. A great many people do everything but trust. They spread the wing of surrender and flap it vigorously and wonder why they do not mount up, never dreaming that it is because the wing of trust is hanging idle by their sides. It is because Christians use only one wing that their efforts to fly are often so irregular and fruitless.

Or perhaps the soul is in a prison and therefore cannot fly. No walls, however high, can imprison an eagle if there is an open way upward; and earth's power can never hold the soul in prison while the upward way is kept open and free. Our enemies may build walls around us as high as they please, but if we "mount up with wings" (Isa. 40:31), we can fly higher than any walls can ever reach. The only thing that can imprison the soul is something that hinders the upward flight, some barrier between itself and God.

If we find ourselves imprisoned, we may be sure that it is not our earthly environment that constitutes our prison house; our own "iniquities" have separated us and our God, and they must be put out of the way before we will be able to fly. As well might an eagle try to fly with a hundred-pound weight tied around its neck as the soul try to mount up with the weight of the smallest indulged sin. (*WS*, 3)

DECEMBER 10
MOUNTING CHANGES SEEING

The soul that "mounts up with wings" (Isa. 40:31) looks at everything from the divine standpoint not from the human. In forming a judgment about any matter everything depends on our point of view. Things appear very different when looked down on from above than when viewed on their own level. What seems like an impassable wall on its own level, becomes an insignificant line to the eyes that see it from the top of a mountain. The faults in others which assume such immense proportions while we look at them on the earthly plane, become insignificant little motes in the sunshine when the soul has mounted on wings to the heavenly places above them.

How changed our lives would be if we could only fly through our days on the wings of surrender and trust! Instead of stirring up strife and bitterness by figuratively trying to knock down and walk over our offending brothers and sisters, we should escape all strife by simply spreading our wings and mounting up to the heavenly region where our eyes would see all things covered with a mantle of Christian love and pity.

Our souls were made to live in this upper atmosphere, and we stifle and choke on any lower level. Our eyes were made to look off from these heavenly heights, and our vision is distorted by any lower gazing.

It is a great blessing, therefore, that our loving Father in heaven has mercifully arranged all the discipline of our lives with a view to teaching us to fly. (*WS*, 2)

DECEMBER 11
FLYING, NOT FLEEING

Our souls were made to "mount up with wings" (Isa. 40:31), and they can never be satisfied with anything short of flying. Like the captive-born eagle that frets at its imprisonment, hardly knowing what it longs for, so do our souls chafe and fret and cry out for freedom. We can never rest on earth, and we long to "fly away" from all that holds, hampers, and imprisons us here.

This restlessness and discontent develop themselves often in seeking an outward escape from our circumstances or from our miseries. We have not found out that our only way of escape is to "mount up with wings," and we try to "flee on horses" somewhere on the earthly plane.

"But ye said, No; for we will flee upon horses; therefore shall ye flee: and, We will ride upon the swift; therefore shall they that pursue you be swift" (Isa. 30:16).

258

Our "horses" are the outward things on which we depend for relief, such as a change of circumstances or some help from men. We mount on these and run east or west, north or south—anywhere to get away from our trouble—thinking in our ignorance that a change of our environment is all that is necessary to give deliverance to our souls.

But all such efforts to escape are unavailing, as we have each proved hundreds of times; for the soul is not made so that it can "flee upon horses" but must make its flight always on wings. Moreover, our "horses" generally carry us out of one trouble only to land us in another. (*WS*, 1)

DECEMBER 12
LIVING BY DYING

The only way out of one life into another is by a death to one and a new birth into the other. Die, then, that you may live. Lose your own life that you may find Christ's life. The caterpillar can only enter into the butterfly's kingdom by dying to its caterpillar life and emerging into the resurrection life of the butterfly. Similarly, we enter into the kingdom of God by dying to ourselves and emerging into the resurrection life of Christ.

Let everything go, then, that belongs to the natural—all your own notions, plans, ways, and thoughts—and accept in their stead God's plans, ways, and thoughts. Do this faithfully and do it persistently, and you will come at last to reign with Him in an inner kingdom which will break in pieces and consume all other kingdoms and will stand forever.

There is no other way. The kingdom of new life cannot be entered by pomp, show, greatness, or strength. He who humbles himself and he only will be exalted. To mount the throne with Christ requires that we will first follow Him in suffering, loss, and crucifixion. To follow Christ in regeneration will surely bring the soul to His crown and throne. (*KK*, 4)

DECEMBER 13
HUMBLING BRINGS REIGNING

Perhaps you will say, "How can I enter into this kingdom, if I am not already in?" Let our Lord himself answer you: "Came the disciples unto Jesus saying, Who is the greatest in the kingdom of heaven? And Jesus called a little child unto him, and set him in the midst of them, And said, Verily I say unto you, Except ye be converted, and become as little children, ye shall not enter into the kingdom of heaven. Whosoever therefore shall humble himself as this little child, the same is greatest in the kingdom of heaven" (Matt. 18:1–4). The kingdom of heaven is a kingdom of childlike hearts, and only those who have such may enter it.

To be a "little child" means simply to *be* one. I cannot describe it better than this. We all have known little children and have delighted ourselves in their simplicity and their trustfulness, their light-hearted carelessness, and their unquestioning obedience to those in authority over them. To be the greatest in the divine kingdom means to have a guileless, tender, trustful, self-forgetting, obedient heart of a child.

It is not saying but doing that will avail us here. To be a child means to do the Father's will, since the very essence of true childhood is the spirit of obedience united to the spirit of trust. Become a little child, then, by laying aside all your greatness, self-assertion, self-dependence, wisdom, and strength, and consent to die to your own self-life and be born again into the kingdom of God. (*KK*, 2)

DECEMBER 14
GAINING BY SERVING

What grander kingship can be conceived of than that which Christ sets forth in the Sermon on the Mount: "But I say unto you, That ye resist not evil: but whosoever shall smite thee on thy right cheek, turn to him the other also. And if any man will sue thee at the law, and take away thy coat, let him have thy cloak also. And whosoever shall compel thee to go a mile, go with him twain'' (Matt. 5:39–41). Surely only a soul that is in harmony with God can mount such a throne of dominion as this!

This is our destiny. We are made for this purpose. We are born of a kingly race and are heirs to this ineffable kingdom—"heirs of God, and joint heirs with Christ" (Rom. 8:17). If only we could realize this and could see in every act of service or surrender to which we are called an upward step in the pathway that leads us to our kingdom and our throne!

I mean this in a very practical sense. I mean that the homely services of our daily lives and the little sacrifices each day demands, will be, if faithfully fulfilled, actual rungs in the ladder by which we are mounting to our thrones. If we are faithful over the "few things" of our earthly kingdom, we will be made ruler over the "many things" of the heavenly kingdom (Matt. 25:21).

He that follows Christ in this ministry of service and suffering will reign with Him in the glory of supreme self-sacrifice and will be the "chiefest" (Mark 10:44) in His divine kingdom of love. Who would hesitate to "turn the other cheek," for in turning, a kingdom is to be won and a throne is to be gained. (*KK*, 2)

DECEMBER 15
REIGNING DESPITE SURROUNDINGS

Our King essentially rose superior to His surroundings; and it is given to us who are reigning with Him to do the same.

Just as Christ was not a king in outward appearance but only in inward power, so will we be. He reigned, not in that He had all the treasures and riches of the world at His command but that He had none of them and could do without them. And so will our reigning be. We will not have all people bowing down to us and all circumstances bending to our will, but we will walk in royal triumph of soul through the midst of opposition.

All this is contrary to the human thought of kingship. The only idea the human heart can conceive is that outward circumstances must bow to the soul that is seated on a throne with Christ. Friends must approve, enemies must be silenced, obstacles must be overcome, affairs must prosper, or there can be no reigning. If we had handled Daniel's business or the matter of the three Hebrew children in the fiery furnace, we would have said the only way of victory would be for the minds of the kings to have been so changed that Daniel would not have been cast into the den of lions and the Hebrew children would not have been cast into the furnace. But God's way was infinitely grander. He allowed Daniel to be cast among the lions in order that he might reign triumphant over them in their very midst; and He allowed Shadrach, Meshach, and Abednego to be cast into the fiery furnace in order that they might walk through it without so much as the smell of fire on them. (*KK*, 1)

DECEMBER 16
KNOWING, NOT HOPING

Uncertainties are fatal to all true progress and are utterly destructive of comfort and peace. Yet it has somehow become the fashion among Christians to encourage uncertainties in the spiritual life as being an indication of the truest form of piety. There is a great deal of longing and hoping among Christians, but there is not much knowing, yet the Bible was written for the purpose of making us know. The object of a revelation is to reveal. If nothing has been revealed to us by the Bible beyond longings and hopes, it has failed in its purpose for us.

A large proportion of God's children never get beyond these hopes and longings. "I hope my sins will be forgiven some day"; "I hope I may be favored to reach heaven at last"; "I hope God loves me"; "I hope Christ died for me." These are samples of the style of much Christian testimony in the present day. Indeed, I have even known Christians who could never get further than to say, "I hope that I have a hope." If this word is used in the sense of firm expectation as the Bible always uses it, it may be all right; but if it is used in the sense I have described, there is so great an element of doubt that it does not amount to a Bible hope at all.

We need sometimes to bring our words out into the light of common sense to see what we really do mean by them. In many cases we would find that the word "hope" would mean, by interpretation, "doubt." (*EDR*, 1)

262

DECEMBER 17
ABIDING AND GUIDING

I am being taught what the guidance of the Holy Spirit is.
Now that Christ is dwelling in my heart, His voice speaks and
I can hear it; and oh, what an unspeakable privilege this is! May
I be wholly given to hearing and obeying His voice. I desire to
present myself as a living sacrifice to Him, to do His bidding;
but He alone can make me do this, and to Him I commit it.

Lord Jesus, You died to make me wholly Yours. Now, I pray
You, accomplish this mighty work and let *no* hindering thing
remain!

How blessed it is to know myself "dead to sin" and "alive
unto God" (Rom. 6:11)! It is such a wondrous blessing that, if
God had not declared it, I would not dare to dream of it. But
oh, praise His name! He has declared that for this very purpose
Christ died, so that I, being "dead to sins might live unto righteousness." And, taking my place at the foot of the cross, I
boldly declare that what He died to accomplish *is* accomplished.

It is all *in Christ*. Oh, how my soul hangs upon this! Christ
in me and I in Him! All is in Christ; there is nothing out of
Him; I myself, out of Him, am nothing. But oh, the blessed
truth—He died to make me one with himself, and to make me
die to every life but His.

Since He is living in me, He must be working there. And if
He is working, I have nothing to do but *yield* myself to Him.
Oh, how I love that word *yield*; may it be my meat and drink
continually, as I make it my practical life.

He is within me; my soul knows it; and my soul can trust
Him! (*Diaries*, 1867)

DECEMBER 18
UNITING FOR LIVING

Love takes different forms in our lives and regards its object
in many different ways. The love of the bridegroom and the bride
is the highest and closest and most tender that human hearts can

know, and it pictures the affection between Christ's heart and ours. It is one of the last revelations to come to the soul. At first we seek His *gifts* only, but at last we seek *Him*. At first we are occupied with our needs, but at last we lose sight of the gifts in our longing for the Giver and can be satisfied with nothing short of Him. In response He declares that we are one with Him.

"That they all may be one" (John 17:21)—one with the Father as the Son is one! Similarity of thought, feeling, desire, love, hate—we may have it all, if we will. We may walk through this life so united to Christ that our cares and interests, our sorrows and joys, our purposes and wishes will be the same. His will alone will govern us and His mind alone will lead us.

He in us and we in Him will then be our living, until at last our lives will become so intermingled and conjoined that we will be able to say in very truth, always and everywhere, "Not I but Christ." Self will vanish in such a union as this, and the great "I" of ours, which so fills up our present horizon, will wilt down into nothing before the glory of His overcoming presence! Be one with Him, then, and let the power of that oneness be lived out in every moment of your existence. (*VU*, 142–43)

DECEMBER 19
CONQUERING BY RECKONING

Have we, like the children of Israel, permitted some of our enemies to live in our midst? Are we letting them pay tribute instead of driving them out? If we are, we shouldn't wonder at the slavery and misery that oppress us; it couldn't be otherwise. In the Lord's order, only those who reckon themselves dead not only to a few sins but to every sin can gain continual victories and live the life of uniform triumph.

This is the great difference that arises in the experience of those who enter into the land of promise now. For some, self seems to be swallowed up at once by the revelation of Christ and to lift up its head no more, while for others, the death of self is accomplished only by slow degrees and through great conflicts. The triumphant experience of the Israelites under Joshua is a type of the first, and the failing experience of the time of the Judges is a type of the second.

Through death to life is always God's way, and there is no other. To live we must first die. We must lose our own lives to find the life that is hid with Christ in God. We must reckon ourselves to be dead before we can reckon ourselves to be alive; and the more thorough and wide-reaching the death, the more all-pervading and victorious will be the life.

Is it not a grand proposal of the gospel, then, that we should put off at once the old man of sin and put on forever the new man of Christlikeness. (*OTT*, 139–40)

DECEMBER 20
BELIEVING FOR CLEANSING

We are to receive Christ by faith for our sanctification just as we receive Him by faith for our justification. In receiving Christ for sanctification, the soul sees that Jesus delivers from the *power* of sin as well as from the *guilt* of sin, and he learns to trust Christ to keep him from evil and deliver him from temptation. He ceases to make resolutions or to rely on his own efforts to be made holy. He gives himself unreservedly to Christ to be dealt with according to His will, *believing* that Christ is able and willing to keep him from falling and will do so. Like a weak and helpless child he falls back exhausted into Christ's arms and leaves *all* his cares in His hands.

The sanctified believer will testify that Christ really does cleanse his heart from inbred sin and does a work of grace in his soul so as to make his Christian life a triumphant and exalted one.

I have been used to hearing this view much objected to, but it seems to be the only experience that can supply my needs. I do give myself up unreservedly to God to be and to do just what He wills, and I do trust only Jesus to keep me moment by moment, to preserve me blameless, to purge me and cleanse me and to sanctify me wholly. I know He is able, I believe He is willing, I believe that He will. (*Diaries*, 1868)

DECEMBER 21
SAVING FROM SINNING

A life hid with Christ in God! How wonderful that this should be mine—not judicially only but really and actually, so that I can in truth say that God *is* working in me "to will and to do of his good pleasure (Phil. 2:13).

Ever since the definite step of faith when I was enabled really to reckon myself "dead indeed unto sin, but alive unto God through Jesus Christ our Lord" (Rom. 6:11), I have had a very different experience from ever before. The center of my being was reached at last; the inner citadel was taken possession of by Christ; and the strong man who kept the house before was bound and his goods spoiled. I am now abiding in Christ, and I find that according to the measure of my abiding are fulfilled to me the promises made to those who abide: (1) "Whosoever abideth in him sinneth not" (1 John 3:6); (2) "He that abideth in me, and I in him, the same bringeth forth much fruit" (John 15:5); (3) "If ye abide in me, and my words abide in you, ye shall ask what ye will, and it shall be done unto you" (v.7).

What a blessed life it is to be actually "dead . . . unto sin but alive unto God through Jesus Christ our Lord" (Rom. 6:11). I used to take this statement as altogether judicial, and of course it had no power over me. I knew I was polluted in my own eyes, that I was alive to sin and under its dominion, but I believed that God looked at me only *in Christ*, that He saw me pure, holy, just, and righteous in His Son. The only benefit that I had received from the death of Christ was deliverance from the *punishment* of my sin but not from the *act* of it. Now I see that the purchase of Christ's death was infinitely more valuable than this. (*Diaries*, 1867)

DECEMBER 22
COMMITTING, NOT WORKING

If we continually commit all to Him and leave it in His hands, our lives will become lost in His, and the pure life of God will work in us that which is pleasing to Him. Our only part in this great work is to stop working. Abiding, resting, believing—these are our responsibilities; Christ does all the rest.

Whether in temptation or in service, if we cease from our own plan and our own activities, leaving the care and ordering of our work to Him, He will plan for us, work through us, and use us as His instruments to accomplish His own purposes of love and mercy. The responsibility will be all His; we need only be obedient. Who can understand the sweet rest of soul to be found in this, except those who have experienced it? Everywhere and in everything we are nothing and Christ is all!

How I wish that this truth might be sealed home to the heart of every child of God! The promise is sure that they who hunger and thirst after righteousness shall be filled (Matt. 5:6), and the fulfillment is all in Jesus. We will not be filled with any goodness of our own nor with any righteousness to which we can lay claim as an independent possession. Instead we will be filled simply with Jesus and His righteousness. For He himself says, "I am the bread of life: he that cometh to me shall never hunger; and he that believeth on me shall never thirst" (John 6:35). Our hunger and our thirst are all satisfied forever in Him! (*Diaries*, 1867)

DECEMBER 23
GIVING AND CARING

Christ's work is a *finished work*, and I rest in it. I was like a lost sheep in the wilderness, and He sought and found me and is carrying me home. Shall I not trust Him entirely? Oh, I do trust Him! I am living now on a word of exhortation connected with a precious promise: "Humble yourselves therefore under the mighty hand of God, that he may exalt you in due time:

casting all your care on him; for he careth for you" (1 Peter 5:6–7). The Greek word that refers to our care signifies "distraction of mind," but the word that means God's care for us signifies "fixation of mind." How complete and inexpressibly comforting this makes the thought. It is our privilege as God's children to cast *all* our care on Him, and today I have been enabled to do it without any reserve.

My peace is therefore perfect. "Thou will keep him in perfect peace whose mind is stayed on thee: because he trusteth in thee" (Isa. 26:3). I realize this to be true. How could it be otherwise when we are trusting God? Christians often do not realize this. They forget who it is they are trusting and become full of anxieties and fears. But surely, as God's children, we may trust Him entirely, and indeed He tells us to do so. He promises us that if we will trust Him our peace shall flow as a river (cf. Isa. 66:12).

I long more and more to lose all sight of self and to be completely swallowed up in God's love as manifested in my precious Redeemer. I feel that I am less than nothing, the very offscouring of the earth, yet Christ has redeemed me and I am an heir of God and joint heir with Christ. Oh, what a free gift it is! (*Diaries*, 1858)

DECEMBER 24
GIVING AND FORGIVING

The thought of the freeness and fullness of the gift of God in Jesus Christ our Savior is at times overwhelming! Even now my feelings are almost inexpressible. How rich and free is His grace to me! He is filling my heart with His fullness and is daily leaving less and less room for self. God's gift has been to me such peculiarly free grace. I had nothing to recommend me to His favor—*nothing*—not even a merit of earnestness or of much sorrow for sin, no love or joy or inward grace, no trace of fitness for the heavenly; yet He knocked at the door of my heart, my utterly impure heart, and when I opened He came in. I know that He lives there and that He will purify and cleanse it and make it fit for His dwelling place.

"Herein is love, not that we loved God, but that he loved us" (1 John 4:10). This is the rock on which I rest. "He is made of

God unto us—unto *me*—wisdom, and righteousness, and sanctification, and redemption" (1 Cor. 1:30, para.). He is made this, and all I have to do is rest in Him. I trust simply to the promise, "Him that cometh to me I will in no wise cast out" (John 6:37). I come, and therefore I know that He receives me. Whether I feel happy or unhappy, whether I seem to be walking in light or darkness, Christ's love is unwavering and unchangeable.

"O the depth of the riches both of the wisdom and knowledge of God!" (Rom. 11:33). The apostle Paul, after making this exclamation, goes on to say, "I beseech you therefore, brethren, by the mercies of God, that ye present your bodies a living sacrifice, holy, acceptable unto God, which is your reasonable service" (Rom. 12:1). May the Holy Spirit so engraft this truth into my heart that it will bear rich fruit! (*Diaries*, 1858)

DECEMBER 25
WANTING HIS WILLING

I have been reading Upham's *Madame Guyon* this morning. How full of religious truth is every page! One quotation from Fenelon struck me particularly. It seems to embody such a deep spiritual truth and is so like what I have often thought but could never express. He is speaking of souls that have arrived at a state of perfection and says:

Such a soul not only desires and wills in submission but absolutely ceases, whether to desire or will, except in cooperation with the divine leading. Its desires for itself, as it has greater light, are more completely and permanently merged in the one higher and more absorbing desire of God's glory, and the fulfillment of His will. It desires and wills therefore only what God desires and wills. Its desires are not only submission to the divine desires and purposes but are identical with them. It may desire everything in relation to the correction of the imperfection and weaknesses, its perseverance in its religious state, and its ultimate salvation which it has reason to know from the Scripture or in any other way that God desires. It may also desire all temporal good, houses and lands, food and clothing, friends and books, and exemption from physical suffering, and anything else, so far, and only so far as it has reason to think that such desire is coincident with the divine desire.

The holy soul not only desires particular things sanctioned by the known will of God but also desires the fulfillment of His will in all respects unknown as well as known. Being in faith it commits itself to God in darkness as well as in light. And to this I must attain if I would be perfect. (*Diaries*, 1858)

DECEMBER 26
ABIDING AND DELIVERING

There is a deliverance! Paul knew it and answered, "I thank God through Jesus Christ our Lord!" (Rom. 7:25). George Fox knew it and said, "I clearly saw that all was done and to be done in and by Christ; and that He conquers and destroys this tempter the devil, and all his works, and is atop of him. My living faith was raised that I saw all was done by Christ the life, and my belief was in Him." Thousands of Christians in all ages have known Christ's great deliverance and have rejoiced to testify of its wondrous blessedness.

Christ's death purchased for us not only the forgiveness of our sins but also victory over them—not only freedom from their guilt but freedom from their power as well. Faith in Christ will bring us much besides salvation from eternal condemnation. Because we try to live our lives apart from Him we fail. We realize that He gives us life in the first place, but we do not see that He also must live it for us. We trust Him for the forgiveness of our sins, but we trust ourselves for the daily conquering of them. We pray for divine aid and for the influence of the Holy Spirit, but still our thought is that they are to be given to us that *we* might fight and conquer. This is the secret of our failures.

We are as helpless in the matter of sanctification as in the matter of justification. We are as thoroughly cast on Christ for the control of an irritable temper as for the pardon of all our sins. Christ must be all in all to us every moment. "Without me," He says, "ye can do nothing" (John 15:5). This is the secret of peace and victory. (*Diaries*, 1867)

DECEMBER 27
DYING BUT LIVING

Christ died to give me actual holiness as well as judicial; He died to make me really dead to sin and really alive to God in Him. He died in order that He might become my life—the only life I have—and, living as one, He might work in me that which is pleasing in His sight. I therefore die voluntarily that I may be alive in Him. I lay down my own life and declare myself to be dead in order that Christ may become my life. With Paul I say, "I am crucified with Christ: nevertheless I live; yet not I but Christ liveth in me: and the life which I now live in the flesh I live by the faith of the Son of God, who loved me, and gave himself for me" (Gal. 2:20).

So I am abiding in Christ and He is living in me. All I have to do now is yield myself to Him as one alive from the dead and allow Him to do with me whatever He pleases!

I do not always abide in Him. Alas, no! Satan sometimes succeeds in enticing me out and making me take up my old life in the flesh again. But thanks be to my mighty Savior, His blood avails to atone for even this, and again and again He forgives me and cleanses me afresh from all unrighteousness. I find that daily I learn more and more to hang on to Christ by a naked unfaltering faith, and as a result I find myself more and more confirmed in abiding in Him.

And why should not the time come even for me, when I will be so established and settled there as to go out no more? (*Diaries*, 1867)

DECEMBER 28
LIVING BY BELIEVING

"The just shall live by his faith" (Hab. 2:4). We get life by faith and we must live it by faith. We must cease from our own works in living just as we did in getting life; Christ must be the

One who does it all. He must work in us to will and to do His good pleasure. We must no longer live, but Christ must live in us. Words cannot express the possibilities of a life where His abiding is known.

Surely here is the secret for which your soul has been so long seeking in vain. If we are dead, and Christ alone is our life, then His wisdom, power, and righteousness are all engaged for us, and we cannot possibly lack any good thing. If we will cease to frustrate the grace of God by our strivings; if we will come at once to the end of self and all self's efforts; if we will acknowledge our utter helplessness and commit our all to the Lord Jesus Christ; if we will trust Him to fight our battles for us; if we will, in short, reckon ourselves to be dead and take Him as our life—then the work will be done.

Christ never refuses to take possession of the soul that truly abandons itself to Him. Let us then no longer keep possession of ourselves. Abandoning ourselves and confessing our absolute helplessness and nothingness, let us commit the daily and hourly and even momentary keeping of our souls to Jesus. Let us come to Him saying: "Lord Jesus, I commit myself to you. I cannot help myself. I cannot save myself from sinning or make myself holy, but you can and will! I cast all the care of it on you." We will find that He will not fail us. (*Diaries*, 1867)

DECEMBER 29
RECEIVING HIS BLESSING

To some the promise of the Father comes as a mighty and overwhelming power; to others He comes as the tender and gentle presence of love. But either way, He always makes His presence manifest; and at that day, whenever it comes, the words of our Lord which He spoke to His disciples concerning this wondrous gift, are invariably fulfilled: "At that day ye shall know that I am in my Father, and ye in me, and I in you" (John 14:20). We may have believed it before because God says it is so in the Scriptures, but from the moment we receive we know it by the testimony of an inward consciousness that is unassailable by any form of questioning or doubt.

The Israelites had believed the Lord was in their midst all

along in their wanderings and in their years of bondage, even when no sign of His presence was seen among them. But when the temple was built, when they all saw how "the fire came down from heaven, . . . and the glory of the LORD filled the house" (2 Chron. 7:1), they *knew* it. We cannot wonder that at once, without the need of any command from Solomon, they bowed themselves with their faces to the ground and worshiped and praised the Lord.

Words fail in seeking to tell of the blessedness of this inner life of divine union, and the spirit stands amazed before such glorious possibilities of experience! With Solomon we exclaim, "But will God in very deed dwell with men on the earth? behold, heaven and the heaven of heavens cannot contain thee; how much less this house which I have built!" (2 Chron. 6:18). And the Lord answers, as He did to Solomon, "I have heard thy prayer, and have chosen this place to myself." (*OTT*, 216, 221)

DECEMBER 30
BELIEVING AND FORGIVING

The fact of forgiveness is preached to us. We believe the word preached. And as a result we have peace.

But some may ask, "Is the fact true until we believe it? Are my sins forgiven before I believe they are?" Certainly they are. We could not believe it unless it were already true. In the heart of God there is always forgiveness just as a mother is always ready to forgive the sin of her child. But this forgiveness cannot reach us until we believe in it. Our faith does not induce God to forgive us; it is in no sense the cause of our forgiveness. Faith is only the hand by which we lay hold of the forgiveness that is already ours in Christ.

Our sins do not separate God from us but only us from Him. Our forgiveness is a fact in the mind and heart of God toward us before we believe it. We do not make it true by believing it, but we believe it because it is true. And peace is the result of believing, not believing the result of peace. (*VU*, 127–28)

DECEMBER 31
RELYING AND RESTING

God's existence is all the warrant your need requires for its certain relieving. Nothing can separate you from His love—not death, life, angels, principalities, powers, things present, things to come, height, depth, nor any creature (Rom. 8:35). Every possible contingency is provided for here; and not one of them can separate you from the love of God which is in Christ Jesus our Lord.

After such a declaration as this, how can any of us dare to question or doubt God's love? Since He loves us, He cannot exist and at the same time fail to help us. Do we not know from experience what a necessity it is for love to pour itself out in blessing on the ones it loves? Can we not understand that God, who is love, cannot help blessing us? We do not need to beg Him to bless us, He simply cannot help it.

Therefore, God is enough! God is enough for time; God is enough for eternity. GOD IS ENOUGH!

> *Only to sit and think of God,*
>   *Oh what a joy it is!*
> *To think the thought, to breathe the Name,*
>   *Earth has no higher bliss. (GAC, 41A)*

ABOUT THE AUTHOR

Hannah Whitall Smith was the spiritual mentor of many, including Catherine Marshall. Born into a Quaker family in Philadelphia in 1832, she grew up tirelessly investigating the religious life. She and her husband, Robert Pearsall Smith, immigrated to England to become one of America's most famous expatriate families. Their lay ministry was known as the Higher Life Movement, and in 1875 Hannah wrote THE CHRISTIAN'S SECRET OF A HAPPY LIFE, which originally was conceived as an article for her husband's inspirational magazine. The book became a worldwide bestseller and has influenced generations.